CW01645257

MATILDA SWINNEY

The Girl Who Jumped

CHAPTER EIGHT

First published by Chapter Eight Publishing 2022

First edition

ISBN: 978-1-7399024-3-8

This book was professionally typeset on Reedsy.
Find out more at reedsy.com

To the man who taught me how to jump.

Acknowledgement

This book brought great joy and purpose into my world. I owe its completion to many wonderful people. Firstly, to S for teaching me how to embrace the beauty of life and trust the universe. Next to Sophie, for being the first person to ever read The Girl Who Jumped and for transforming the plot so brilliantly. To Lili, for being the kind of friend every person needs. Michelle, for your patience and meticulousness. Anne for truly understanding the heart of the characters and for your unbelievable attention to detail and to my parents, for always supporting me. Lastly, thank you to my babies Amalia and Millie. You ended my twenty five years of procrastination and made me focus long enough to finally finish this story. You will always be my motivation in life.

Chapter 1

I had an eighty percent chance of being murdered. Mum would have a heart attack if she knew. I'd called Amelia yesterday to warn her. She'd sounded calm on the phone, if a little proud. We'd agreed she'd raise the alarm if she'd not heard from me by nine a.m. tomorrow.

Before I could start imagining my funeral, my phone vibrated in my hand: *Are you on time? You may answer yes or no.* I closed my eyes briefly and stopped walking but a crowd of people spilling out of the Underground, propelled me forwards. I came to the side, out of the way. I put my hand on the cold metal railings overlooking the park and breathed out shakily. I texted back, *Yes.*

My phone vibrated instantly, *Is your heart beating quicker?* I gulped. It was. The tension over the last few hours had built to a fever pitch. I was having a tough time keeping calm. I replied, *Yes.* It was a blunt response but he liked it that way. The deal was no initiation of conversation or long-winded replies. He had a lot of rules.

I started walking again but stopped to look up at the sun shining through the thick canopy of trees above me. The day was cold and sunny. I should be glad to be alive. The next few hours were entirely of my own making. I'd visualised what I was about to do for months, dreamed about it for years and masturbated myself to sleep thinking about it. It was supposed to be fun.

I checked my phone. I had another message: *You will check in first, as you want to get ready.* I replied, *Yes.* He answered, *Do you know where to go?* I rolled my eyes and texted, *Yes.* Of course I knew where to go. How old *was* he? That's why phones existed. I'd already checked the hotel's location this morning. It was exactly two minutes from the Underground. I typed the postcode of the hotel into the map app, just to be sure, and followed the directions out of the park and across the main road.

One minute later, I stood in front of The World's Tallest Hotel. Ivy clambered all the way up it. I looked down at my old blue suitcase and leggings. I was massively under-dressed. There was no point backing out now, though. It was now or never.

As I pushed open the heavy glass doors, a man waiting inside in a top hat and tails bowed deeply.

"Ma'am."

I looked behind me in confusion.

"Ma'am?"

He meant *me.* I didn't realise they welcomed everyone so nicely. I wasn't rich or a celebrity.

"Hello, thank you." I whispered, wishing my Yorkshire accent wasn't so strong. "I'd like to check in please."

"Yes, just this way, ma'am."

I carried my suitcase in my arms so it wouldn't damage the shiny marble floor and followed behind the man to reception. He motioned for me to sit at a large desk. I put my suitcase down carefully on the floor and nudged my plastic bag behind it. I looked down at my trainers. I was bringing the hotel down a whole star.

"Ma'am?"

He was waiting. I'd missed something.

"Yes?" My cheeks flushed.

"The booking name please."

I paused. I'd never said my date's name out loud before. A rising look of suspicion in Hotel Man's eyes told me he was considering throwing me out. Perhaps, he thought I'd stolen the identity of the richest man in London and was attempting to check in. Or maybe, he thought I was a prostitute. That was more likely.

I spoke as slowly and as confidently as I could. He raised his eyebrows. His pause was everything—I must have pronounced the name wrong.

"We've upgraded you."

What?

"To a town-house residence."

He was serious. A grin spread across my face.

"Thank you," I said, wanting to hug him.

"Your suite's not quite ready yet, so if you don't mind taking a seat, we'll sort that out for you as soon as possible, ma'am."

There was only one man in the lounge, sitting confidently on a pistachio armchair near the floor-to-ceiling windows. I could see the edge of his shoulder clad in an impressive jet-black suit and the glint of a watch. I froze. I stopped breathing altogether. My fantasy had begun. It was him. He was here already. Maybe he'd cut his day short and arrived early just to watch me walk into the hotel. He was obsessed with me already. I knew it. I'd read about this online – the devotion, intensity, adoration of a man who knew The Game.

I sank down onto the nearest sofa to gather my thoughts. I wasn't ready to see him yet. My biggest problem was my old grey jumper and red face. I'd imagined meeting him for the first time in a tight dress and immaculate hair and makeup. He wasn't going to fall in love with me when I looked like this. I glanced at my phone. I had one message: *Are you in?*

I shivered, deliciously. This was the closest I'd ever get to being in a James Bond film. I was on a mission. A sex mission. My heart was racing, my hands were sweaty and I actually felt a little bit sick. But it would be worth it. If I faced my fear of meeting an online stranger for the first time, I'd be rewarded. In a few hours from now, I'd be tied to a hotel bed having the most intense orgasm of my life.

I texted back, *I'm in.*

The next few seconds happened fast. Black Suit stood up and turned towards me. His dating profile photo hadn't done him justice. He was George Clooney with blue eyes. He looked rugged like he'd been through every war the world had seen. He'd said he was forty one but his profile name was *51grey* and from the deep furrows on his forehead, I was guessing he was fifty one. It would make more sense.

His eyes were so blue, I couldn't look away. He was stronger than I expected. His legs looked muscular and his shirt clung to his arms. It was just the right amount though, like he had muscles because he was a hunter-gatherer who fought tigers during the day and flung his cave-man wife over his shoulder at night. Not because he took a bunch of body-building selfies and ate nothing but chicken and broccoli. I pulled at my old grey jumper self-consciously. He should have given me more warning of how handsome he was.

He was still striding towards me, showing no signs of

stopping. Were we about to shake hands? Perhaps, he was a double kiss kind of guy. Before I could work out whether I should do two kisses on each cheek or just one, his stubble brushed against my skin and an expensive fragrance wrapped around me. I took a deep breath in. I'd never smelt anything that good before. For a second, my brain shut down. I forgot how to move my mouth. His lips brushed mine. I felt a jolt of electricity run through me.

He sat back, satisfied, in an over-stuffed armchair next to me. He looked calm but I was reeling from his perfect lips. They were soft but hard. I looked at his hands. He had thick thumbs, like really thick. I gazed down slowly at his suit trousers, wondering whether Amelia's theory about big hands was right. Everything about him was so powerful. Self-assured. His grip on my body would be tight. He'd throw me across the hotel room easily.

I pulled my eyes away from his legs. His stare was burning into me. He was so close, I could see the whites of his eyes. His groomed facial hair was speckled with grey. His tanned skin made his blue eyes even brighter. He didn't seem to care how long he looked at me. I stayed totally still. Sweat was building on my upper lip. I watched his eyes to see if he'd noticed. He was busy studying me as if I was a scarf he'd found in a designer sale and he couldn't believe his luck. It *was* unusual. This situation. Me. In a Mayfair hotel asking a man I'd never met to tie me to a bed and fuck me. The truth was, I might look innocent with my Disney eyes and long blonde hair, but I had a desire inside that was aching to be met. And I couldn't wait any longer.

"You're so beautiful."

His voice was calm and well-spoken with an edge to it -

something I couldn't place. He smiled but I didn't smile back. My mouth wouldn't stretch that way. My face felt frozen.

"You're so beautiful." He said it again.

"Thank you."

"What's your favourite drink?"

I paused. I loved a porn star martini but I couldn't say it. It was too cliched.

"So, you got us an upgrade?" he asked changing the subject.

"Yes," I said.

I appreciated the compliment but we both knew it was him who got us the upgrade. He must be famous or a billionaire.

I fanned myself self-consciously, hoping to displace the sweat on my upper lip. He looked questioningly at my flapping hands.

"It's hot," I said.

No response, just that same curious look in his eyes that made me want to explain myself.

"I'm so hot. You're making me nervous."

"Good. You're so beautiful, Tilly."

"Thank you," I whispered. He'd called me beautiful three times in the space of one minute. My grey jumper clearly hadn't ruined his first impression of me.

He raised one eyebrow expectantly.

"I need to say it here?" I asked.

"You really should say it every time."

I nodded but stayed quiet. Unless he started spanking me on the sofa here and now, he couldn't exactly make me say the word. I'd say it later when we were drunk. It would feel less jarring that way. It was the only part of The Game that I wasn't sure about.

"It's rude to stare, isn't it?"

I stifled a laugh. I hadn't expected him to make jokes.

"What do you drink?" he asked again.

"Cocktails. Sweet ones."

"Of course, you do," he said with a smile, his eyes lighting up. "Which ones?"

I searched my mind for a more innocent sounding cocktail than a porn star martini but Slippery Nipple and Multiple Screaming Orgasm were the only ones I could think of.

"My favourite is a porn star martini," I said finally.

He laughed. "Yes, Tilly."

He fell silent, tapping his polished oxfords against the wooden leg of the sofa, making a loud click each time. He glanced at his watch.

"I never wait. How long does it take to get a suite ready?"

I looked around, there was no one in sight. We'd only been waiting a few minutes though. He must be one of those guys who's super busy. He probably had a PA.

"Your suite is ready. May I accompany you?"

Hotel Man had appeared next to us, as if out of thin air, like a magician with his hands clasped behind his back and his head bowed.

"The lady will go first. I have some work to do."

I stood up and his intense stare left me immediately. I felt surprisingly bereft. I followed Hotel Man as he carried my plastic bag and suitcase through the glass foyer.

Chapter 2

My phone vibrated and I glanced over without touching the screen: *10 minutes to be in front of me.* I shook my head, adrenaline rushing through me. George didn't need a response. I was running out of time. The last thing I wanted was a text conversation. I checked my reflection. I looked so grown up. I'd given him a choice of two dresses, and he'd chosen the longer one I'd never normally wear. It was less slutty and more demure. It sang, *I have my life together* and *I've inherited millions of pounds from my rich but loveless family.*

My heels were eight inches high and a big mistake. It took all my concentration to walk quickly without falling over. I felt the smooth floor of the lift under my feet change to the marble of the foyer. It was now 6:02 p.m. I was late. I'd have to text him. I'd be breaking the rules by initiating conversation, but I had no choice. I sent a quick message, *I'm coming.*

He texted back, *You will be late anyway so slow down. Don't rush.*

Surely, two minutes didn't count? I was normally half an hour late for everything. I speed-walked into the hotel bar and typed back, *I'm here now. I'm sorry.*

I teetered over the carpet, my heels sinking into the thick pile. The hushed bar was like a glamorous library where the readers were all millionaires and sipped from crystal glasses. I flipped my bag around so the Prada label was visible. It was the only thing that made me belong here.

I spotted George sitting in a velvet chair shaped like a scallop. He checked his watch impatiently as I walked towards him as sexily as I could without falling over. My heels were way too high. I'd broken two of his rules already—no initiating texts and no lateness. How would he punish me?

"Sit."

I sat like a trained dog and stared at the cocktail in front of me, willing him to tell me to drink.

"Drink."

Yes. We were already communicating telepathically. I clutched at the steel cup but, in horror, noticed a steel straw sticking out of the liquid. I had no idea how a steel straw would work. I drank the glass of water next to it instead. It was better he thought I had a passion for water than absolutely zero knowledge of fancy drinks.

"You may look at me."

I glanced up and immediately regretted it. His blue eyes locked on to mine. My breath caught in my throat. I stifled a whimper. We'd barely even met yet. How did he have this effect on me already?

"Can I sit closer to you?" I asked, feeling an urge to smell his gorgeous scent again.

"Please do."

I edged along the velvet sofa, looking back at my bag as if it were an item of unidentified luggage.

"At least make it look like your bag belongs to someone."

I giggled, as elegantly as I could without snorting, and pulled my bag closer.

"Nice. Prada."

George's nod of approval was everything I'd wanted but I did not deserve it. My bag was from MBK shopping centre in Bangkok where I'd got a strange haircut, bought lots of cheap bras, and haggled for fake Celine bags for my best friends, Amelia and Sarah and a fake Prada one for me.

"Thank you."

"You should call me 'sir.'"

The moment I'd been dreading was finally here. I'd never called a man "sir" before. I felt like a waitress or a shop assistant. I guessed it was an important part of The Game, though. It showed I was inferior to him. During my extensive research, I'd discovered three ways to address a dominant man: "Daddy", "master" or "sir". "Master" and "daddy" were beyond weird. "Sir" was mildly better. Plus, George preferred it.

"Even in public?" I asked.

"Yes, Tilly, even in public."

"Is it to mark my inferiority?" I asked, unable to contain my suspicion.

"Pardon?" He said. His mouth moved into a straight angry line.

I gulped nervously, but in the name of feminism, pressed on. "Calling you Sir. Is it to show I'm inferior to you?"

He shifted forward in his seat, his face deadly serious. "You will never be inferior to me." He paused, waiting for his words to sink in. "Never. It's merely for theatrical effect. It emphasises our roles. It acts as a constant reminder of The Game."

"The Game" was our agreement of submission and domination. I nodded, satisfied. I liked how seriously he'd taken my question.

"Eat," he ordered, sitting back in his chair.

The salad looked like a work of art. It was chopped within an inch of its life and drizzled artistically with dressing. But the last thing I wanted to do was eat.

"I'm not hungry," I whispered. My feminist bravery had evaporated. I'd been left with clammy hands and a churning stomach. How could I *not* feel nervous when we were sitting so closely together?

"You must eat Tilly."

I obeyed reluctantly, forcing a small mouthful of chicken and lettuce into my mouth. I felt his eyes on me and sat up straighter, angling my face in, what I hoped was, a sophisticated way. I noticed a flicker of amusement in his eyes. His gaze fell to my bare legs. As he stared, I felt an involuntary flutter of pleasure. I pressed my thighs together.

"You're so beautiful," he murmured.

"Thank you." I felt heat spread through my cheeks, wishing I didn't blush so easily.

With a sudden surge of confidence from his compliment, I sucked the steel straw. Success. A flow of ice-cold, bitter liquid hit my mouth. I flinched. I preferred sweet ones.

A flicker of disapproval flashed across George's face. The cocktail was probably fifty pounds. I wanted to apologise but he spoke before I could.

"Do you know what this is?" he asked, gesturing to a small jug of wine.

I frowned. It had to be a trick question. Perhaps, this was the second initiation—first the steel straw, and now this. I stared at its long, thin neck and wide, round bottom.

"It's a carafe. Crystal," he said, answering for me.

"Yes, Sir." I nodded, dutifully. I thought a 'carafe' was a knitted hat.

"I only drink French red wine," he said as he poured. I watched the heavy red liquid tumble into his glass.

"It's all in the detail. Tilly. I. Control. Every. Detail."

I bit my lip, remembering the way his stubble had brushed against my skin when he kissed me. Was it socially acceptable to close my eyes and get him to talk to me? His voice was too sexy. I watched as he caught the attention of the bar staff. He turned back to me without warning.

He paused, pleased to find me staring at him. "You like my words, don't you, Tilly?"

"Yes, Sir." I said, moving an inch closer.

He tutted lightly and shook his head. "I'll tell you if I want you to move closer."

Was he trying to scare me or turn me on? Because both were happening right now.

"You have a lot to learn."

I frowned. I didn't have *that* much to learn.

A waiter arrived and Sir pointed several things out to him on the menu. I waited impatiently. Was he implying I didn't know what I was doing? Sure, I didn't have any experience in being dominated, but I had a lot of desire. I wasn't naive. Finally, the waiter disappeared to the bar.

"You're only twenty-four, aren't you, Tilly?"

I nodded.

His face softened. "When are you twenty-five?"

"In February."

"I'll buy you Jimmy Choos, if I'm still your sir."

I felt my jaw drop. All irritation at being called inexperienced evaporated. Jimmy Choos? How much money did he have?

A drink landed in front of me with a passionfruit on top.

"I hope that's more to your taste."

I blinked at it.

"Drink."

I obeyed, and my mouth came alive with sweetness. He'd picked a winner.

"Slow."

I stopped gulping and placed the glass back down on the table.

"Good girl."

I felt a warm glow in my heart at his praise. The words "good girl" should've annoyed me but somehow everything he said turned me on. He shifted closer, reaching out to grip my neck. His hand felt cold against my skin as he pressed my windpipe. The intense look in his eyes made me hold my breath. He was enchanting and terrifying all at once. He pressed tighter. My breath got stuck in my throat. I wanted to take a big gulp of air but I couldn't. He was applying more pressure by the second. He was going to strangle me to death.

I dragged my eyes away from his and glanced around the bar in panic. Could he kill me without anyone noticing?

"Look at me."

I turned to look back into his eyes. He released my windpipe and I gasped for air. Without warning, he pushed his thumb roughly inside my open mouth. As my heart rate subsided, I made eye contact and sucked on his thumb as sensually as I could. It was time to claim back control. I pushed his thumb deeply into my mouth, caressing his rough skin with my tongue, watching the horniness in his eyes grow.

He stopped me, abruptly. "Do you think the family opposite us will complain?"

The family was, thankfully, talking quietly amongst themselves. They'd seen nothing.

"I bet they'd have a heart attack if they knew what I was going to do to you tonight."

"You'd be surprised," I murmured, looking at the way the husband gazed at the strict wife. He definitely got tied up to their four-poster bed every night.

Sir didn't reply. I scanned his face. The straight line of his mouth was back again. I'd said something wrong. Maybe, I should have agreed with him instantly. It wasn't just us who had kinks, though.

"Take your thong off."

His jaw was clenched, his face serious. This was the third initiation. I had no choice. There was no way I could do it. We'd get chucked out. Everyone would look at me in disgust. Maybe the police would be called. People didn't do things like that in bars like this. I was supposed to be demure. But, his eyes locked onto mine and without another second's hesitation, I began a method of high-speed panic wiggling to pull my thong down past my bottom.

"Take your time. Don't rush."

"How?" I snapped.

Great advice. It's not like I'm attempting to get completely naked under my dress without anyone seeing. Now you've said those words, I'll just relax and stop rushing. The only way this was going to happen was if I rushed. At some point, I had to get my thong off from under my bottom and past my thighs. Surely, a quick side wriggle was the best way to do that?

"Use a cushion."

I grabbed an overstuffed cushion. As I stood up, I pulled my thong from under my bottom as quickly as I could. It fell to my ankles and I lunged forward to hold my underwear safely in my hand.

I'd done it. I resisted the urge to whoop loudly in triumph. I wanted to stand on the table and swing my knickers in the air. My crotch was naked in a five-star hotel. In under five seconds, I'd triumphed. I felt a rush of laughter threatening to bubble up to the surface. Removing thongs should be a mandatory part of all first dates. I felt amazing.

"Give it to Sir," he whispered, holding his hand out, waiting.

I paused. Did I want to give him my only matching lingerie set and the precious evidence of how wild I was? His jaw tightened. I handed my thong over reluctantly, watching, mortified, as he held it in his large open hand. People would see.

"Everyone's wrapped up in their own little box, Tilly. No one will see." He shook his head.

Just like the bitter cocktail before, he'd read my mind. He was right, though. Everyone was ignoring us, happily absorbed in their own evenings.

"Everyone lives in a box, Baby Girl, trapped by their ideas of who they think they should be and what they think the world should be."

There was nothing sexier than a visionary, apart from George Clooney, and Sir was both.

"Very few break out of their box, Tilly. They stay inside their box life, box job, box future, never questioning anything. They follow the rules. Always. It's all anyone's ever been taught. It's an illusion."

In the flickering candlelight, his face was alive with excitement. I felt as if we were in *The Matrix.* His passion was contagious. My heart was still hammering in my chest from my thong removal victory and now he was making idealistic claims on a first date. He'd skipped the small talk and jumped straight in at the deep end. I found myself nodding. We *did* all live life in a box. A box that was never to be broken out of or questioned. Go to school, get a job, find a partner, have kids, go on a few holidays and die.

This man clearly knew how to break convention, how to live life fully, embracing everything and questioning anything that didn't suit him. *And he told women to take their thongs off on a first date.* I looked at his black leather shoes, perfectly shiny and polished. I admired his Rolex. This had been the most thrilling night of my life so far, and we'd not even got to the sex part yet. I shook my head in disbelief.

"Tilly?"

"Has anyone ever told you, you have big thumbs?"

His laugh was a deep rumble, much louder than I'd expected. I jumped in surprise and smiled proudly at the same time. I'd made impenetrable Sir belly-laugh.

"No, I can say honestly that in my fifty one years of life, not one person has said I have big thumbs."

For a fleeting moment, he looked lighter, younger, less serious.

But then, he placed his glass down on the table, his eyes darkened and he said, "When we enter the room, you will go first. You will place a cushion down on the floor in front of the window. You will stand and wait, facing the curtains."

The cheerful hum of the bar suddenly muted. I could hear a ringing in my ears. The moment had arrived. Somehow, I'd never expected this time to come. The train journey here, our unexpected meeting in the lobby, my panic to get ready and the luxury of our surroundings had all sped by in a blur. Now,

The Game was about to become my reality and I had no idea whether I was ready.

Chapter 3

"Breathe, Tilly, breathe," Sir whispered, taking off my blindfold.

I closed my eyes and listened to his soothing voice. My heart rate, which had been beating loudly in my ears for the last hour, began to slow down. I stretched out deliciously, my brutally spanked skin grateful for the soft cloud of duvet.

I blinked my eyes open, taking in his naked body. He was *very* muscular. I ran my fingers down his broad chest.

"Tilly," he warned.

My eyes widened. Was I not allowed to touch him?

He shook his head and tutted gently. "Not without my permission."

I looked around the room—everything looked blurry. The last hour had been amazing. His thumbs had not disappointed. I'd stood naked and blindfolded by the curtain, waiting to see what he would do next. He'd kissed me, clamping down hard onto my bottom lip. A noise had escaped me, half-gasp, half-moan. I'd wanted to apologise for my trembling body but the heat from his skin told me he felt the same.

When we'd finally made it to the bed and I'd recovered from his merciless spanking, he'd pressed his body into me roughly. I'd thrust myself against him as he entered me. His tempo increased. My body melted. A slow explosion of each and every one of my senses had forced all thoughts out of my mind. Drunk with lust, an earth-shattering orgasm had shook through me. I'd stared at him in wonder afterwards, blood coursing through my body, tears threatening to spill over. What was happening? We barely knew each other. I'd not even orgasmed the first time I'd had sex with my first boyfriend.

"Lie on me, Tilly."

He beckoned me over gently. I moved closer to him on the bed and placed my head on his chest. As his panting subsided, his heartbeat became steady and rhythmic lulling me into a blissful state of relaxation.

He sighed and whispered softly to himself. "I feel like I've not slept in months."

I wasn't sure whether he was talking to me or not. I always slept well. Did being an entrepreneur mean he never slept?

"I don't want to leave, you understand?" he said, moving suddenly. I sat up too. He took my head tenderly in his hands. "I have to go into a room of people who I don't want to be with. They're expecting me, though, Tilly. It's important that I go."

An apology was etched across his face but I didn't know why. This had been the plan all along. Maybe he felt the unexpected connection too. The intimacy was palpable. My moans had filled the room just seconds before. His body had molded into mine worryingly perfectly. None of this fitted in with my plan to explore my deepest sexual fantasy with no strings attached. Love wasn't supposed to be a possibility. I was done with boyfriends.

The sooner I was alone, the better. I needed to work out what on earth was going on in my head.

"I understand, Sir."

He rubbed the small of my back and ran his fingers lazily across my thigh. I looked at his face, trying to analyse his expression but he stood up from the bed, and walked into the other room. I strained my ears to pick up his movements. It sounded like he was talking to someone.

"Pardon Sir?" I called through, cheerfully.

There was a low hum of talking and then a muffled noise and he said, urgently and loudly, "Don't come in."

Perhaps, he didn't want me to see him half-dressed. It would ruin his "sir" persona. I stretched out sexily on the bed, arranging myself provocatively on top of the covers while I waited. I was ready for round two. I had to make the most of his amazing thumbs. I pressed my head down into the duvet and pushed my bottom up high in the air. He wouldn't be able to resist me.

A few minutes later, he walked back into the bedroom in his black fitted suit and polished shoes, looking like our wild sex session had never happened.

"Tilly," he laughed under his breath, admiring my accidental-on-purpose position. He walked over to me, and I crawled playfully towards him on the bed. I was Baby in *Dirty Dancing*.

There was a beat of silence. The expression in his eyes told me he was going to stay but then he leaned forward and kissed me on the forehead. "I've got to go."

"Bye, Sir," I said ruefully.

"You should enjoy this." He waved to the room. "Get some friends round, have a party."

The door clicked shut behind him. I sat stunned on the bed. I wasn't a huge fan of cuddling after sex but I would have liked a few minutes more. Listening to his slow heartbeat had calmed me down. Where was he rushing off to anyway?

I stood up. Sir's final words ran through my head: *Get some friends round, have a party.* I didn't have any friends I could ring up and invite round to a suite in Mayfair at eleven o'clock on a Saturday night. My quiet friends would be tucked up in bed, and my party friends would be so drunk they wouldn't be able to remember how to use a phone. And none of them lived in London anyway.

I knew Amelia would jump on the last train and travel the two hours from Sheffield to be with me, though. So would Sarah. They'd love to see this suite. In fact, they were the whole reason I was here.

You should try Sexy Kittens, Amelia had told me two months ago.

Sexy Kittens? I'd asked, looking in confusion at Sarah and then out of the window of our favourite coffee shop. What was Amelia talking about? I'd spent the past hour hopelessly complaining to them both about how rubbish dating sites were and now Amelia was recommending kitten websites.

"I'm running out of time. I've got to do something in the next few months."

She nodded. She knew how important it was that I got over my ex-boyfriend Darren.

"Trust me. Sexy Kittens is a good idea. It's a sex website. Move on in style. Make an occasion of it. Do something you've always wanted to do. You could find a dominating guy on there if you still like the idea of that."

I shook my head in mock horror. Was now really the time to talk about our kinks?

"What?" she asked, wide-eyed. "You said you've always wanted to be dominated. It's your idea, not mine. I'm just giving you the tools you need to get started." She pushed her long, glossy hair behind her ears and took a slow sip of coffee.

"It's easy. You create a profile online and done." She made a flourish with her hands. "Guys message you who are interested. You'll be inundated."

I loved that Amelia included me in her liberated attitude, but I was not cut out for sex sites. My domination fantasy would have to stay as that - a fantasy.

I glanced over at Sarah again to see what she thought. She'd always been the sensible one: Ever since we'd all met over the sandpit in year one at infant school. First, Sarah was the one telling us not to put too much sand on the floor, now, years later, she was our go-to for all dating and career advice.

"Do it." She nodded, happily.

"Really?"

Wasn't she supposed to tell me to spend more time alone or get counselling or something first? My past relationship had been tough. Hardcore domination wasn't exactly the typical antidote to trauma. It sounded like a risky idea.

"You've done eight months of being alone. You've done the finding yourself while travelling-"

"Now it's time for the hot sex," Amelia interrupted, loudly.

Sarah glanced around the coffee shop self-consciously to see if anyone was listening, before continuing in hushed tones. "Seriously, though. Amelia's right. It's time to put you first. Indulge. You're mentally ready to move on, so why not make it an experience of a lifetime?"

"Imagine how good it would be to live out the one fantasy you've always wanted. This is your chance. No more faking orgasms," Amelia added.

Was this an intervention? Sure, the only real orgasms I'd

had were solo-ones but I didn't know they were keeping count. And yes, I'd always fantasised about being dominated, but I wasn't sure if now was the time. My confidence had been massively dented by Darren. It would take a huge amount of trust. Plus, there was no way I'd find someone online who could dominate me properly and respect me.

"We'll do your profile now," Sarah said decisively, picking up her phone. Amelia nodded enthusiastically, scooting her armchair over so she could see.

I'd committed to creating a profile *and* finding a dom before I'd barely said one word.

Back in the suite, I walked around the empty luxurious room thinking about Amelia and Sarah. Technically, I'd done well. I'd had a mind-blowing orgasm and now all I could think about was Sir. Mission complete. They'd be pleased. I stepped into the waterfall shower in the sparkling white bathroom and ran a deep, hot bath immediately afterwards. I sat in the comforting water, playing absentmindedly with the bubbles, wondering whether my sudden love of hygiene was a red flag. I'd never had a shower and a bath before. The enormity of what I'd just done hit me. I got out of the bath quickly, grabbing a thick, fluffy towel from the heated bathroom rail. The less I thought about it, the better.

As the silky softness of my towel rubbed my skin, I thought of our threadbare brown ones at home. They were a world away from this. Mum said they were exfoliating though, and the thick fluffy ones didn't dry you properly. She had a point. As I turned to dry my back, I noticed just how marked my bottom was. My phone vibrated. I picked it up to reply. He'd sent two messages, *You were amazing xxx.* And the next message twenty minutes later, *In hindsight. I should have stayed.*

His three kisses didn't go unnoticed. I texted back, *Thank you. I would have loved nothing more. I know you're busy, though. Good night, Sir.* The simplicity of his rules stopped me from rambling. I was grateful for that. Now was not the time to discuss my constant rush of adrenaline when I thought of him or my double hygiene response to having sex with him for the first time. If *he* was one big red flag, then I shouldn't discuss anything with him. That's what Amelia and Sarah were for.

He messaged back immediately. I raised one eyebrow. He didn't care how quickly he replied or how eager he looked. He wasn't playing games. *We'll discuss everything tomorrow. Sleep well.* He sent a rose emoji, which was secret code for "you're dismissed," so feeling relieved to be truly alone, I put my phone down and padded across the thick cream carpet to the kitchen. I was hungry.

The fridge was impressive. Endless delights of mini champagne, whiskey, wine, luxury chocolates, and salted caramel popcorn smiled back at me. Sugar was exactly what I needed. And, hello, what was that? A tin of sweets on the side. I lifted the lid and breathed in its fruity smell, but I put it down immediately. There was no way I was paying thirty pounds for glorified Haribo. Instead, I found a free glass bottle of water and five sorry-looking fluffy almonds at the bottom of my bag. That was better. I was saving money *and* being healthy.

At 2:07 a.m, I sank into bed, pressing my face against the cool silk of the pillows. Silk was amazing for dewy skin. I'd read that somewhere. I'd wake up in the morning with a fresh face. I'd probably still have the mark under my eye, though. Was it OK to have bruises after sex? We did have a safe word; plus, I *had* specifically asked for everything that'd happened. It felt like domination made red flags blurry, though. Nothing was clear. I didn't want to jump headfirst into a bad situation.

I picked up the heavy bound welcome book on the glass bedside table and read about the beds the hotel used. My mattress was the same as the Queen's. Along with my silk pillows, I would have the best night's sleep ever. Thoughts about confusing, bruise-inducing, orgasmic sex could wait until the morning.

Chapter 4

Good morning, Baby Girl. Go to the mirror. Photo your bare arse. Show me. And your shoulder, please. I opened one eye to read Sir's message before covering my eyes with a pillow and groaning. It was too early for tasks and the word "arse" made me want to giggle. I dozed for an hour longer, appreciating the delicious warmth of my bed. I wasn't moving anywhere. That was for sure. After my week of sleeping under a scratchy duvet in a grungy hostel in Brighton, the Mayfair suite's luxury felt unbelievable.

I'd stayed in the Brighton hostel for the whole week of my acting course. It was scruffy but perfect: a short walk along the coast to my drama class, *and* it had a kitchen. I'd cooked porridge in the mornings and prepared my dinner in the evenings. Even though I'd made a good choice in terms of location, it could easily have felt lonely. The people staying in the hostel were friends. They lolled about on the sofa together watching films on a projector, drinking wine, and decorating pumpkins for Halloween. I'd felt like an outsider, but it'd been OK. I'd had a distraction. Sir had kept me busy with his texts every night.

Where are you? Wearing what? His messages were always formal. He rarely used abbreviations, and he liked to know exactly what I was wearing and where I was. I loved the intensity of it all. I'd sent a long reply back to make sure I didn't miss out any details. *I'm in a hostel near the sea in Brighton watching a film on a projector with the people there. I'm wearing black leggings, a black top, no socks, and the underwear I showed you.*

To my delight, his answer had been instant, *I'm totally infatuated. Totally. You are intense as you are beautiful. My voice needs to fill your soul. When I eventually touch you... Naked... You will be light-headed... Adrenaline high... Your mind a blur...*

I shivered. Over the last few days, the heat of his messages had gone up a notch. My phone vibrated again, *You thought long and hard about your rules. We need to discuss marking. I want to mark you. You would enjoy a crop.* I stared at the screen. "Marking" sounded too hardcore. I didn't want any permanent marks. Wasn't a crop for horse riding, anyway? Clearly, he needed to read my contract again.

1. *No love bites above the shoulders.*
2. *No extreme choking or anything that puts me at risk of death.*
3. *No permanent marking.*
4. *No videos or photos to be made of me without my permission.*
5. *Both the sub and dom will take an STD test and keep proof of the results afterwards to show no STDs.*
6. *The safe word is "red box."*
7. *When one of us does want to end our arrangement, we are able to do this at any point. The other person will be polite, respectful, and keep everything 100 percent confidential. We text* STOP.

It was a first draft but I was pleased with it. It was a collection of my sub and dom research, ideas from Amelia, and some rules Sir already used, like the safe word being "red box" and the idea of sending *STOP* in a text. I'd spent a lot of time on it.

I took a deep breath and replied, *Do you mean permanently mark me?*

No, Tilly.

I frowned at the screen, feeling confused. I typed back, *So how would you mark me? Does a crop make a bruise? I like spanking and biting. I've never been cropped before. How long would the marks last?* I watched the three dots, impatient for his response. I was eager to learn and I could even be persuaded to change my mind. There wasn't many areas of domination that *didn't* turn me on.

I shook my head in disbelief as his rudely short reply arrived, *We should discuss in person. It's late.* That was it? He'd started the discussion and now he was stopping us midflow for no reason. I looked around the hostel, feeling annoyed. As I watched the hostel friends happily enjoying their black-and-white film, totally oblivious to my alter ego, I decided it didn't matter. Two could play at that game. I'd be even blunter than Sir from now on. I texted back, *Goodnight* and turned my phone off.

* * *

When I finally got out of bed an hour later, in my gorgeous five-star suite, my head was pounding. This was the hangover to end all hangovers. I texted Amelia to let her know I was still alive before sending photos of my bruises to Sir. The mark on my face looked better than it did last night, but I had no idea how it was even there, and the marks on my bottom were angry red and purple splotches. I felt secretly proud of those ones. I'd never been spanked hard enough to be bruised before.

My phone pinged, *They'll heal quickly. What time are you leaving the hotel?* His lack of concern was worrying. The mark on my face was a big deal for me—but for him, it might as well be a paper cut. I typed a response, *I didn't want my face to be marked. That breaks my rules.* I pressed Send but looked around the plush hotel room and immediately felt guilty, so I sent another message, *But I know it's not that bad. And I do feel like your Baby Girl here, Sir.*

You are my Baby Girl. I miss you this morning. I rolled my eyes. He was totally sweet talking me. You can't miss someone you've only spent a few hours with. My phone pinged again, *The marks technically were made by the floor and not my hand? Therefore no breach?* He was getting close to an apology, I could feel it. It was important I got one. I *had* asked for the full experience, but I'd also made it clear I didn't want to be permanently marked. Surely, being regularly bruised from sex wasn't a healthy addition to my life? I wouldn't be able to go swimming or wear a bikini on holiday without my mum worrying. I'd have to wear a full wetsuit that covered every inch of my body and meant I had offensively pale skin for the rest of my life.

I watched the three dots dance. A long message was coming my way. Finally, my screen lit up, *Apologies, Tilly. I will be more careful. All marks should be gone within a week. If you need me to be more lenient, then we can discuss? I have made you my ONLY sub. You have a role to play. If you can't do it, then now is the time to say.*

It wasn't *X Factor*. I didn't have to feel grateful for making it to the next round. I was pretty sure he only ever chose one sub anyway. I typed back quickly, *Do you always choose just one sub? Don't get rid of everyone just for me—it's a lot of pressure.*

He replied, *No pressure. I'll look after you always. In the scene, were you not excited and a little scared? You came so often. The sex was hard but not unreasonable. This is what a dom does. You are my sub. Taking your thong off was brilliantly done, by the way.*

I nodded proudly to myself. My thong disappearance act *had* been good. I texted, *Thank you, Sir. Your fingers felt amazing. I didn't want a mark on my face but I did love the sex.*

There was no response and no dots, so I carried on getting ready for the day, relishing the experience. Doing my makeup underneath a glittering chandelier was a whole lot better than squinting in the mirror of my dimly-lit, tiny bedroom at home. After a few minutes, my phone finally pinged, *Have you left the room yet?*

Suite, I corrected him.

Apartment, He came back with. I laughed. He messaged again, *I suggest you take a good look around. Remember the details of the scene. A life experience, Tilly. Bye for now.*

I looked around the room. It *had* been a life experience. I caught sight of a menu on the side. My stomach rumbled. Who knew when I'd ever be somewhere this glamorous again? It was time to sample fine dining. I picked up the phone to order room service.

"May I have the four-egg omelette and the mate tea please?"

"We don't have mate tea."

I looked back at the menu in confusion. It was right there.

"But it's on the menu?" I said tentatively.

The man on the other end of the phone sighed. He was not Hotel Man. He was angry Kitchen Man.

"You mean 'maté,' I suppose. Shall we charge it to the room?"

"No, I can pay now," I said hurriedly, finding another almond in my bag as I grabbed my card and read out the long number. I'd spent twenty pounds on an omelette and pronounced "mate" like it was my new friend. Of course, it wasn't mate tea. I bet the whole kitchen was laughing at me.

Half an hour later, an omelette arrived on a silver platter. It was cold. I sat facing the wall of mirrors and made a face at myself. The magic was gone without Sir. I leant forward onto the cool glass table to soothe my pounding head. I liked to stay curled up on the sofa eating pizza when I was hungover, but there'd be no chance of that today. I was travelling to an Airbnb in London and managing a three-day promotional job tomorrow.

Before I left, I kissed the wall goodbye. It felt smooth, so I rubbed my face against it and then pulled back in horror. There was now a foundation mark on the immaculately painted wall. I wasn't made for luxury. I turned the handle of the heavy mahogany hotel door - it was time to return to normal life.

Chapter 5

It'd been one week since my submissive experience with Sir. I was now in a grimy burger bar watching my new date, Simon, pick his teeth with a business card from the restaurant. He was not the handsome graphic designer with a love of skiing and patterned socks that his online profile had said he was. He was a whole lot safer than a man who insisted on being called Sir, fulfilled all my sexual fantasies and made me orgasm the first time I met him, though.

A loud noise, more broadly associated with a zoo or sewage system than a restaurant, ripped through the air.

"Meat always makes my stomach a little dodgy," Simon explained, shifting in his seat.

"Perhaps you could become a vegetarian?" I suggested helpfully, putting my fork down to give myself a small break from eating. My cheese-soaked burger was no longer tempting.

"Yeah, and start wearing sandals and meditating." He snorted.

A piece of beef shot out of his mouth and landed on my plate. I stared at it, outraged. His profile should have said: *negative outlook, bad habit of picking teeth at the table, and high chance of farting or burping when eating meat.* This is what I got for trying a "normal" dating app. I'd thought it might be good for me—help me stop obsessing over Sir—but I should have known that nothing would seem exciting after our night together.

"I wrote my will a few days ago," Simon announced.

I raised my eyebrows. "That's very organised of you."

"Well, we've not got long now, have we?" he said, shrugging his shoulders.

I looked at him in horror. "I'm twenty-four."

"I know. I remember your profile. As soon as you hit thirty, though, it's all downhill from there. I should know," he said sadly.

"You're only thirty-one," I pointed out, taking a sip of my cocktail.

"I feel old, though. That's why I did my will. I've been getting strange pains in my hips."

I picked up my fork and started to eat again. Was seven too early to call it a night?

"What can I get for you guys?" the waitress asked brightly, appearing at our table with a small blue notebook and pen.

"Time for dessert already?" Simon looked up.

"The cheesecake would be perfect please," I said, smiling at the waitress.

"Decisions, decisions, decisions." He sighed loudly, spreading out the huge menu on the table. "I like a good apple pie, but you can't argue with a classic cheesecake. But then, there's always the chocolate fudge cake. That's a personal favourite. What to do, what to do."

The waitress forced a smile. I looked around, it was a busy night. I could see couples tucking into burgers and chips and guys sharing pizza and beer.

"Shall I come back?" she asked politely.

"I've made a decision," he announced. "I'm gonna go with the apple pie and custard."

She scrawled down his choice in her notebook.

Simon shook his head. "Hold that thought. Could I just have custard? A big bowl of custard, but not too hot. I don't wanna make these any worse," he said, pointing to his chapped lips.

I surreptitiously glanced down at my phone in my lap. I'd noticed the screen light up a few seconds ago. It was Sir. He'd sent one message, *OK, so we can agree on no marks above the shoulders ever, but spanking, biting, and scratching anywhere else are fine.* We were still negotiating terms so we could move forward and meet again. I was happy for the delay. I still hadn't worked out my feelings, yet. I messaged back, *Yes, Sir. Agreed.*

I looked up to see Simon applying lip balm from a small, clinical-looking tub in front of him. The waitress was gone. I was being rude.

"So, do you have any brothers or sisters?" I asked politely, putting my phone down.

"Yeah, just one brother, Clive. He's dead now."

"That's terrible. I'm really sorry."

"It's fine. He was a stepbrother and we were never that close anyway. If I'm honest, he was a bit of a miserable so and so," he said, reaching for the lip balm again. "How about you?"

"I've got one older brother who lives in Spain now. We're really close, though—we grew up together." I smiled.

Simon nodded so I took it as my cue to carry on talking. All I had to do was fill the next ten minutes.

Luckily, a detailed comparison of British ice cream and Spanish ice cream made the minutes fly by. When my cheesecake arrived, I ate it quickly. I reached over the table to pass Simon's custard to him, which had been confused as a side dish. He put his spoon into the bright-yellow custard and held it there before putting it to his lips and slurping it into his mouth. I flinched. I couldn't hold out any longer. It was time to call it a night.

In the taxi going back to my Airbnb, I breathed a sigh of relief. I checked my phone. I had two more messages, *We are agreed. You can add the new rule to your contract.* And five minutes later, *What's holding you back from meeting a second time? What are you scared of?*

The truth was, I didn't know the answer. He'd given me the world's best orgasm and made me feel exhilarated. I loved the way he looked at me, and the way he talked but I couldn't shake my uneasy feeling.

My phone vibrated again, *I want you to be 100% safe and secure, Tilly.*

It was important I acted overly-cautiously for once. I couldn't enter into another toxic situation. Plus, I had a burning question but Sir wasn't the person to ask. I would wait until I had spoken to Amelia and Sarah and then I'd replied properly. There was no rush. I answered, *Yes Sir. May I have time to think before I answer your question?*

Of course. Take as much time as you need. Dismissed until nine a.m.

* * *

"He farted when he ate beef?" Sarah asked, taking a step back from her pyramid of bottles.

It was eight the next morning, and we were setting up a stand at a fruit festival in the centre of Leeds. We were brand ambassadors for a new orange juice brand, Alive. Our job was to hand out free samples to as many people as possible in the hope they'd buy some. I was the manager, which sounded more impressive than it was. All I had to do was turn up thirty minutes earlier than Amelia and Sarah and write a report at the end of the day.

"It could have been a burp," I added quickly.

"Oh, that's alright, then," Amelia said, outraged, from her place on the floor where she was organising crates of juice.

I sighed. "Online dating is a train wreck."

"It *is* the way you do it. Where do you find these people?"

"Hey!" I said, whacking Amelia. "I just got unlucky this time."

"*This* time?" Sarah quipped. "Remember Limp Lewis?"

Amelia laughed. "Yeah, and Dodgy Darren."

I shushed them. "Guys. Keep your voices down. I've told you, those nicknames are unfair. Lewis just didn't know what he wanted."

"Apart from asking you to be his mum in bed," Amelia snorted.

"Ewwww," I cringed. "It wasn't *his* mum specifically. It was the general fantasy he wanted to try." I shuddered, remembering.

"Well, the point is, he wanted to be dominated," Amelia carried on.

"True," I said.

"Which is not what you want to do," Amelia finished.

I nodded.

"And Darren. Is he out of prison yet?" Sarah asked.

I swallowed. My throat felt instantly sandpaper dry.

Noticing my pale face, she said, "Let's not talk about that."

"You're right," Amelia said hurriedly. "We've got something wonderful to discuss."

Sarah nodded determinedly, relieved to change the subject. "It's the perfect next step for you. Girl solo-travels around South East Asia, has an epiphany with Buddhist monks and returns to the UK to find her true sexual calling."

I looked at Amelia's playful expression and Sarah's excited face, feeling a surge of gratitude for their limitless support. My past relationships were a train-wreck. It was true. My friends knew how important it was that I moved on. They were one hundred percent behind my Sir Mission and I loved that.

"Honestly. I'd want a sir if I didn't have a Dave," Sarah said, focusing on finishing her pyramid.

"Really?" I asked in a high-pitched voice.

"Seriously. I want to hear everything. Don't leave anything out. You have to tell us every detail."

We were nearly ready for the day. Our stand was a mock old-fashioned greengrocer. It had a green-and-white-striped awning and big wicker baskets full of oranges. We were currently modelling brown baker boy hats and aprons. It wasn't our finest hour, but we'd looked worse.

"So, did you really have sex straightaway? I can't believe you didn't meet at least once first," Sarah said, placing the final bottle of orange juice on top of her pyramid.

"That's why I was so scared. He said that most people meet him first to talk, but I couldn't be bothered with that. I wanted the real deal, I didn't want to wait."

"You sent him the contract before you met him, didn't you?" Amelia checked.

"I did, but I feel like he's only paying attention to it now."

"What do you mean?" Sarah asked, narrowing her eyes.

"One of the rules was no permanent marks, and I had a mark

on my face the morning after."

"I guess that's part of it. And they *are* gone now," Amelia said, nonplussed.

She was right. They'd faded much faster than I'd expected.

"But Tilly should get exactly what she wants," Sarah said firmly.

"Plus," I said, sighing heavily, "aren't I undoing the work of all feminists everywhere?"

Amelia frowned. "No." She shook her head. "Absolutely not. You're reinforcing the work of all feminists everywhere. You ask for what you want, and you get it." She took a passionate glug of juice.

"You're not afraid to embrace your desires," Sarah added.

Feeling encouraged, I continued, "What about - like how do you know whether a relationship is a healthy one or not?"

"What do you mean?"

I closed my eyes to gather my thoughts, feeling a little sick. "My question is, can you spot a toxic relationship before you get involved?"

Amelia stopped to consider. Sarah said carefully, "It depends. You might not know at first."

"There are signs though," Amelia said. "Like how does he make you feel?"

"Excited," I replied without thinking. I frowned. "But what's the difference between butterflies and dread? What if-" I paused. "What if he's like Darren?"

Saying my biggest fear out loud made me want to cry.

Sarah took my hand. "You will feel it in your heart."

Amelia looked into my eyes. "You know the doom feeling you got with Darren?"

I nodded.

"Do you get that?"

"No," I shook my head, vehemently.

"OK, well if you ever get that feeling, run away."

"Even if you're in the middle of nowhere," Sarah added.

"Or super late at night," Amelia continued.

"We'll come and rescue you," Sarah finished, looking deadly serious.

"And then we'll kill him," Amelia announced.

"Amelia!" I laughed, half-scared, half-pleased.

"We *will*," She insisted.

Sarah nodded, satisfied with Amelia's plan. She sank into a deck chair at the front of the stand and said, "OK, start from the beginning. I want to know every detail."

I laughed. My friends were crazy. And I wouldn't have it any other way. I stood next to the pyramid of juice and launched into a detailed account of the night, including the huge hotel suite, taking my thong off in the bar, Sir's box life speech, amazing sex and hardcore spanking. Talking about him made me feel more confident. If Amelia and Sarah weren't worried, maybe I shouldn't be either. What I was feeling was a healthy amount of trepidation and nothing more.

Chapter 6

I opened the black iron gate to our garden, avoiding the handle so I didn't get rust on my acrylic nails. I narrowly missed the low-hanging branch above the gate before slipping in the mud on the grass. Mum's plan of creating a paving-stone paradise needed to happen soon. This was like an episode of *Jungle Run* where I had to overcome obstacles to collect bananas and get monkey statues.

Mum wanted to find old stones of special meaning for the path. She said she'd look in skips and ask neighbours. She said it would add character to a normally soulless series of paving slabs and enhance the vibe of our dry stone wall. I put the key in the lock, pushing the door hard with my foot to open it, avoiding the rotting bit of wood at the bottom.

"Darling."

Mum flung her newspaper aside and gave me a hug. I sank into her arms. She smelt of the garden and a soft familiar scent I couldn't pinpoint.

"How was the festival? And the course? And the job in London?"

It'd been nearly three weeks since I'd seen her. A lot had happened. There'd been the acting course in Brighton, London with Sir, a promo job in London, and then the fruit and vegetable festival yesterday.

"It was great to see Amelia and Sarah. And the course was amazing. The teacher was brilliant, Mum. She knew so much."

I made a quick mental promise to myself to talk about my acting course in excessive detail so I wouldn't mention Sir once. I couldn't let anything slip out.

"What did she think of your monologue?"

"She preferred the first one—in fact, she gave me a whole new monologue for my other speech."

"Did she? Let's hear it. We'll have a cup of tea and you can read it to me, even if you don't want to act it."

"Thanks, Mum. It's not a light one, though. It's a bit upsetting."

"Excellent," she said cheerfully, "you know I prefer that to comedy."

I walked into our tiny kitchen to make tea. Mum sat down at the table and picked up her newspaper again. She hummed *The Great Escape* theme tune under her breath while she read. I grabbed my favourite Winnie the Pooh mug out of the cupboard and picked a blue flowery one for Mum. I squashed down my urge to tell her about the heated bathroom rail in the five-star suite. She wouldn't care, anyway. She preferred camping and fresh air to luxury hotels and cities. Plus, it would inevitably lead to questions about why I'd been in such a nice hotel in the first place.

My phone vibrated. It was Sir, *97% in my head, Tilly.* The higher the percentage, the more he was thinking of me. It was like our own private language. I was dismissed so I waited for his permission before I replied. He sent another text, *You may speak.* I typed back obediently, *You're in my head too, Sir.*

I opened the cupboard and looked at the stack of herbal teas.

There was way too many types to choose from. My phone vibrated, *Once you have slept in your own bed and taken stock, you will smile, I hope, and remind yourself what an amazing night it was.* I messaged back quickly, *I think you're right, Sir.*

I chose the raspberry and echinacea tea before glancing at my phone again. He'd sent one more message, *That makes me happy, Baby Girl. I feel, in hindsight, I pushed you too far, too soon. You know I'll look after you?* I scrunched up my face. Did dragging me across a hotel room count as looking after me? I ignored my thoughts and texted back, *Yes, I think this now. I just need to trust and learn.* He replied, *Good, Tilly. I have many wonderful memories.*

He had good memories already? I texted, *Yes, me too. I want more, Sir.* He answered, *More memories? Or more intensity?* More intensity was surely impossible. I meant more memories. No more tepid dates with online guys like Simon. Talking to Amelia and Sarah had made me realise just how much I wanted to see Sir again. I answered, *Not more intensity, just more of the game. I thought about what I want. I want to satisfy my desire to be dominated.*

I poured boiling water over the herbal tea bags as I waited for his next text. It took longer than normal. But it was worth it, *You are my Baby Girl. I will satisfy your desire. Look at your calendar for the next five weeks and tell me when you have a weekend free, please. You have a week to deliver this. Dismissed until eight a.m.*

I nodded. I knew the drill now: Reply politely and briefly even if I wanted to scream at him, "*why do you cut our text conversations short?*" Hopefully, it was some kind of technique to keep me interested because he was falling in love with me already and felt insecure. I could forgive him for that. I replied,

Thank you, Sir.

"Tilly," Mum called through.

I looked up from my phone. She wasn't in the dining room anymore. She must have stopped reading her newspaper. Through the ajar door, I could see her sitting on the sofa in the living room. She was wrapped in a blanket waiting for her tea. I'd not even notice her move. Sir's messages were all-consuming. I picked up the mugs and walked carefully through into the living room.

"I thought no chocolate because we're still on our health kick?" I checked, balancing a cup of tea on the sofa and one on the windowsill.

"Yes, darling."

My mind was full of Sir. Was he planning a weekend away for us? How did sub-dom holidays work? He'd probably book the whole floor of a royal suite in Paris. We'd take a private jet there and drink champagne and eat caviar.

"*Bake Off* or *Gogglebox?*"

I crashed back to reality.

"*Bake Off*, please."

"You look tired. You can show me the monologue tomorrow."

"Thanks, Mum. We're on bread week, I think."

Chapter 7

A week later, I was on my way to Tring for my long weekend with Sir. I'd never been to Tring before but it was hardly Paris. My phone vibrated with a long message from Sir, *Good morning, Tilly. Room 225. Second floor. There's a card key at reception. Champagne is in the bathroom. Help yourself. Stand with your back to the door in the marked point. Curtains closed, side lamp of the bed on only. Pink heels for the opening scene please with your new white lingerie. Blindfold on. Hands by your side. Any questions? You may answer with yes or no.*

I answered, *No, Sir* and got a quick message back, *Good girl.* I sat back happily in my seat, looking longingly over the top of my book of monologues at the guy's headphones opposite me. Headphones would block the rattle of the train out. Silence would calm me down. The continuous roar of the carriage made my heart beat painfully fast. No one could feel relaxed with an engine that loud.

Two hours later, when the train pulled into Tring there was a total lack of coffee shops, or *any* shops for that matter. Plus, the taxi that arrived to pick me up was alarmingly rickety. It'd break down any second now, and I'd be stranded in a field of sheep with no phone signal. This was nothing like our London experience. Tring didn't seem like the sort of place to have an efficient car breakdown team. Why were we meeting in the middle of nowhere?

The taxi pulled up at the front of a country mansion next to a fountain of water dancing in the sun. This was more like it. I walked briskly over the manicured lawn. My heels sank into the grass with every step. Croquet players glared at me as if I'd grabbed their little croquet bats and hit their poodle dog on the head. I must've broken an unspoken rule.

I reached the marble steps and collected my key card from reception as coolly as I could, resisting the urge to confess my lawn sin to the receptionist. It would be my first blunder of many, so there was no point in wasting her time.

I got to my room with only twenty minutes left, so I rushed straight into the bathroom where I found my nemesis. Waiting for me in the sink, surrounded by ice, was the bottle of champagne Sir had mentioned. He'd casually said, *Help yourself*, as if he were being generous and not putting me at risk of a serious cork-related injury or a thousand-pound bill for damaging the hotel.

I took a deep breath, peeled off the wire, put my thumb over the cork, and wiggled it off. I braced myself for impact and jumped when it popped loudly. A happy gush of champagne fizzed into the sink. I grabbed the glasses and poured two, feeling proud.

I looked around the bathroom, noticing Sir's messy toiletries. I thought the room was supposed to look like no one had ever arrived? I took a big gulp of champagne. The bubbles caught the back of my throat. I took another swig, admiring the black tubs and expensive labels. No wonder he looked so good.

My heart skipped a beat as I walked into the bedroom and spotted the handcuffs and blindfold waiting dangerously on the bed. They weren't fluffy pink; they were industrial strength and looked ominous. In front of the bed on the floor, there was a sheet of white paper. Sir had written on it in black biro: *Stand here, you slut.*

My blood ran cold. Was it possible to feel terrified and horny at the same time? "Slut" was secretly my word of choice. If I had to pick one name to be whispered in my ear during sex, it would be "slut." I gulped down the rest of my drink, wishing it was vodka. I straightened my hair as fast as I could, put on more mascara and lipstick, and inspected my reflection in the full-length mirror by the door. It would have to do. I didn't have time for anything else. I had three minutes left.

I ran to the piece of slut paper and stood on it. I'd broken the world record for getting ready. I'd clawed back precious seconds and done everything right. I looked down, admiring my new white lacy underwear. Two days ago, a huge La Perla box with scented tissue paper and hundreds of rose petals had arrived at home. I'd had to hide it under my bed. If Mum had seen it, she would have been outraged by the money he'd spent.

I shifted my shaking legs, feeling the crispness of the paper under my feet. The paper felt strange. My heart stopped. *My heels.* I sprinted back to the wardrobe. I pulled hard to free them from the mesh of the suitcase. I slammed myself down onto the floor in panic. If Sir entered now, he'd take one look at me and leave. He didn't have time for disorganised girls who had no clue what they were doing.

I put everything away at lightning speed before checking the time on my phone. By some miracle, I still had one minute left. I could use my last sixty seconds to sprint to the bathroom and down the second glass of champagne. But, instead I chose the sensible course of action. I put my blindfold on and stood on the piece of paper, hearing it rustle under my heels. I smiled to myself. Peace restored.

The door clicked open. The room fell silent. I imagined Sir standing in the doorway, taking his time, drinking in my lingerie-clad, quivering body. My legs were shaking uncontrollably. I heard a sharp intake of breath. Was he blown away by my beauty or seriously worried about my trembling legs?

I felt his breath on my neck. He put his hand around my windpipe, just as he'd done in the hotel bar. The dull pain of his fingers around my throat fused with a rising panic inside me. He pressed down hard. He either had a thing for strangling, or his plan all along had been to kill me. I was a few seconds away from death. I wouldn't go down without a fight, though. I'd spit in his face, kick him hard in the balls, and run for the door.

Before I could launch my attack, he released my neck and moved away. I straightened up in relief. I searched for his breath in the silence. Strangely, now his hands were gone, my windpipe missed them.

Minutes felt like hours as I waited. I kept my back straight, hoping I looked elegant and not a nervous wreck.

Without warning, I felt his hand on my left inner thigh. My body came alive. Goosebumps spread across every inch of me. His tongue forced its way inside my mouth. I kissed him back passionately, leaning into his body.

"Stand up straight," He ordered, his voice cold.

I righted myself, feeling a pang of disappointment in my heart. He was so strict. He moved away. I let out a cry. I pressed my lips together hard. Why had I done that? I was supposed to be completely silent during a scene. Plus, there were too many things wrong with that noise. It definitely wasn't a sexy cry.

He was gone again. I felt like stamping my foot in frustration. I understood the power of teasing, but he was taking it too far. I wanted him on me. The room was eerily silent. Maybe the room was empty and he'd left immediately when I made my awful, not-sexy moan.

I heard a soft rustle of clothes. He was getting closer. His hands gripped my hips and he was back, kissing my neck and teasing his fingers under the lace band of my knickers. I pressed my mouth shut so I wouldn't make any more unattractive noises. He'd returned to tease me to an earth-shattering orgasm and I wasn't going to let anything get in his way.

In one quick motion, he pulled my knickers down and expertly unhooked my bra. I felt the relief as my bra came off. I stood naked, feeling shy, my nipples hard, my mind a blur.

A hush fell in the room. I stood tingling in anticipation. I could hear a clock ticking but nothing else. I flinched. My mind told me he was about to spank me, but I was wrong. He wasn't even near me. The sound of liquid pouring into a glass made me relax my shoulders. It was like music to my ears. I released my hands from their tight fists. There would be no spanking for now. I was safe.

"Drink," Sir said, bringing an ice-cold glass to my lips.

I drank thirstily, grateful for the alcohol. Standing blindfolded, waiting, was a vulnerable position to be in.

His soft lips replaced the flowing champagne as he kissed me deeply. His hand in my hair pulled just roughly enough to make me whimper into his mouth. I kissed him back, harder now, aching for more. He teased his fingers up to my thigh. I held my breath as he moved along, edging between my legs.

His finger brushed against me, and I gasped.

He tutted. "Wait, Tilly," he whispered into my ear.

I reeled in disappointment. I couldn't wait for much longer.

"All fours, please," he ordered quietly with an authority that made me obey instantly. Trembling with anticipation, I was no longer my normal self-conscious self. I felt for the end of the bed and climbed on blindly, moving as far into the middle as I could.

"Now spread yourself open for me, Baby Girl."

I opened myself for him, aware of how wet I would be.

"Good girl," he murmured. I felt his gaze inspecting the most private part of me. He traced his lips up to my thigh, stopping to kiss me softly. I bucked into him. He held my body still, stroking his fingers along my wetness.

"Oh dear, Tilly. You really need me, don't you?"

"Yes, Sir," I panted.

As soon as the words left my mouth, I knew my mistake. His fingers left my body.

"You never talk during a scene, no matter what I ask you. That was a test, and you failed," he muttered.

In a second, that felt like it would last forever, he pulled back his hand. I flinched as he made contact. The searing pain of his rough hand set fire to my skin.

"Nine more," he said calmly.

I couldn't catch my breath. My mind screamed at me to move away but my body stayed still. I wanted to fight back or escape but I knew how much harder he would spank me if I did.

By the fourth hit, my skin was raw. I cried out in pain. It was impossible to stay silent. "Please, Sir, stop please."

"Not until you say your safe word," he said, the force of his spank coming through his words. "We both know this is what you want."

I pressed my head into the duvet. The pain was unbearable but it subsided quickly. And as soon as the sting left, I needed more. It was the strangest feeling. As each spank got harder, the pain melted away. The sharpness of the hit was somehow absorbed. I pushed through into a quiet space in my mind. He hit me harder still, but I could no longer feel it. I was floating somewhere else.

"You can do it, Tilly," He whispered, cutting into my peace.

A final hit and the pain was gone. Just like that. He rubbed my hot skin as I writhed in pleasure and relief. I ached for his fingers inside me, but instead he pressed the palm of his hand against my clit. The coolness of his skin felt amazing. He teased one finger gently inside and paused.

"You're dripping, Baby Girl."

There was no sense in arguing that. As it turned out, spanking made me peaceful *and* super horny.

He took my hips roughly and whispered, "you're getting what you want, you little slut."

He thrust himself hard inside me. I drifted away into a blissful corner of the world where only Sir's touch existed. He pulled out, flipping my body over easily and entering me again. My legs locked around his body as I clawed blindly at his back, my nails digging into his skin. He thrust hard and fast. A low moan escaped me as I pressed myself desperately against him. I needed him to crawl inside me. I could feel him throbbing and pulsing as I began to clamp helplessly around him.

"Please can I come, Sir?" I begged.

"Yes, Tilly, yes, you can."

I shook under his strong body, holding onto his back for dear life, pressing my face into his chest as my orgasm took over.

Chapter 8

Sir peeled the blindfold off. “Welcome to the room, Baby Girl.”

I blinked my mascara-clogged lashes open. Everything was hazy. I gazed over at Sir to admire his Daniel Craig body, but a soft purple T-shirt obstructed my view of his abs. That was strange. I was sure he’d been naked during sex.

“Hi, Sir. I love your top.”

He laughed. “I’ll get you a towel.”

He came back with a fluffy white towel and wiped me down gently. I moaned at his touch, remembering my complete abandon just seconds before. How did he have such an effect on me?

His eyes met mine. “Are you good?”

“Yes, Sir.”

He smiled. “I can’t get over you saying Sir all the time.”

“I should, though?” I checked, feeling suddenly embarrassed. I didn’t want to get anything wrong.

“Yes. Perfect, Tilly.” He nodded in approval, before turning the TV on with the volume down low and placing the remote next to my right hand. He tied my hands together with a short piece of rope from his bag and began a call.

“Hugo. How are you?”

There was silence. I stared at Sir indignantly. Was now really the time for a business meeting?

He ignored my expression as he laughed appreciatively. He said, "Let's see what they say Monday." He ran his hand over the chaise lounge slowly before turning to face me. I lay naked on the bed, waiting. Who the hell was Hugo? Stuff being an obedient sub who waited happily. The ropes were digging into my wrists and I was hungry. I didn't want to lay here. I forced my hands apart angrily, but they wouldn't budge. He must have taken a knot-tying class or something.

"I'm just focusing on what's in front of me today," He said, smugly, walking over to stand above me. He watched me struggle. He frowned. I couldn't work out whether he was concentrating on his phone call or annoyed about my attempt to escape. Fury could be fun. Maybe he'd spank me again and we'd launch into another sex session.

"OK. I'll have that over to you by end of play today," he said before putting the phone down. He began untying me, immediately. I made grateful noises to encourage him.

"Stop bleating. You're a wriggly little fucker, aren't you?"

I stopped. "Yes, Sir."

"I'd leave you tied up, but you're too loud. I have important calls to make, Tilly."

Surely, it wasn't the best time to sort out business matters while I was naked on the bed? I rubbed my wrists for dramatic effect. I could see red marks on my skin, but I knew they wouldn't last. They weren't deep enough. He passed me a banana and a bottle of water. I peeled the banana, gratefully.

"The glass of champagne didn't go unnoticed, Tilly. That was very thoughtful."

I took a bite of my banana. Did he mean the second glass I hadn't had time to drink? I smiled but didn't say anything.

He would prefer it that way. He made a second phone call, sounding even more authoritative. Imagine if he were the CEO of a major company and this was his guilty pleasure—*I* was his guilty pleasure. I chewed slowly on my banana, imagining being tied up all day in his plush apartment. He could spank me every time he made a million pound. I'd be his lucky charm.

"You have one hour to get ready."

I looked up in surprise. His call was over. He was fully dressed in a dark-blue suit, standing in front of me with his phone and hotel key card in his hand.

"One hour," he repeated.

Before I could say goodbye, the door clicked shut. Once again, he'd left almost straight after sex. We hadn't cuddled, talked about how the taxi had nearly broken down during my journey here or discussed his work. But, what did I expect? He wasn't my boyfriend.

In the bathroom, I breathed in the fruity scent of my cleanser as I removed my makeup. I felt shaky, but more from the force of my climax than anything else. There were no marks on my face or anything that worried me. I was getting used to Sir's way already. I was a newly converted spankee.

Forty-five minutes later, my heels clicked on the stone spiral staircase as I walked. This was definitely a private health club for secret oil tycoons to relax in. The staff would take one look at me and ask me to leave—there was no way I was a tycoon of any sort.

An open door led to a big room with high ceilings where Sir was sitting at a polished dining table in a bay window. I sped towards him before anyone could ask for my room number and chuck me out for not knowing. My mind had gone blank.

My heart fluttered as he looked up from his phone, his jaw

tense, eyes bright. He gave me the slightest of nods.

"Please sit."

I sat down.

"Sir, madam, tea, coffee?"

I looked in surprise to see who knew Sir. A waiter in a crisp white shirt and black waistcoat hovered next to us, holding a metal jug. I smiled to myself—obviously, "sir" was a normal way to greet customers.

"Coffee for both of us, please," he answered.

A stream of boiling-hot liquid spilled into my white china cup.

"Do you drink coffee?" Sir checked.

I stayed silent. The waiter would be gone in a few seconds, so I'd reply then. I didn't want to say "sir" in front of a stranger. Also the answer wasn't exactly simple. The truth was, I *did* drink coffee but I was weaning myself off. I'd drank far too much on a recent holiday to New York. I'd insisted on having a coffee with every sweet treat I tried. I was now on a coffee ban so, technically the answer was no. One more day of caffeine wouldn't hurt, though—plus, if Sir thought I didn't drink coffee ever, it would be a nightmare. Every time we'd meet, I'd have to survive with no coffee. The perfect answer would be "sometimes," but he wasn't a middle-ground kind of guy. I'd have to commit with "yes" or "no."

He looked at me expectantly, waiting for my reply.

"Yes, Sir," I smiled.

He nodded. "I will be with my client for the rest of the day, Tilly, as planned. He is paying good money and expects a lot from me."

I sat up straighter in my chair. What, exactly, did he expect from him? I *had* to ask him what his business was.

"I expect you to keep busy and be quiet."

"Of course," I said. I liked being alone. I'd done a ten-day meditation trip alone recently, while I was travelling around South-East Asia. I'd been a model student during the retreat, too. I'd definitely *not* napped in my room at five a.m. instead of meditating or piled extra cushions on my wooden mattress so I could sleep. It would be easy for me to keep quiet. I had lots to do, anyway. I needed to go over my lines for my drama school auditions and read two plays.

"Follow me."

I stood up immediately, but he was too quick. He'd already disappeared out of the door. I tripped against the corner of the table and followed behind him briskly, rubbing my hip as I walked. I'd banged into some kind of wooden-encased steel table. It would be a lasting bruise, for sure. He strolled down the corridor, and I jogged on my heels to catch up.

We walked into a room with the sun pouring through a glass roof. French doors opened wide onto the lawns of the spa. No one was playing croquet now. Sophisticated people breezed past outside. A handful of women sat inside, sipping celery juice and reading the *Financial Times*. Everyone wore the same white flannel dressing gown and slippers. I looked anxiously down at my skirt and jumper. Why hadn't Sir warned me about the dress code?

He pulled a chair out for me. "Sit, Tilly."

I sat down obediently, and he walked away to a glass counter full of food, coming back moments later with cake and coffee.

"The banana is the best."

I licked my lips. Sir went outside on his phone, so I ate my cake alone. The first bite was yummy and moist. I closed my eyes as I entered a higher level of bliss. Mary Berry would bow down to whoever made this cake. What was in it? I tried to stop guzzling. I couldn't be finished when Sir came back. I was supposed to be graceful and sub-like.

In between modest nibbles of cake, I recited lines in my head. My habit of ruining every drama school audition I'd ever attended over the past two years was about to end for good. I would eliminate all nerves by living and breathing Shakespeare so it'd be second nature. The audition would be effortless. The acting course in Brighton had definitely helped. My luck was about to change.

I watched Sir pace up and down on the lawn outside. I could see his breath in the icy air. He was jerking his hands about angrily. Had a business deal fallen through? He sat down at a wrought-iron table, more subdued now as he looked at the grass and nodded repeatedly.

My phone vibrated. I glanced down and instantly wished I hadn't. My stomach tightened. Adrenaline rushed through me. I breathed out shakily. I had to stop the terror I felt inside. It was Amelia.

Darren's out. I've just driven past him.

I rubbed my forehead hard. Why was Amelia even telling me? It didn't matter. We'd split up a year ago. He had no way of contacting me. I breathed out, shakily. He *did* know where I lived, though. I scanned the room desperately, looking for anything to calm me down. But the composed expressions of the people around me only made me feel worse.

I studied a floral teapot on a nearby table. It sat in the middle of plates of carefully cut sandwiches and tiny cakes. I focused on the blue pattern of the porcelain, willing my fear away. There was no point in panicking. Everything was OK. I was safe here.

"What did you think?"

I stared at Sir, blankly. Where had he come from?

He was standing in front of me, pointing at our cakes. "Do you want to try mine?"

I forced a nod, unable to speak.

He stopped talking and scanned my face. "Are you OK?"

"I'm fine."

Worry flitted across his expression but he didn't press. Instead, he asked again, "Do you want to try mine?"

I smiled, gratefully. "Yes, please."

I sunk my tiny fork into his cake, happy to have a distraction. It was carrot cake with a small layer of cream cheese on top. It melted in my mouth. He watched me closely as I devoured it, his concern lifting when I smiled again.

"It's delicious, Sir."

"We'll have lunch here."

I nodded happily. I'd ignore Amelia's text for now. If I focused on Sir and our beautiful surroundings, I knew my fear would fade. Bad news didn't belong here. I watched the white- robed people milling around the grounds of the spa and sitting serenely in the Winter sun. They didn't look like they'd ever worried about anything. Their minds must be full of chandeliers and roll-top baths. I longed for their blissful lives. I watched a lady sip a black coffee and write a precise note in her leather-bound journal. She'd *definitely* never made terrible relationship decisions or been scared of an ex-boyfriend. She looked naturally composed and totally immaculate. She oozed confidence. One thing was for sure, I'd never belong in a place like this.

Chapter 9

"Would you eat chicken curry?"

I had no idea what to say. It was the next evening, and we were eating out in a gorgeous restaurant. I thought the deal was I didn't decide anything for myself and sat elegantly while Sir did everything for me. I didn't want any responsibility when I was with him, not even choosing food.

"Tilly?"

I panicked. I had to commit. I *was* hungry. Hopefully, the curry would come with poppadoms and a massive naan bread dripping with butter. "Yes, Sir. I love curry."

"Excellent, Tilly," he said, a glimmer of surprise in his eyes.

Perhaps, I didn't look like the curry type. What *did* a curry lover look like? I took a swig of my third cocktail. I had so many questions. It was time to learn more about the elusive Sir. There was so much I didn't know.

"Sir, can I ask a question?"

"Yes, Tilly."

"How many relationships have you had?"

He folded his napkin and placed it next to his plate, thoughtfully. "Long ones?"

I nodded.

"I've had two seven-year relationships and one nine-year

relationship."

Nine years? I'd expected Sir to be a naughty Casanova who breezed through life spanking women but never committing. I opened my mouth to ask more questions but thought better of it. I counted silently in my head instead to give him time to reply. I normally rushed conversations and talked too much but I had a sense he was the kind of person who needed more time to respond.

I was right. I'd reached four when he broke the silence. "I've been lucky enough to have some truly wonderful women in my life. My first girlfriend did some brilliant things for me. I'd never read a book before I met her."

I looked into his eyes as he spoke.

"She basically gave me a list and said you have to read these books. *Love in the Time of Cholera*, *Birdsong*, *The Wind-Up Bird Chronicle*."

The evening had turned intimate. It was one thing to have amazing sex, but I'd never expected Sir to be a book lover. My Casanova image of him evaporated, and a handsome, shy man who loved to dominate in the bedroom but buried his head in books throughout the day replaced it. He definitely wasn't toxic. That was for sure. My heart was melting.

"Will you send me the list, Sir? I want to remember."

He'd mentioned a few books I'd not read yet. We could hold a monthly book club and discuss our favourite characters while kissing. Maybe he could spank me if I disagreed with him about plot lines.

"I'd love to." He smiled.

I fought the urge to profess my undying love for him. We were clearly made for each other. I was categorically not allowed to fall in love though. I had promised myself that.

This was about sex and nothing else.

"I was cheated on in my first relationship," Sir said, sipping his wine calmly.

I opened my eyes wide. Maybe heartbreak was the reason he'd chosen to become a dom—he'd abandoned normal relationships because he was sick of being cheated on and would never be able to trust another woman again.

"Have *you* ever cheated?" he asked.

I was temporarily speechless. That was a big question.

He waited silently for me to answer, an unreadable expression across his face.

Before I'd realised I was talking, I replied, "Many times."

Many times? Why on earth had I said that? I'd cheated a terrible amount of times in my first relationship, but that was down to neglect and lack of love. Lewis had been useless at texting. Plus, he'd refused to use public transport so when I'd gone to university we'd not seen each other for months. I'd sunk into a destructive spiral of one-night stands in order to win back his attention. I'd only been nineteen at the time—surely, I could be forgiven and it could be put down to a naive first experience of love?

"We're the same, Sir," I said with a sudden surge of emotion.

"We're not," he said, shaking his head firmly. His jaw was tight.

I should never have said I'd cheated many times. It made me look bad. Normally, I was loyal. We *were* the same.

"You are my sub," he added, matter of factly.

I downed my drink and tuned out his voice. He couldn't say we weren't the same because he had no idea what I was like. He knew nothing about me. Reminding me I was his sub was basically his way of saying he'd never have feelings for me. His rejection shouldn't hurt, but it did.

"For two straight years, I did nothing. I didn't have sex, I didn't even look at a woman in a sexual way. I just meditated and focused."

He was a book lover *and* an enlightened monk? That was me. Or at least what my aim had been when I'd set out travelling.

"I did that too," I said excitedly. I didn't need to tell Sir I'd ended up finding a shop that sold Cornetto ice creams on the monastery grounds and stuffed a nonspiritual amount into my mouth every day.

"What's that?"

"*That* is meditation and not having sex, Sir. Obviously," I said surlily.

"Nighttime Tilly has arrived," he retorted, his eyes sparkling.

"What do you mean?" I laughed. *He had a name for me?*

"You're super quiet and obedient during the day, and then when it comes to the evening, you turn feisty and argue back and say whatever you want."

Nighttime Tilly sounded fun. I scooted closer to him.

He tutted. "You should wait for my permission to move."

His hand lightly gripped my neck for three seconds. I studied his stubble, not daring to look around at the restaurant, in case anyone was watching. I breathed a sigh of relief when he let go. I didn't want to make people feel uncomfortable.

"Nighttime Tilly. Can you change your train ticket?"

"What?" I asked blankly.

"Pardon, Sir," he corrected me.

"Pardon? My train ticket, Sir?"

"Yes. I would like you to change your train ticket. Don't leave so early in the morning. We should have breakfast together."

I turned to get my phone out of my bag. My train left at seven tomorrow morning. I would change it now.

"Not now, Tilly."

"Yes, Sir," I said, bowing my head.

Why not now? What if there was an unexpected spike in train ticket cancellations and, by tomorrow morning, all tickets were sold out? Or perhaps I had to switch my ticket a certain amount of hours before my original train left.

"You're so beautiful, Baby Girl." He muttered to himself, "Be careful what you wish for."

I giggled politely but wondered what he meant. There was no bad side to our situation together, was there?

"I bet men go crazy over you," he murmured.

An unwanted image of Darren shot into my head and I closed my eyes, pushing it to the back of my mind. Tonight was not the night for bad memories. Being with Sir was like an escape. I wouldn't allow anything to ruin it.

"Baby Girl?"

"Nothing Sir." I smiled brightly, opening my eyes quickly.

He watched me carefully but I sat up straighter and kept smiling. And, to my relief, at that exact moment, our food arrived. There was no dripping naan bread, but it smelt amazing. I waited as Sir checked his phone and took a photo of his plate. He finally picked up his cutlery to start.

"Just showing people your food, Sir?"

"Yes, Tilly," he said, looking up in surprise.

Maybe he had a secret food blog.

"You may begin," he said.

Finally. I grabbed my cutlery. There was no time to worry about whether it was OK to eat with a spoon here. I was starving.

After a few mouthfuls, Sir began to talk. "Historically—"

I savoured the delicious flavours of the curry, barely able to hear him. I was in food heaven.

"Here we go," he continued. "Historically, I've never taken a sub here. Not one. You're the first."

I made a face. Was I supposed to feel special? All it did was remind me I was one of many. I wasn't the first and I probably wouldn't be the last.

"I can have other subs, you know," he said pointedly.

My heart stopped. My quiet book-lover Sir was gone.

"You can have *other* subs? Normally, in the past? Or now?" I asked, gulping my cocktail down in order to keep calm and not screech too much.

"Now."

I thought the rule was we could date romantically but we couldn't have another sub or dom. He'd specifically said, *I've made you my ONLY sub.* Plus, it was in my contract. I never would have chosen him if I knew he wanted to have other subs.

"You said you were getting rid of everyone, that I had a job to do."

"I love how you quote me," he said admiringly.

I ignored him. "It's in the contract, Sir."

"Look at it."

I took my phone out of my handbag, but from his expression, I had a bad feeling he was right. I'd made a contract, but he'd made one too, and the truth was, we hadn't exactly been organised. We should have mixed both into one document straight away and signed it. I opened my notes. There was his contract. *Clause three: I am not messing about. I will have only one other sub.* I read it again. My eyes stopped on the last four words. My heart fell. One *other.* Not one. How had I missed that?

I laughed in shock. "Sir. The way you wrote it, it was misleading, you—"

I stopped midsentence and fell silent. He'd tricked me, but this restaurant wasn't the place to have an argument. People were happily eating their food and enjoying their evenings together. I could feel anger fizzing inside me. Did one other sub mean he had someone specific? Was he having sex with someone else?

"I can't help the way you read it," he said coldly.

I looked at my bag longingly—a smack to the face wouldn't go amiss. I could knock him off his smug seat easily.

"I'm your Sir, you're my sub. Really, I can have as many subs as I like. It's up to me."

That wasn't true. I looked around the restaurant. Were there any witnesses to this madness?

"Baby Girl?" he asked. "Are you having a meltdown?"

And now he was goading me. I shook my head in disbelief.

"This doesn't suit you," he snapped.

I frowned. No way was he annoyed at *me*. How had he switched from wonderful to an absolute cock, in an instant? I couldn't let him get away with this. I had to say something.

"But why did you say you had made me your only sub?"

"Go to the bathroom and sort yourself out."

I stood up, my blood boiling. People who ignored questions were not to be trusted. How could he leave a question hanging in the air without giving it a satisfactory response or at least telling me he'd answer another time? He handed me my handbag. I snatched it and walked away.

In the toilets, I looked at myself in the mirror. I would not crumple into a ball and sob. I brushed my hair and applied more lipstick. I looked around the bathroom, noticing tiny marble birds on the sink taps and hand-painted patterns on each cubicle door. I would definitely have a bathroom like this when I got my own house, minus the cubicles. The birds were a work of art. I couldn't let this wonderful place be ruined by the world's biggest dickhead.

I marched back through the restaurant. I controlled this night. I'd do what I wanted and I wouldn't let Sir make me feel sad.

"Better?" he asked as I sat down.

I felt a flash of fury. *Better?* Technically, I wasn't better because he was still a cock; however, I had chosen to rise above his cruel confession and have an amazing night anyway. He admitted no responsibility for his actions. He was either having sex with loads of other women or saying it simply to upset me. Either way, he was being heartless and rude.

I nodded silently.

"Good, let's enjoy ourselves." He smiled.

I ignored the temptation to throw my drink in his face. I wanted to grab him and squeeze his cheeks until he apologised. But, instead, I placed my hands in my lap, straightened my back, and looked beyond him as if there was something of great interest in the distance. I would become the world's best sub so he'd fall hopelessly in love with me and cry when I broke his heart. He had it coming.

Chapter 10

I woke up the next morning with a feeling of sleepy happiness. Sir was snoring gently next to me. The velvet curtains were thick. Our room was pitch black. The hotel was silent. No sounds of people walking by in the corridors. And not a sound from outside. Not even the occasional bleat from a sheep.

I watched Sir sleep for a few seconds. He snorted loudly before returning to his gentle low hum of snoring. With a sinking heart, I remembered his other sub revelation. I loved that it was somehow my fault because I hadn't read the contract correctly. *What a dick.* I sat up in bed, suddenly wide awake. As I looked daggers at him in the dark, he rolled over and farted. I gasped. The outrage. He was unravelling before my eyes. First, the sub revelation, now loud snoring and farting in bed. Where was my Hollywood romance? I peered at the clock on the bedside table. It was 6:07 a.m. If I left now I could still catch my original train. He'd wake up alone and deeply sorry. I wanted him to feel the same sting of rejection I had felt last night.

A couple of hours later, I opened one eye. I'd fallen back asleep. The room was lighter. The bed was empty. I could hear water running in the bathroom. He was having a shower. Faint shapes of the furniture, now visible, told me it was much later.

I glanced over at the alarm clock: it was 7:41 a.m. I closed my eyes, my head still throbbing.

Minutes later, the door clicked shut. He'd not said goodbye. He was gone.

I walked into the bathroom, noticing the frost lacing the window. Was Sir somewhere outside in the icy morning making important phone calls? Perhaps he was doing an early-morning motivation session with a high-profile client.

I treated myself to a waterfall shower. It must be a mandatory element of all luxury hotel bathrooms. It was a blissful way to start the day. It felt like hundreds of firm hands giving me an all-over body massage. As I closed my eyes to enjoy, the conversation from last night entered my mind. Sir had gone from vulnerable to emotionless in an instant, "*Really, I can have as many subs as I like.*" He'd been so sure he was right, and the truth was, his contract *had* been clear. It'd said he could have more than one sub. I squeezed the shower gel extra hard. I'd never made a mistake like that before. I was an excellent reader.

My phone pinged so I grabbed a towel and checked my messages. I had one from Sir, *Twenty minutes. See you in the breakfast room. No need to dress up. Black cardigan. Black skirt.* I sat on the heated marble floor to dry my toes. Obviously, I was going to dress up. Unless he wanted me to appear in a tracksuit and no makeup.

When I got downstairs, Sir was sitting at the same table as yesterday. Outside the bay window, I could see the cold sun peeking through a heavy grey cloud. It would rain soon. As I walked closer, he looked me up and down. I placed my hands stiffly by my side, doubt seeping into my heart. My clothes were right. I'd been careful to follow his orders. I was wearing my black cardigan and skirt with black pull-ups and heels. I'd mastered doing my hair and makeup in record time. I'd not forgotten anything.

He exhaled sharply. "This place isn't good enough for you. Come with me."

A luxury five-star spa wasn't good enough for me?

He stood up and held out his hand. I took it breathlessly, rushing along behind him as he dragged me along. The thickly carpeted reception muted the sound of my heels. Outside, the cold air made me shiver. I wished I'd brought a coat.

"We won't be outside for long," he assured me.

A few seconds later, we jumped into the cosy softness of his Mercedes. He flicked a switch on the dashboard, and the leather chair began to spread delicious warmth throughout my body. This was a world away from Mum's car with the plastic seats that stuck to my back in the summer and felt uncomfortably cold in the winter. Green fields flashed by as we drove to a nearby village. We got out of the car and I followed closely behind him into the most stylish coffee shop I'd ever seen. He sat on the edge of an over-stuffed sofa and looked at me. I sat on the edge, too, so I could keep my back straight and look serene. The silence between us hung in the air. There was no music or background noise of people talking, it was still so early. His line from last night about crazy guys came into my head. I pushed it away. I hated unwanted thoughts ruining wonderful moments.

He noticed. "Whatever is in your past, you're safe now Tilly. I want you to know that."

He reached out to take my hand. I blinked away tears furiously. We didn't know each other well enough for tears over breakfast.

His face looked softer than normal as he carried on speaking. "We have the power to feel and create whatever we want, Tilly."

He rubbed my hand with his thumb. His skin felt rough against mine. I watched, mesmerised. I didn't want our time to be over. I didn't want to say goodbye.

The waiter arrived and the magic was broken. Sir ordered scrambled eggs, smoked salmon and black coffee. He started reading the newspaper. I looked out of the window.

"Back to normality," he said, glancing up from the paper.

"Yes, Sir."

"So surreal," he muttered.

I watched raindrops race each other down the glass. I still had a lump in my throat. I hadn't expected him to care about my past. We barely knew each other but I *did* feel safe when I was with him. I felt spaced out as if I'd been part of another world for the last few days, but it was probably just the offensive number of cocktails I'd drunk. It would be good to get home. I'd have a rest from alcohol and wear no makeup for a bit to let my skin breathe.

"We'll get your suitcase now. I'll drive you to the station," He said, standing up.

I rushed to grab my handbag, feeling a pang of disappointment. The morning had raced by.

"There's no point you waiting on a cold platform."

I shook my head. "No, Sir."

"Have you got your ticket?"

"Yes, Sir, it's on my phone."

"Clever, Tilly."

A smile spread across my face. He looked genuinely impressed, like I'd invented the idea myself and created the app over the weekend.

"Wait here," he said, walking away to the counter to pay.

He came back a few minutes later with a small paper bag. "You need to eat." He pushed it into my hands and turned to leave.

"Thank you, Sir," I whispered, clutching the bag and following behind him.

When we got to the train station, he parked and stopped the engine. "You can have these for next time."

He pressed three condoms into my hand. I frowned at the shiny red foil. Why couldn't *he* take them? I looked up to see what he meant, but he'd already got out of the car and walked round to open the door for me.

"Tell me you're home safe." He kissed me hard on the lips.

I opened my mouth to say something, but nothing came out. Where would I put them? It made way more sense for him to take the condoms. I walked away to the train platform, rolling my suitcase behind me. I stopped to look back, catching a final glance of his Mercedes as it sped away down the country lane. I opened the paper bag in my hand. Two bright-yellow bananas stared back at me.

Chapter 11

Splinters of glass lay on the bed. It was early the next morning. I was back at home. I was shaking. The glass sparkled in the weak morning light. Every muscle of my body tensed. I had to keep still. If I moved I'd seriously hurt myself. My heart was racing. I closed my eyes to think. As long as I stayed still everything would be OK.

I breathed deeply, trying to work out what had happened. Someone must have broken the window. We lived in a really safe area, though. Nothing like this had ever happened before. Mum had even left the keys in the front door once and we'd found them the next morning, hanging in the lock exactly as she'd left them. Plus, the strange thing was, my bedroom felt warm. If the window was smashed it would be icy cold in here. It wasn't Summer yet.

Suddenly, images came flooding into my mind. Darren's house. He'd been angry. He'd taken my phone. I'd searched upstairs, looking for a way out. I could hear him shouting. He was somewhere in the house. He was getting closer. His footsteps boomed on the stairs.

I'd spotted an old flowery rug on the floor and pulled hard at it. Relief had flooded through me at the sight of a trapdoor underneath. I'd forced it open as quickly as I could, staring at the tunnel below. I was saved. I'd jumped down and sprinted back home in seconds. But when I'd returned, a heavy cloud had hung around the house. Darren was coming. I could feel it. That's when the splintering noise had shot through me.

I opened my eyes blearily as my nightmare began to fade. It wasn't real. There was no glass on my bed. I stretched my hands out, running my fingertips along the soft duvet cover. A sigh of relief escaped me. I glanced over at the window. It was intact, like new. Nothing had happened, but it had felt so real. My brain was torturing me. I had to talk to Amelia and Sarah to work out why. We should make a promise never to talk about Darren again. I couldn't keep going like this. For a year I'd been fine, but now memories were hitting me all at once. I needed to change my head. A walk to the bathroom and a cold splash of water would do it for now. Hopefully, I'd dream of something else when I closed my eyes to sleep.

* * *

"So, he said he could have other subs?" Amelia asked.

I breathed in the musty smell of my borrowed jumper and shrugged my shoulders. "It was in the contract all along. I just read it wrong."

"Well, that's a load of shit. It's not your fault. He knew what you wanted. He should have told you outright instead of hiding behind a stupid set of rules."

I handed out a sample to an old lady walking past in a red coat and hat. It was two days later, and I was working on a one-day shortbread sampling job with Amelia and Sarah.

"Feed your desires," Amelia said, handing a shortbread to a passing man in a dark-grey suit.

"Pardon?" he asked, examining the blue cellophane in his hand, his brow furrowed.

"Feed your desires. You know, feed your desires with the shortbread, because it's delicious," Amelia explained, smiling politely.

He turned the small package over in his hand, intrigued. I sighed. Amelia had this kind of effect on guys. She ignored him and carried on handing samples out.

"Thank you," he said finally, holding up the shortbread with a big grin as if she'd given him a diamond ring.

As he walked away, she said, "There's always one."

"It's clearly a strapline," I said, shaking my head.

I pulled at my purple jumper. It was too big, and the musty smell was starting to get to me. I guessed I should count myself lucky, a big purple jumper and our own dark-blue jeans were much better than our last outfit with the baker boy hats.

"So, do you agree?" Amelia prompted.

"Yes. But I think there's more to it. He'd literally just told me he'd been cheated on in his last relationship."

"That's interesting," Sarah said. I hadn't realised she'd been listening. She'd been handing out samples at high speed next to us. We had a lot to get through, and she had another promo job on the other side of town in a few hours.

"He's peacocking you," she said.

"What?" I asked, staring at Sarah. Weren't peacocks blue with big, fancy feathers?

"Yes," Amelia breathed. "He's peacocking you, showing off, reminding you who's boss. It's an amazing sign."

"It is?" I asked in relief.

"He's in love with you." Sarah said excitedly.

I looked at her in disbelief. That was a bit far, we'd only met twice.

"It's not about love, it's purely a sexual arrangement," I said, firmly. But, as the words left my mouth I wasn't so sure.

Sarah and Amelia exchanged knowing glances before ignoring me completely and carrying on with the conversation.

"Sarah's right. He's falling in love with you and doesn't know what to do. He said he had other subs to try and claw back control and keep being the cold Sir he wants to be," Amelia said, taking a bite of shortbread.

I found myself smiling.

"He's probably never really been in love before," Amelia added.

I shook my head. That couldn't be true. Sir was older than us and he'd had loads of long relationships. He'd definitely been in love before.

"Dave peacocked me when we first met," Sarah confessed.

"Really?"

I'd never heard the term "peacocked" before, but maybe they had a point. Sarah and Dave had an amazing relationship. They'd been together since school and shared everything with each other. If *he'd* peacocked her, it had to be a good sign.

"Dave said he could ask someone out on a date if he wanted to because we weren't exclusive," Sarah recalled, still sounding angry.

I raised my eyebrows. She never spoke badly about Dave.

"A last-ditch attempt! Like a stag night. He's scared, but he knows this is the final hoorah," Amelia yelled, grabbing another piece of shortbread.

I laughed.

"You know you shouldn't eat the samples," Sarah said disapprovingly to Amelia. "I wasn't going to say anything, but you've had five now."

"I didn't know you were counting," Amelia said. "Anyway, we're celebrating Tilly and Sir right now."

I helped myself to some shortbread, feeling elated. Sir wasn't a cock. He was overwhelmed. His gentle words the next morning entered my mind. I opened my mouth to speak. I had to tell Amelia and Sarah.

"There was something else," I said quietly.

Sarah stopped handing out samples, noticing the seriousness of my voice.

"Are you OK?" she asked.

Why did Sarah's big brown eyes of concern immediately make me want to cry? I looked up at the sky momentarily, feeling annoyed with myself. I wanted to explain without getting tearful.

"When you texted about Darren," I paused, looking at Amelia.

She nodded, gravely.

"It made the bad memories come back even faster. I know it's been a year and I should be over it already but I've started getting sudden flashbacks of him shouting or I see the wild look in his eyes when I knew he was out of control. Knowing he's out of prison now and walking about makes me so scared." I stopped talking. Amelia took my hand. I could feel Sarah's hand on my arm.

I took a deep breath and carried on. "I feel terrified as if I'm right back with him and I can't get out of the relationship. I don't understand why I still think about him so much."

Silence fell. I felt a mixture of relief at saying everything out loud and dread because I hated bringing it up.

"Did you tell Sir?" Amelia asked, gently.

I nodded. "I mentioned it."

"What did he say?" Sarah asked.

"He said I was safe now."

And that's when the tears fell. I couldn't hold them in any longer. I wiped them away quickly.

"I know, we've only met twice and I barely told him anything about the flashbacks really. But, the way he said it. It was like he knew. Like he understood," I whispered.

Sarah wrapped her arms around me and Amelia hugged us both. We stood in the middle of the street, still holding samples of shortbread with stressed commuters rushing past us, looking bewildered at our public show of affection.

"People will think we're doing a flash mob."

I snorted, laughing through my tears. Amelia always knew how to lighten the mood.

"One, two, three," Sarah shouted and we spun out of the hug. I looked at Amelia's jazz hands and Sarah's big theatrical smile. They always made me feel better.

"Jazz hands are the answer to everything," Amelia said.

"Always," Sarah agreed. She paused and then said tentatively, "What do you think about trying counselling?"

"It might really help," Amelia nodded.

I pushed my hair out of my eyes. Therapy sounded serious, but maybe they were right. I didn't want to keep having nightmares forever. Darren coming out of prison could be the motivation I needed to take control of my fear and get the help I needed.

"I'll think about it," I said, tentatively.

Sarah and Amelia knew better than to push the topic any further. We'd always turned to each other for advice and they knew I usually listened in the end. It'd been that way ever since our first sleepover together when we were eleven years old. I smiled fondly. We would spend an hour putting face masks on and sharing our deepest secrets, before learning the dance moves to our favourite band, *Steps.*

"So. . ." I smiled, pushing the topic of counselling out of my head for now. Enough about Darren. "Do you think Sir might have been testing me to see whether I cared or not when he mentioned other subs?"

"Yes. Exactly," Amelia said. "Don't say a word, though. Let him come to you."

"Like in *Hitch*," Sarah added easily.

Hitch was our favourite film. In the beginning, Will Smith made the clueless guy wait even though he was desperate to call the girl he loved. And it worked. The girl ended up calling him and eventually falling head over heels in love. All I had to do was wait and Sir would explain himself.

Chapter 12

I stood in the train station staring impatiently at my phone. I had all the self-discipline in the world when I was with Amelia and Sarah, but alone, it was impossible. I couldn't wait much longer. Why hadn't Sir called me already to apologise and profess his undying love for me? I pressed my phone screen off determinedly and walked to the train station's coffee shop. It was time to forget all about him.

I pushed open the door, making the cheery bell ring as I entered. A waft of coffee and croissants drifted over, and I felt immediately happier. Sugar and caffeine would make everything better; plus, if I ate slowly enough, I'd kill at least ten minutes.

As I handed over a five-pound note for a fudge bar, my phone lit up. *I recall the first time we met.* I punched the air in joy. I'd done it. That'd been easy. He'd probably reminisce for a bit and then apologise about the other sub confession, and I wouldn't have to do a thing. The cashier gave me a funny look as she handed over my change, but I didn't care. Sir had texted me. I skipped out of the shop holding my phone tightly. It vibrated again, *How happy I was when I saw you.*

I sat down on a metal bench smiling dreamily, unaware of the loud clatter of trains trundling past me. Within a few seconds, he'd apologise *and* tell me how much he loved me. I was sure of it. Before I could reply, he sent another message, *How you kicked and screamed through our first scene and how shocked you were. Magical times, Baby Girl.* Our first scene felt so long ago already. I typed back happily, *Haha. I was so shocked. It was everything I had ever asked for amplified by about a thousand. I was out of my depth.* I remembered the way he'd marched towards me in the hotel lobby and kissed me hard on the lips. I typed another message, *When you came up and kissed me immediately, Sir. I keep thinking back to that moment. That's when I knew I was in over my head.*

But you didn't run, Tilly, he texted. I shook my head. I was never going to run. His sexy authoritative air was too perfect. Everything about him was perfect. I knew he'd pin me against a wall and punish me for being a bad girl. It was the moment I'd been waiting for, since forever. It didn't matter how terrified I'd felt. Nothing would have stopped me. I replied, *I wanted to be in over my head, Sir. For you to take full control.* I thought of his recent sub confession, and sent a final, more sombre line, *All I have to do now is trust you.*

He answered quickly, *Trust is everything, Baby Girl.* I sighed. How did he not know what I was talking about? I'd wanted this to be easy, for him to take the hint and explain himself, but clearly, I would have to say more. He should be launching into a heartfelt apology already and asking for my address to send me a dozen red roses. But, this was real life. I'd have to press him for an explanation. The truth was, I couldn't carry on seeing him knowing he had other subs. Sure, I shouldn't care what he did in his own time. We were supposed to be about sex and nothing else. But I *did* care. I took a deep breath and started to type, *That's why I got scared about the other sub thing, but I'm cool now.* I shook my head in frustration. Why did I always dilute everything I said? I should have left out the cool bit.

My phone vibrated, *Supercool sub.* I smiled in disbelief. Now he thought I was being a cool dude. Maybe it was a good sign that he didn't know what I was talking about. If he'd forgotten what he'd said already, it was because he'd made it up in the moment and it meant nothing to him. But then the clause in the contract had existed from the beginning. I shifted in my seat, feeling impatient. Enough of being polite. I had to find out what was going on. I typed my response and pressed Send before I could stop myself, *I meant the other sub thing. Not being a sub.*

Sir sent a question mark back. I rolled my eyes. This was painful. He was making me spell it out. I tried again, *I meant I got scared and tried to put barriers up because of the thought of you with someone else, but I'm cool now and know that chemistry will only make this even more exciting and different.*

I waited for his response. Maybe I shouldn't have sent such a long message. If he dismissed me now I'd have to call him. There was no way I could wait any longer. I needed an explanation. My phone vibrated in my hand, *I don't have another sub.* My heart stopped. That was it. The words I'd been waiting for were right there on the screen. I should screenshot them. Sir didn't have another sub. No loopholes this time. But, why had he mentioned other subs if he'd never had one in the first place? Maybe Amelia and Sarah were right. He was peacocking me.

I typed, *I didn't expect to care, Sir. That's why I was so surprised. I guess I'm still naive about this and learning.* He replied, *You are beautiful, Tilly.* I waited with my heart in my mouth for him to finish typing. Was he about to explain everything? *And sweet and not naive at all. Caring is just an inevitable consequence of being super intimate.* I smiled as I texted back, *That's true, Sir.*

I looked up at the departure screen. My train would arrive in two minutes. My phone lit up, *You are a perfect sub, the best and only. I must go, Baby Girl.* He never normally repeated himself. He was definitely telling the truth. I texted back, *Thank you, Sir. Bye for now.*

When I arrived home an hour later, there was a huge pile of paving slabs in the garden leaning against the shed. I walked over to inspect them.

"They're good quality." Colin's voice carried over the wall. I straightened up and turned around to see our next-door neighbour watching me with a big pile of laundry in his arms. The light drizzle of rain must have prompted his wife, Margaret to order him outside to save their clothes, which had been hanging on the washing line.

"We gave them to your mum. They're old stone. They've seen better days but they're good quality," he repeated.

"They look great." I smiled, enthusiastically.

"Good luck lifting them, they're heavy. We had to borrow Bob's wheelbarrow," He called cheerfully, disappearing into his house.

We'd always lived next door to Margaret and Colin, since as far back as I could remember. We were lucky. Our house was on a quiet country lane in a nice part of Sheffield. We were a tight-knit community. It'd been fun when I was younger but now, I had to admit, it was suffocating at times. No one could ever know about Sir, for example. They'd be dining out on the controversy for years.

Mum gave me a thumbs up when I walked into the house.

"How was Colin?" She asked.

"He was good," I laughed. "Good find on the stones by the way."

"Thanks darling. When you're free one weekend we should look in some skips together."

I looked at her. Skip window-shopping wasn't something I'd ever imagined for us.

"It'll be good to get some fresh air," she continued. "You'll be surprised what you can find in skips. Do you remember the programme we watched about the kids that survived on skip-food alone?"

"We should eat first before we go," I said quickly. She was not about to convince me to save money by snacking on food we'd found in skips.

"A lot of it is still within it's expiry date. It's like new."

"Do you want a cup of tea?" I asked, changing the subject.

"Yes please, darling. I got us a new flavour - peach and orange."

I made a "mmm" sound in appreciation as I admired the new fruit tea.

"You should seriously think about skip-food."

"Yes Mum," I said, putting a tea bag into each mug.

My phone vibrated. It was Sir. *Diary please when you can, Tilly.*

I squealed.

"What darling?" Mum called through.

I paused. "A good job just came through."

She seemed pleased with my response, "That's good. Let me know when you're free. We should definitely spend a few days looking in skips."

"Definitely Mum," I said. As long as we weren't eating food

we'd found, I was happy to go. It would be fun.

I focused back on the screen. So far, Sir had booked a night in a Mayfair hotel and three nights in a luxury country spa. How on earth could he top that? I looked at my calendar. I was working a lot this month, but I had a few days spare next week because my drama school audition was on the twenty-third. I hadn't told him yet. He'd insist on booking a hotel for me, and I couldn't let him do that. I texted back quickly, aware Mum was waiting for her tea, *27th and 28th, Sir. There will be an earlier date too. I'm still confirming it. I'm trying to find another date in case that doesn't work for you.*

I was tempted to tell him about my audition. Surely, I couldn't turn up in London secretly and stay in a hostel while texting him and pretending I was in Sheffield? That wouldn't feel right. I typed another message, *Also 22nd and 23rd. Any of those dates I'm free, Sir. I have an audition on the 23rd for drama school so I'll be in London anyway.*

A minute went by. I poured boiling water over both tea bags and watched steam raise from the mugs. I'd talked too much again. It was impossible to keep some messages short though. My phone vibrated, *Baby Girl. Why did you take so long to tell me? I'll book a hotel for the 22nd. What time is your audition?* I smiled. I knew he'd do that. I replied, *I didn't want to bother you. I know you're busy. Ten a.m.*

I picked up the mugs and walked through to the living room. Mum was absorbed in her newspaper, so I sat down on the edge of the sofa to check my phone. I had three more messages, *I'll attempt to stay over, but you need to focus. Have you already booked somewhere? Don't tell me you're in a hostel.* I swore he could read my mind. I typed, *I've booked a hostel but I can cancel it.* He replied instantly, *Tilly does not stay in hostels.* I shook my head. Sir's Mayfair life probably made hostels seem unbearable, but they weren't that bad. I did prefer hotels though. I texted, *Thank you, Sir. That's really kind of you. I would love you to stay if you're able to, but I know you're busy. I'll look at trains now.*

I stopped texting and opened my train app. Sir sent another message, *Aim to get to London for 6:30 p.m.* I replied, *What will I be wearing?* He sent a long message back, *Your black VS as the first scene in London, pull up stockings and your hair super straight. Pale lips, French manicure, your short leopard skirt and a pale-blue cardigan (if you have one?) open to show the strap of your bra. Clear?*

Mum had stopped reading her newspaper and was picking up the TV remote so I texted back, *Yes, Sir. Clear. I don't have a blue cardigan.* And then I put my phone down.

"*Bake Off*?" Mum asked.

"Definitely." I settled myself on the sofa and pulled half of the blanket over my legs. My phone vibrated but I ignored it. I'd text Sir in a bit when Mum was asleep. *Bake Off* was our ritual. It was a time just for us, when we put aside everything and sat together for an hour. We temporarily became baking experts, guessing what the judges would say and providing the programme's full narration.

Chapter 13

An hour and a half later, I checked my phone. The TV was off and Mum was upstairs getting ready for bed. Sir had sent two messages, *Buy one please. Baby blue.* I texted back, *Yes, Sir. I'll look now.* He replied quickly, ignoring my long delay, *Check Benetton.*

I snuggled down into the blanket and opened my internet browser. I loved clothes shopping. I'd never bought anything from Benetton before. I could see cashmere and wool knitwear. I couldn't see any baby-blue cardigans so I checked Hobbs instead. Hobbs was out of stock online, but I could order one and collect it in person in London.

My phone vibrated, *In fact, don't buy one now. Wear the purple jumper I got you with the black skirt. I'll send you to Benetton in London.*

That wouldn't work, though. Benetton didn't sell baby blue cardigans. *They don't have any, Sir. I can reserve a light-blue cardigan extra small to pick up from Covent Garden from Hobbs if you approve.*

He replied, *Why are we still discussing cardigans?*

Wow. That was abrupt. What was his problem? I'd saved him a tonne of time by doing research, but instead of being grateful, he sounded irritated. Stuff one-word replies, he was about to get an essay on cardigans. I'd make him apologise for his rudeness *and* agree with me. I typed furiously, *Because you said you will send me to Benetton, but there's no point because I checked online and they don't have what you want. Hobbs do, so I can reserve one to make it easier for you.* He couldn't argue with that.

He messaged back in seconds, *I told you what you will do. You'll shop after your audition. Then you'll wait for me at the hotel in your white lingerie and new cardigan. Kneeling for your Sir. Am I clear?* He wasn't backing down, but the question was, how on earth would I be wearing a new cardigan if I couldn't buy a cardigan? Unless I planned ahead and ordered one for him, he wouldn't have what he wanted.

I gave myself a moment to calm down before replying, *Yes, Sir. I was checking that was OK because Benetton doesn't sell what you want.*

His response lit up the screen, *Enough about the fucking cardigan. Dismissing you until eight a.m. tomorrow.* I gasped. That did it. He was so obsessed with controlling everything, he'd lost the ability to listen. I turned my phone off. I wouldn't reply at eight a.m. He'd have to wait and wonder where his obedient little sub had got to.

* * *

"How rude," Amelia said with her hands on her hips.

It was nine the next morning. I was leafletting with Sarah and Amelia in Sheffield. So far, Sir had sent one message and I'd not replied.

"I know," I said, grateful for Amelia's outrage.

"He's peacocking you again," Sarah said.

"Yes," Amelia breathed, turning round to stare at Sarah as if she'd just discovered gravity.

"Guys you can't keep using that phrase."

"But, he is," She insisted. "He's constantly trying to keep you in line and control the situation. He doesn't want anything to get too familiar or normal because then he'll be out of his comfort zone."

"He feels confident when you're within the sub-dom perimeter," Amelia added.

I frowned. Was that peacocking? The definition was getting a little hazy.

"Why don't you ask him for a collar?"

"Are they getting a dog?" Sarah asked, looking confused.

Amelia shook her head. "No, it's a symbol in the BDSM world. It means he owns Tilly."

"He owns Tilly?"

What was going on? Being owned was a totally different subject. It had nothing to do with Sir being rude.

"People can't own each other," Sarah continued, her voice sounding shriller than normal.

"It's the best way for Tilly to find out what he's thinking," Amelia explained. "It puts everything out on the table. No more secrets or peacocking. It means you're committed to each other. You know what to expect. The theatre of being owned is there for dramatic effect. Essentially, it's an eternity ring."

I smiled. OK, I understood now. Amelia had it sussed. She understood The Game better than me. It would be the best thing to do. I'd have physical proof that Sir was serious *and* loyal. Plus, maybe he'd stop being so rude once he knew I wasn't going to break out of our sub-dom agreement and turn what we had into a domestic relationship.

"You gave me three flyers," a woman said, pushing them into Amelia's hands.

"Whoops. Thanks so much," she called casually, putting the leaflets in the bin as the woman turned to walk away.

"Isn't it too early for an eternity ring?" Sarah asked.

"What kind of collar would I get? Is it an actual dog collar?" I said at the same time.

Amelia nodded. "It could be. You should ask him. See what he prefers. It could be anything - a bracelet, a necklace or an actual collar."

"How do you know if you can trust him, though? He's been so rude," Sarah said, looking worried.

I paused. She had a point. His rudeness could be forgiven though, especially once I'd made him apologise in person. Plus, I had a good feeling about him. Sure, he spanked me in the bedroom and was as dominating and hardcore as I'd always dreamed of, but during the day he was so kind and thoughtful. I remembered his gift goodbye in Tring.

I smiled. "He gave me bananas."

"What?"

"He gave me bananas. The last time I saw him before I got on the train, he gave me two bananas to eat."

Sarah stared blankly at me.

Amelia started to laugh. "Bananas?"

"Yes," I said impatiently. What was the big deal? Bananas kept you fuller for longer. They were a thoughtful gift. "The bananas gave me a good feeling."

Amelia carried on laughing. Sarah turned on the spot to hand out more leaflets. "Give Tilly a couple of bananas, and you own her."

Amelia snorted. "Imagine if he'd given her a banana cake."

I shook my head in disapproval. "Let's focus on the job, guys. We shouldn't even be talking, anyway, we need to watch out for secret shoppers."

When I got home after the leafletting job, I walked past the growing pile of paving slabs by the shed and unlocked our front door. I had two messages from Sir. One four hours ago, *I hope your morning's going well, Tilly.* And one a few minutes ago, *Is my little slut OK?* I closed the door behind me and took my shoes off. He was so insanely inappropriate. I'd missed texting him though and "slut" *was* my favourite word. I picked up my phone and typed back, *Hi Sir. I'm good. I was working.*

I liked being aloof. I walked through into the living room and flopped down on the sofa. He sent a message back straight away. *I've missed my little sub today.* I smiled and, before I could stop myself, texted back, *Have you ever given a sub a collar before?* There was a pause but he was still online. A few seconds later, he texted, *Yes, once. But in the game. Not as ownership.* My heart sank. Trust Sir to have done it already. Did in the "game" mean during sex? I hated the thought of his skin rubbing against somebody else's.

He texted, *We start in the scene. I've used rope before too. This requires a lot of trust. A soft collar is where you start. I can use a restraint. It will mark less.* I put my phone down. He was missing the point, the collar was supposed to be a symbol of loyalty. He was getting overly technical and making me nervous. I couldn't have marks on my neck.

I took my time replying. *Sir, I only wanted it because I like the idea of being owned by you. I don't like the idea of it hurting my neck or marking me.*

He answered, *I know, Tilly. Do you want to be totally owned?*

You are anyway. The collar would mean completion. You only have sex with me until either of us walk away. At this point, you have the freedom to fuck who you like.

I pulled the blanket over me. He was saying everything I wanted, but I had to be ninja-like with my next moves. If he thought I was jumping in too soon, he might run away and be a Casanova forever. He was like a rabbit playing in the grass—if I got too close, he'd skip away. I replied casually, *I would like to think about it, Sir.*

Yes, no pressure. You brought it up. I raised my eyebrows. Now he wanted it more than me. I'd successfully planted the seed in his head. I texted him back, *But to be honest, I like the idea of it. Plus, I'm not going to fuck anyone else so it doesn't make any difference, Sir.*

He replied, *My thoughts too. Dismissed for one hour, Tilly.* For once, I didn't care. It would be good to be dismissed. Our collar conversation had gone well. There was a lot to process from the past few weeks. Maybe, I'd make myself a peach and orange tea and sit on the sofa quietly.

As I moved to stand up, I heard a loud rap at the door. Time stopped. The knock came again. Angrier this time. I could hear a low voice. Could my movements be heard through the wall? I couldn't sit back down and if I moved forward, I'd be seen through the window. I'd have to stand in a half-squat and not move an inch. I held my phone tightly in my sweaty hand. If he smashed the window, I'd call the police first and then Mum. I wasn't sure I'd be able to talk on the phone though. My throat had clamped shut.

"Tilly," came the unmistakable male voice.

My vision went black. My knees felt weak. I should move or hide or do something but fear had completely paralysed me.

"More paving slabs here," the voice called again.

Paving slabs? It was Colin. I laughed loudly, the noise jarred me out of my frozen squat position. I walked through into the dining room, feeling dizzy with relief. As I opened the door, I felt suddenly embarrassed. Who ignored their neighbours like that? At least I'd been out of sight.

"Thanks Colin," I said, as cheerfully as I could.

"Was that a new fangled workout?" he asked, peering round the door.

"What?"

"The squats you were doing. You shouldn't fall for these fads you know. A brisk walk and a few vegetables are all you need."

"Thanks Colin," I smiled weakly, wishing I could hide my blushing cheeks.

"Tell your mum we have a few more if she wants them," he said, pointing to the two slabs he'd leaned against the wall. They were smaller than the last ones and baked orange in colour. Mum would love them. I closed the front door, feeling silly. When was my brain going to catch up with reality? I was safe now. There was nothing to worry about.

Chapter 14

A few days later, I sat on the train feeling proud. I'd become a super sub. I'd packed my suitcase the night before, put on a face mask, straightened my hair twice, and even shampooed and blow-dried my makeup brushes. My phone vibrated. *Are you on schedule? You may reply in two words.* I answered, *Yes, Sir.* He replied, *Are you excited?* He never normally asked whether I was excited. Maybe he was feeling guilty about being such a cock about the cardigan. I hadn't forgotten. He still hadn't apologised properly. The collar conversation had distracted things.

I texted a quick, *Yes* and glanced around the train carriage. It was empty. I plugged in my hair straighteners and ran them through my long blonde hair at lightning speed. I was sure I wasn't supposed to do this, but I wanted to look like I'd stepped out of a magazine. The models were always so sleek and perfect. It took a lot of commitment to be that shiny. I'd tried this morning but one step outside and my hair had gone immediately frizzy. I was like Monica on holiday in *Friends*.

Steam rose into the air, and I heard a crackle. My hair must be wet somehow. I smelt a faint whiff of smoke. Any second now, the fire alarm would go off and the sprinkler systems would kick in and I'd be back looking like Monica. I turned off my straighteners quickly, balancing them precariously on the pull-down plastic table so they would cool down without melting it. I pulled out my book of monologues and started to read in what I hoped was a relaxed way. I didn't want to be told off for disorderly conduct on a train. I was sure the plugs were only for laptops. If anyone asked me why my hair straighteners were hot, I'd play dumb and say I had no idea and was seriously considering complaining to Babyliss. It was a health and safety issue.

The train pulled into St. Pancras station. I emerged from my carriage, swishing my hair and strutting along, pulling my suitcase behind me. I looked like a combination of a magazine model and an *Apprentice* star. I felt my phone vibrate. It was Sir, *Walk along the platform to the end of the train station. Turn right into the Renaissance and straight through the bar into the lobby. I'm already there. Clear?*

I typed back, *Yes, all clear, Sir.* He sent another message immediately, *How long will you be?* He was so impatient. Really, it was only a thirty-second walk to the far end of the platform, but I couldn't take the risk. He'd definitely be keeping a tally of the seconds I was late so he could spank me in the hotel suite. And as sexy as that sounded, the pain was real. I texted back, *Four minutes.*

I slowed down as I got to the end of the train station and looked around for an elegant bar. I'd presumed there would be a sign for the Renaissance, but there wasn't. I checked my phone again. He'd said turn right. I turned right immediately and banged into a man in a thick black wool coat. He was basically a wall. I was lucky I'd not been knocked out. What was he doing standing silently wearing clothes that felt like bricks? I looked up accusatorily at him, but he smiled politely and reached out to open a door.

It was as if the wall of the train station opened. I crept through the huge door and whispered, "Thank you."

Clutching my suitcase, I shrank away from the stylish women working on laptops by the bar. I stole a glance at them, hoping to catch at least one person online shopping. Maybe they were *all* pretending to do professional stuff, and I shouldn't feel like such an imposter.

As I entered the lobby, sunlight streamed through the high windows. A soft scent from huge pillar candles hung in the air and mixed with fresh fragrance of lilies. There were fewer people working in the lobby and a loud hum of talking and clatter of glasses and china on tables. I looked around for Sir, but I couldn't see him anywhere.

"Tilly."

I heard his smooth, self-assured voice before I saw him.

"Here."

I turned around. There he was at a round table set for two with crystal glasses and sparkling silver cutlery. He stood up from his chair and kissed me. He was wearing a freshly pressed white shirt.

"Hi, Sir," I said.

A waitress appeared out of nowhere and placed a glass of red wine and the brightest blue cocktail down on the table. I narrowed my eyes. That better not be for me. The cardigan texts came whooshing back into my mind. He'd been so impatient and rude, and now he'd bought me a blue drink. Standards were slipping. He knew I liked porn star martinis. I shook my head in disbelief, but he didn't notice. He was talking to the waitress.

"Can we get the dinner options for today, please," he ordered authoritatively before settling himself in his velvet chair.

As the waitress walked away, he pointed to a chair opposite. "Sit."

I sat down, tapping my foot restlessly. I'd have to bring up Cardigangate. Seeing him in person was reminding me just how rude he'd been.

"Hands."

Time slowed down as he inspected my French manicure. I swallowed nervously and scanned his face. I wished I could read his mind, like he seemingly could mine. It was impossible to work out what he was thinking. He would totally win at poker. His face was expressionless.

"Good girl," he said finally, with a nod of approval.

I smiled in spite of myself.

"How is your world?"

How was my world? Well, the blue drink wasn't doing anything for me and Cardigangate was still vivid in my mind. Other than that, I was fine. The last few days had been interesting. I'd gone skip-browsing with Mum and helped her carry another pile of slabs home. And after my scare with Colin knocking at the door, I'd started researching counselling sessions. Enough was enough.

I looked at Sir wordlessly. He probably wasn't even expecting an answer to his question. His lightly tanned face looked peaceful. He gazed up at the arches above us and then back to me. The last thing he wanted was me rambling on about my life. Just a simple nod and a smile would do it.

His expression turned serious and he said, "For all I know, you could be with lots of other men in Sheffield."

I blinked in surprise. That was the last thing I'd expected him to say. We'd been thinking completely different things. It was true, though, I *could* be a female Casanova with countless dates lined up in my diary, wild sex every night, and a boyfriend at home.

"That's true." I nodded casually.

He stared at me, demanding more with his eyes, but I didn't elaborate. He didn't need to know that he was the only man I was sleeping with, the only one I was even talking to.

"I hope work went well."

"Yes Sir."

"Good girl."

He was dying for me to say more, I was sure of it, but I didn't. I liked having the control for once. His other sub confession had really hurt.

"They didn't have any other cocktails that looked good, Baby Girl. I had no idea it would be blue."

His eyes were shining with laughter.

"Thank you, Sir."

I clung desperately onto the last of my anger about his rude cardigan texts, but he was making me smile. Maybe he'd been super stressed with his businesses and that was why he'd got so snappy about knitwear. Our texts had been normal after that but now that I was with him, I couldn't ignore how hurt I'd felt. I took a sip of my cocktail. It was surprisingly delicious.

"We can get you another one, Tilly."

"No, Sir. It's fine, I like it."

"Well, OK. We can order a new one when you're finished."

"Thank you, Sir."

Silence fell between us. And then he clicked his fingers in delight. "It's not the blue cocktail. Tilly's angry."

I forced myself to frown. He didn't understand how important Cardigangate was to me.

"There was no need to be so rude," I said, pointedly.

"When was I rude?" His eyes opened in surprise as if he had no idea what I was talking about.

"The cardigan."

He looked blankly at me. It was only three days ago—how could he have forgotten? Whose life was so busy they forgot such an important incident?

"Oh! The Benetton thing," he said. "I'm always like that. You know I like things to be done immediately. I was concentrating on a lot of jobs and speaking to a lot of people. A cardigan was the last thing on my mind."

I shook my head. "No, Sir. You're never like that. You're straight to the point but never rude. There's no room for rudeness in Baby Girl and Sir. It should always be fun."

I had no idea where outspoken me had come from. I wasn't even drunk yet. I sat back in my chair proudly, ready to argue my point.

"Well, I really appreciate your honesty," he said.

He paused. I watched his face. I could see genuine concern in his eyes.

"You're right. I won't ever do it again."

I was speechless.

"I'm sorry Tilly. I never want to hurt your feelings. That was never my intention."

I couldn't muster the words to respond. *He was apologising?* I thought he'd be adamant he was right and we'd argue for ages. I was half looking forward to it.

"Baby Girl was angry," He sang. "I love it when Baby Girl is angry."

I laughed. A weight lifted from my shoulders. I had my apology. I should forget all about my audition tomorrow and let loose. I'd been so focused on preparing for it recently and so annoyed at Sir, tension had built up inside me. I needed a night to relax. I took another drink of my cocktail and scooted closer to him.

"You must ask for permission to move." He tutted, nipping me hard on the upper thigh.

His fingers dug hard into my skin. I squealed.

"We're only just getting started, Tilly," He whispered in my ear, letting his lips trail down the nape of my neck until I shivered.

It was wonderful to be back together.

Chapter 15

"Good morning, Tilly. It's seven a.m."

"Good morning, Sir," I said, squinting my eyes. Why was he not in bed?

"Thirty minutes, please. Meet me at breakfast. We need to be early for your audition. I'll drop you off in the car."

"Yes, Sir."

The door closed behind him and I snuggled down into the duvet. I'd only had six hours of sleep and way too many cocktails. The best place for me right now was bed. We did not need to get up at seven. He was definitely a morning person. He'd probably worked out in the hotel gym already and had two coffees. I'd give myself five more minutes. We had ages before my audition.

Three hours later, I sat on a wooden chair gazing up at a chandelier. I thought the government had made cuts in the arts? The last drama school I auditioned at was freezing cold, and the lights went off in the middle of my monologue. This was a world away from that. The students all wore silk shirts and drawled in confident voices. I needed an invisibility cloak. Why, with all the latest advancements in technology, hadn't they made one yet? It couldn't be that difficult.

I thought of Russell Brand. He'd successfully auditioned

here, and he wasn't rich at the time. He hadn't worn silk shirts. In fact, he'd had a pet mouse living in his hair, or at least that's what I'd read. Perhaps this school was looking for a rough diamond to polish. That could be me.

I sat up straighter in my chair, clasping my hands tightly to hide my Cruella de Vil nails. I'd taken the polish off this morning, but they were acrylic so I couldn't change their talon-like length. I was every drama school's worst nightmare. They didn't like branded tops or glamorous outfits. I was sure they didn't like blonde hair either. I was wearing all black and no makeup to balance out my hair and nails, but I didn't know if it would be enough. Sir had said I looked like I was from the cast of *Fame* when I arrived at breakfast. He'd made me eat porridge and drink loads of water before we left so I'd be full of energy.

The girl at the welcome desk announced the next set of names, "Ryan Mercer. Tilly Wade. Daisy Burrows. John Reece."

I jumped in fright. That was my name. I glanced around, no one was doing anything. Why was everyone silent? Maybe this was the first test—if I copied everyone else and stayed quiet, I'd fail. They wanted to check we weren't sheep and could think for ourselves. I should stand up from my chair and launch into my Shakespeare. That would show initiative.

A confident dreadlocked boy stepped forward. "Hi. You're my group. I'm an MA student. I'm here to give you a tour of this fabulous place."

"Wonderful!" I said.

It was important to be enthusiastic at all times. Anyone could be watching. The MA student could be a mole. He was probably a secret professor or member of the judging panel. I followed briskly behind him as he walked, making sure to ask lots of questions and laugh at any jokes he made.

After the tour, he led us to a small classroom to warm up and prepare for our individual auditions.

"Tilly Wade," a woman said, popping her head around the classroom door.

Trust me to be the first person. I'd had no time to warm up my mouth by pretending to chew a piece of gum that got bigger and bigger or eat imaginary toffee that stuck to my teeth. I'd not even panic-checked my lines.

"How was it getting here?" the woman asked as we walked down the corridor to another room.

"Oh, really easy," I replied, smiling broadly as my heart pounded violently in my chest.

"You live nearby?"

"No. I stayed in a hotel last night. I'm from Sheffield," I explained.

"Oh, quite the journey, then."

I cursed myself. I'd said the wrong thing already.

"Here we are."

I walked into the room, which was much bigger than the classroom. There was a wooden desk at the end of the room with a man sitting behind it.

"Hi, I'm Mario!" the man said warmly. He was wearing a red shirt with little penguins on it.

"I'm Ruth," the woman added.

"Hi!" I said with a big smile. I refused to be put off by their good cop, bad cop game.

"OK, what do you want to do first?" Mario asked.

"I'd like to do my Shakespeare."

"Go ahead," Ruth said as she sat down next to him.

I closed my eyes in a professional way. My first acting teacher had told me to take a moment before an audition to get into character. It was challenging when people were watching, though. I imagined Mario smiling and Ruth tapping her foot impatiently. Would Ruth secretly respect me for taking my time? I took a deep breath. Maybe she'd hate me more. It felt like too many seconds had gone by already. I'd have to start.

"'The quality of mercy is not strained,'" I blurted out.

Ruth struck through her notebook with a big pen. My head whipped round to look at her. Had she just crossed my name out? This was ridiculous. I would do my best acting ever so she'd have to reinstate me on the list. I opened my mouth, but nothing came out. The words had gone. All I could think about was Ruth and her notebook. I paused thoughtfully to stall for time, looking out of the window and repeating the first line in my head to jog my memory.

"'It droppeth like the gentle rain,'" I continued, keeping one eye on Ruth to see what she would do next.

At the end, Mario redirected me, "More urgency, please. What does this mean to Portia?"

"It's life or death," I said passionately.

"Well, play it that way," Ruth retorted.

I hid my anger and remembered that Russell Brand had been redirected in his audition years ago—it was a good sign.

They didn't say anything after my second attempt, so I began my contemporary monologue confidently. The words flowed out of my mouth. I was in character. This was going well. I bowed my head as I finished, the emotion still hanging in the air.

"Not very contemporary."

My shoulders crumpled.

"Contemporary is within three years. You should be looking at recent plays. Not plays from more than a decade ago," Ruth continued.

She was right. My contemporary speech was more than ten years old. I had no idea that was a rule.

"Thank you so much for your time," Mario said kindly.

I left the room, got my things from the classroom, and retreated to the bathroom near the entrance. I sat on the toilet and looked down at my blank acrylic nails. I was doomed to fail from the beginning. I wasn't made for drama school. I checked my phone. I had thirty minutes before Sir was due to pick me up outside. I could take my time getting ready and still be early. I left the cubicle, emptied my bag near the mirrors, and began applying foundation.

Twenty minutes later, I walked out of the front doors, feeling like a new woman. I'd even found a grey nail polish in my bag and painted my nails. As long as I did my toenails to match before Sir saw them, he'd be happy. As I dashed across the road to get as far away as possible from my failed audition, I saw Sir parked on double yellows waiting for me.

"Tilly," he called out of the car window happily.

"Hi, Sir," I said, rushing over.

"How did it go?" he asked as soon as I'd settled into my seat.

"Not good." I felt an urge to bury my head into his shirt and cry.

"Oh, Tilly." He turned to look at me. "Well, you never know," he said hopefully.

"Yes, Sir." I nodded, looking down at the floor. There was no point explaining the good cop, bad cop situation or my out-of-date monologue.

He drove us to a beautiful pub with green shutters and

flowers outside.

"Very close to home," he laughed, looking around quickly.

I giggled, feeling confused. Did I give off stalker vibes? He shouldn't worry. Even if he told me his address, I'd never remember it—all the streets sounded the same in London.

Sir ordered two glasses of champagne, and we stood together near the window. The pub was alive with rich people talking and laughing conspiratorially.

"A lot of celebrities come here, Tilly. This is their local."

I looked around. Who would I see? If Gordon Ramsay walked in and ordered a beer, I'd have to say something. My granny Sheila always laughed when he swore on TV. He was her favourite chef. I shook my head. He wouldn't drink beer, though, surely, he'd drink wine? Maybe his favourite drink was French wine like Sir. We could buy him a bottle and talk to him about his friendship with Victoria Beckham. If I played it right, it could lead to me being adopted into the Beckham's family. That was something I'd always wanted. My mum would understand.

"Don't look. It's important to be discrete. This is their place to relax," He said, noticing how excited I was.

I stopped looking around and stood still. As I sipped my champagne, I began to feel less dazed. I should be proud. I'd done the audition. Sure, I'd not done amazing but I hadn't totally forgotten my lines or made any majorly embarrassing mistakes. I put my hand on Sir's leg.

"Is that allowed?" he asked sternly.

"Sir. I can't help it."

He tutted. "Bad Baby Girl."

I laughed and kissed him on the cheek.

"This is the Tilly I know. You seem much more relaxed today.

You were angry yesterday."

I narrowed my eyes. I would always have told him off about Cardigangate whether I'd had an audition the next day or not. I was annoyed because he'd been rude, not because I was nervous.

"I prefer *this* Tilly." He finished his champagne. "Drink up, I have a special plan for you this evening."

Chapter 16

Sir marched down a busy street while I jogged behind him in my heels.

"Come on, girl," he said.

I felt encouraged but also outraged. I wasn't his dog. Besides, it was impossible to keep up with him. He walked like Batman on acid who'd just had a double shot of espresso.

He came to a stop and I crashed into him at full force. I started to apologise but he hadn't even noticed I'd fallen into him. He'd not budged. He was leaning down talking quietly to a man hunched in a doorway, wrapped in a grey blanket. He handed the man a twenty-pound note and carried on walking.

"There's nothing worse." Sir shook his head quietly. "It's a tough time." He turned to face me. His eyes were full of sadness.

Before I could say anything he looked away and picked up the pace again. The moment was gone. We walked up a block of concrete stairs and over a small bridge. I saw a restaurant in front of us. He pushed open the glass door, and I felt a rush of warmth from inside. I gazed around at the impressive pieces of artwork and expensive-looking bottles of alcohol stacked in colourful patterns behind the bar.

"It's a challenge to get a table."

"I can imagine," I said, in awe.

The restaurant was basically a cube suspended over the river. It was breathtaking. The water shimmered in the night and reflected against the glass. A waitress sashayed over, guiding us to a table near the window.

"Sit," Sir said.

I sat down. How had he got us a table? It was definitely an exclusive place. He ordered straight away. I tried to peer over the menu to see what he'd chosen but he was too quick.

"It's beautiful here, isn't it?"

"Unbelievable, Sir."

"A moment in time. We're very lucky."

We sat together in the middle of the busy restaurant. I could see the lights of the river below as we stayed perfectly still, looking into each other's eyes. He knew exactly what I liked. He ordered little delicious starters, fruity cocktails, and healthy salads. Everything tasted better than normal. The flavours were amazing.

"Let's go and listen to the music," Sir said, once we'd finished our food.

We walked down a grand staircase into a hall where there was live jazz playing and people sitting, watching, with glasses of wine.

"One glass of Bordeaux and one glass of champagne, please," he said as we reached the bar.

We moved out of the way with our drinks and stood and watched the music. He put his hand in mine. "One day, you'll be on that stage performing, Baby Girl."

I looked at the stage. It was possible. They held plays here all the time.

"You must always follow your dream. Don't let anything

hold you back."

I turned to look up at him. He squeezed my hand. "You'll be the star of the show. And you won't know it, but I will be here, in the audience, watching."

There was a beat of silence between us. I hadn't expected him to consider my acting dreams or want me to do well. Maybe, it was what any nice man would do but I hadn't had a lot of experience of thoughtful males in my life.

"I'll know you for a long time," he added.

"I would like that, Sir."

I listened to the soothing jazz at it floated around us. I felt content.

After a while, he said, "I have one final surprise for you. Come with me."

Ten minutes later, we stepped out of a taxi. I looked up at a glitzy sign above my head. The Savoy. My heart rate skyrocketed. I'd heard of The Savoy before, but I thought you had to be ultra-famous to enter. I was wearing a cheap dress. Would they have security gates at the door? Instead of checking for weapons, they'd beep for non-designer clothes under twenty pounds. I'd set off all the alarms.

Sir strode confidently towards a side door. I held on to his hand as a man ushered us inside. It was like a scene in *Goodfellas.* Everyone knew him. Maybe, he was a gangster and I'd unknowingly become a mob wife. I wasn't cut out for that life. Hopefully, he was an oil tycoon instead or a secret celebrity. I'd found some information about him online but not much. It felt like his riches were hidden from the general public. Perhaps, he was an important investor. I had to ask him.

I could see glossy grand pianos, and gilded mirrors everywhere. I was desperate to whip out my phone and start filming for Amelia and Sarah.

We walked past a woman playing the piano and into a smaller, more private area. Sir pointed to a sofa and said, "Sit."

I placed my bag down carefully and sat neatly across from him. My life had turned into a Hollywood film.

"Be careful what you wish for." He smiled.

I giggled. There it was again. He obviously had no clue what that phrase meant. He never seemed to use it correctly.

"I always said you'd be trouble," he continued, shaking his head fondly.

Before I could ask him what he meant, a waiter appeared to take our order. I watched Sir point at the menu. He must have been here before. He knew exactly what to choose. The waiter disappeared and we returned to our silence.

A few minutes later, I looked up to see the waiter marching towards us with a cocktail on a gold tray.

"Here we go, Tilly."

The waiter placed a glass of red wine in front of Sir and the cocktail in front of me. I thanked him as he walked away briskly. My cocktail came with a gold leaf; I bet it was real. I should keep it and sell it for extra money. The headline would read: *Girl starts a side hustle selling gold leaves. Bar offers girl lifetime supply of gold leaves to show support.*

"Go ahead, beautiful."

I took a sip. It was bliss, perfectly sweet with a chocolate undertone.

"It's wonderful, Sir. Thank you."

"You know you can compliment me," he said suddenly. He tilted his head and looked at me, his normal arrogance gone.

"Really?" I asked.

"Yes. I have to have something to work with."

He smiled playfully, but I felt his tension as he waited for my reply.

"I thought subs weren't allowed to give compliments, Sir?"

"You have permission."

I smiled. "I have a long list."

His eyes lit up. "That's good to know, Tilly."

The soft piano music filled our silence. I sat back in my chair and sipped my cocktail. Who knew he needed compliments like any ordinary person?

"I've got you a gift," he said quietly, dipping into a yellow Selfridges bag at his feet.

How had I not noticed the bag before? I saw the red box and my stomach dipped. There was no way.

"I thought this would act as the perfect collar," he said. I was sure I detected a touch of nerves in his voice.

The gold scroll writing was unmistakable. The red was the exact same shade. I wasn't seeing things. My life was about to change forever. Sitting in front of me on the glass table was Cartier.

"Can I?" I asked breathlessly.

"It's all yours, Baby Girl."

My heart was thumping in my chest. I pulled the outer box off, feeling light-headed at the sight of the red leather inside. I stroked it, feeling like Frodo in *The Lord Of The Rings.* I ran my fingers over the gold-embossed lettering. I pressed the small gold button and opened the box. A tiny gasp escaped my mouth: nestled inside was my soulmate. We'd finally found each other.

"Do you like it?"

That was the stupidest question I'd ever heard.

"I love it, Sir."

"May I do the honours?" he asked.

I nodded, wordlessly. He pulled the bracelet open and placed it gently around my wrist. He pushed it closed again and secured it with a tiny rose-gold screwdriver. I'd heard about the screwdriver. It was infamous. I'd buy a little silk bag for it and keep it with me wherever I went.

"I'll take this," he said, slipping it into his pocket.

My heart fell. He must have a craving for miniature tools too. It was rightfully his, though, and it was more ceremonious for him to have it.

"Only the best for my Tilly." He put his hands up and raised his eyebrows as if to say he had no choice. "You're owned, Baby Girl."

My eyes brimmed with tears. This was my eternity ring. No one had ever bought me a gift this beautiful before. I was owned by the most handsome and generous man in the universe. My chain of bad-luck relationships was officially over. No more frogs.

"You can have anything you want in this world, Tilly."

I looked into Sir's bright blue eyes.

"Anything. You just have to ask. Be clear with the universe."

Chapter 17

Hours later, we staggered through the hotel reception.

"More champagne," I called, joyfully.

"No. No more," he said immediately but then he saw my face. "Really?"

I laughed. "Yes, please. It's party time."

"Naughty Tilly," he said admiringly, pulling me close. "OK. We'll order room service."

I held onto his hand as we fell down the corridor together. I breathed in his smell. It was a heady mix of something amazing - both dark and light, soft and hard, all at the same time. Why was everything about him so perfect? I stopped and drunkenly pulled him closer. I ran my fingers down his chest, squeezing his arms and kissing him softly.

"Tilly?"

"You feel so good, Sir."

I grazed my lips across his stubble. He caught my mouth with his and kissed me. I used all my force to playfully press him against the wall, but he wouldn't budge. He pushed me back hard, his eyes flashing.

"Don't switch on me," he warned, his voice low.

"Never, Sir." I shook my head. A switcher was someone who wanted to dominate and be dominated too. He didn't have to worry. I'd never want to dominate him.

"Don't push me then, Tilly."

"I can't help it, Sir. I want you," I giggled.

In one swift movement, he pinned me roughly to the hotel wall.

"You've already got me, Baby Girl."

He stretched my arms above my head, his weight pressed into me.

"More," I said, showing him my neck, goading him. I wanted his hands all over me, I wanted to be tied up and helpless. I wanted to be spanked. It'd been ages.

He exhaled sharply, before releasing my arms as if he'd remembered where we were. He guided me into our hotel room and closed the door behind us.

I sank onto the bed, the drinks of the night hitting me all at once. The room was blurry. Sir joined me. He wrapped his arms around me. I nestled into him. Listening to his rhythmic heartbeat, combined with the ticking clock on the mantlepiece, made me feel calm.

"I feel safe when I'm with you," I whispered.

"Good Tilly. You must always feel safe," he said, hugging me tight.

"Sometimes I don't even feel safe in my own head," I muttered.

He released his embrace and sat up, abruptly. I looked at him. I wanted his arms around me again. I must have said something wrong.

"It's important to be positive. Your thoughts become your reality, Tilly." He warned. His face looked serious.

I frowned. I loved how positive he was but that didn't make sense. "Sometimes you can't help your thoughts being negative Sir."

He stayed silent, sitting on the edge of the bed, watching me, so I carried on. "How can you process your past if you can't have negative thoughts? What if thoughts come into your head that you don't want?"

I stood up, feeling angry. I always tried to be positive but sometimes it wasn't possible. My mind was my worst enemy. "Thoughts alone aren't strong enough to make the whole world positive. If someone is going to do bad to you, then they'll do it anyway, no matter what you're thinking."

Sir shook his head vehemently. "No Tilly. Our thoughts are the most powerful thing we have. We can make the world positive. Anything is possible when we have wonderful thoughts."

"So you're saying if Yoko Ono had only known to think positive thoughts, John Lennon wouldn't have been murdered and they'd still be together now?" I asked, furiously.

"What?" Sir said. "What are you talking about?"

"Internal thoughts can't stop external people. I just think if someone's coming for you, then they're coming for you." A sob escaped me.

"Baby Girl. What's going on?" He watched my tears fall. "Is someone trying to kill you?"

I shook my head, without answering. I stifled another sob. I didn't think Darren was going to kill me. Sometimes I thought he might attack me though. The truth was, he terrified me. Even now. My memory of him was so vivid.

Sir pulled me close. I held on to him tightly, pushing my face into his chest. I wanted to forget about everything. His shirt felt smooth against my skin. I pulled back quickly, worried my smudged makeup would make a mark.

"Tilly?"

"Your shirt," I mumbled.

"I don't care. I'm lucky to have your makeup on my shirt," he said. "Let's go to bed."

He picked me up easily and placed me carefully onto the bed. He pulled the heavy duvet over us. I breathed out slowly, feeling even drunker than before. He pushed a strand of hair behind my ear, and said gently, "No one is coming for you. Not while I'm alive."

* * *

"Let's make one thing clear Tilly. There's plenty of sadness in this world, plenty of bad people. I don't deny that. I've experienced it." Sir tilted his head to one side. "Should I reveal this?" He looked at me, as if he was weighing up whether I was ready or not.

I waited, eager to hear what he would say next. It was the next morning. We were in a bakery two minutes from the hotel. The smell of fresh coffee and pastries had greeted us as we walked in. The sound of the kitchen and people ordering breakfasts, added to the bustling atmosphere. We sat together in the corner sharing a warm almond croissant and a double espresso each. Hopefully, the caffeine would snap me out of my hangover.

I moved forward, placing my coffee cup on the table to show I was completely focused on Sir.

"OK. Here we go," He said, seemingly satisfied. "You have all of me now. My mum's second husband was not nice. Not nice at all. It was a terrible time. They were always arguing. He was violent."

He paused before continuing. "Eventually they split up. We moved out of the house we shared with him, to a safe house. One day, my mum went back to the house to get more clothes. We'd left in a hurry so we didn't have a lot of our stuff. When she arrived, he was there. My little sister was playing in the garden. She didn't see anything at the time. I was at my friends house." He looked down at the floor.

What had happened? I moved another inch forward, staring intently at his mouth. The coffee shop was loud. I'd lip read if I had to. I didn't want to miss a thing.

"I'll never forget seeing her in hospital. Her face was ruined."

My chest felt tight. He looked at me. The pain in his eyes was obvious.

"She was so fragile just sitting in the hospital bed there. The bed was so big and she was so small." His voice caught. "I should have saved her."

"How old were you?"

"Fourteen."

"You couldn't have saved her."

He shook his head. He didn't believe me. "I guess not. Anyway, it's not the point. I'm trying to say, that there's bad in this world but good always wins. When you're positive in your head you attract more positivity. I know you can't win every time, but you can drastically change your mindset and your reality with your thoughts. We all start off good. Most people are seeking connection, love, attention. If you don't give it to them, they go elsewhere, they find someone else. No one is coming for you. It would have happened already."

His words calmed me. I knew he was right. I narrowed my eyes. There was still something nagging at my heart though.

"Go on," he smiled, reading my mind.

"Well, sometimes you have negative thoughts when you're processing something, right?"

He nodded. "That's different. That's fine. It's about intention. When you're processing, you're allowing your brain to sort through bad memories. When you visualise or constantly think about something then you're sending a message to the universe that you want more of what you're thinking about."

"I see," I said. That made sense. If only he'd said that last night. It was OK to process bad experiences, to run through memories. It was simply the brain dealing with trauma. There was nothing wrong with me. All I had to do was let the nightmares and thoughts happen, and in time, they would fade to nothing.

"Don't get stuck with negative thoughts though. Process and move on."

I guessed that was what counselling was for. Enough research. I'd commit to my first session in the next few days.

Sir smiled gently before picking up his phone to work. I watched him, immersed in his screen. He took a sip of coffee occasionally, a peaceful expression on his face. The topic of negative thoughts and scary memories clearly didn't bother him. It felt like such a terrifying deal to me but he had the benefit of hindsight. He *was* a lot older than me. He knew everything was always going to be alright in the end. And I knew in my heart he was right.

Chapter 18

"Can I see it again?" Sarah asked.

I held out my wrist dramatically. On cue, Amelia and Sarah made an appreciative "oooh" at the same time. It was two days later, and we were in our favourite coffee shop. My Cartier bracelet was the first thing I'd shown them after I'd rushed in five minutes late. They were still in total disbelief.

"You know that's six thousand pounds' worth?" Amelia asked.

"Amelia," I said, blushing.

"What? It *is*."

"I know, but we shouldn't shout about it," Sarah hissed, glancing around.

"He must have a net worth of at least six million."

"How do you know that?" I asked.

"Well, if he gave you a gift that was zero point-one percent of his total wealth, he'd be worth six million. It makes sense. It's like me giving you a hardback book."

"Cartier isn't a hardback book," Sarah said, outraged.

"The pricing works, though, because a hardback is about twenty pounds—" I began.

"And Amelia's just been paid," Sarah said, finishing my sentence.

"So, basically Sir gave me a beautiful gift that was a little more expensive than he would normally spend on a date but nothing out of his budget."

"Exactly," Amelia said proudly, taking a bite out of her biscuit.

"Are we forgetting that it was the most romantic gesture in the world? It had nothing to do with his net worth, it was a symbol of his deep and everlasting loyalty to Tilly," Sarah said.

"Tilly's owned now," Amelia said, her eyes dancing.

"Amelia." Sarah winced. She didn't like the idea of me being owned.

I sat back in the worn armchair listening to their gentle bickering. I didn't mind Amelia's clinical breakdown of my bracelet but I preferred Sarah's Disney take. I sighed happily. I glanced across the table at them, remembering Sir's story the next morning about his mum. Amelia was taking another bite out of her salted caramel cookie and Sarah was stirring her hot chocolate. For the first time in my life, I had something I didn't want to tell them. It didn't feel right. It wasn't gossip. It was Sir's life.

"So, your first counselling session starts in fifteen minutes. How are you feeling?" Sarah asked, still stirring her hot chocolate.

A fission of nerves shot through me.

"I'm nervous," I admitted.

"That's normal," Amelia assured me.

"What if she's not nice?"

"Therapists are paid to be nice." Sarah smiled.

Amelia nodded. "She'll ask you gentle questions and somehow help you arrive at an enlightened conclusion yourself. It's always the same."

I laughed at her cynicism. As ever, they were both making me feel better. My shaky hands and nervous butterflies had subsided a little already.

My counsellor, Edith, was based a five minute walk from the coffee shop, so a few minutes later I stood up to go. I wanted to be early. Amelia and Sarah gave my bracelet one last stroke before I pushed the door open and stepped outside into the bright Spring sunshine. I was still a little jangly, but I had a good feeling deep down. Edith's voice had been soothing when I spoke to her on the phone yesterday.

Five minutes later, as I walked into her consulting room, I felt instantly at ease. I admired the candles on the side, happy quotes on the wall and a thick cream blanket on the sofa. It reminded me of Sarah's house.

"Take a seat," Edith smiled.

I sat down on the large oat sofa. It was soft but firm. I looked at the blanket, longingly.

"Make yourself at home," she said cheerfully, nodding towards the blanket.

I pulled it over to me and spread it across my legs. It wasn't a cold day but blankets made me happy no matter the season.

"This is your safe space," She began.

Why did I instantly feel like crying?

"Help yourself to tissues at anytime. For now, let's start at the very beginning. Tell me why you're here today."

I took a deep shaky breath. I could do this.

* * *

The next day, I woke up feeling invigorated, like I'd been at a ten day wellness retreat in Thailand and not a one hour counselling session down the road from my house. I looked at the clock on my bedside table. It was seven a.m. Today was a special occasion. It was my birthday. It didn't matter how old I got, I'd never lose my feeling of excitement. My plan was to relax at home all day before going out for cocktails with Amelia and Sarah in the evening.

As I walked down our narrow staircase, the tempting smell of pancakes and coffee drifted up to me. I opened the door to see Mum standing proudly next to the dining table. It was covered in confetti. She'd used our Christmas napkins and big gold plates to make the table look special. She'd even poured our morning orange juice into champagne flutes.

Sitting in the middle, in a black engraved box, was the biggest bunch of red roses I'd ever seen.

"They're gorgeous, darling. They were outside so I brought them in. He's a nice man."

I stepped closer and ran my finger over the engraved letters on the box. I had no idea Sir was planning to send me flowers or that he would even remember my birthday. I was glad he'd chosen to get "Tilly" engraved and not "Baby Girl," and thankfully there was no mention of Sir anywhere.

"Thank you. This is amazing," I said, giving Mum a big hug before pulling up a chair.

She admired the roses one more time before bustling into the kitchen to retrieve a carefully stacked pile of pancakes. As I drizzled a pint of maple syrup over my plate, my bracelet caught the light.

"What's that?"

"Just a gift, Mum. Can you believe it? He's really kind. He

picked it up from a little shop in London." I smiled, putting my arm down quickly under the table and focusing on my pancakes.

"It's lovely. He must think about you a lot. It can be lonely living alone." Mum smiled, sadly.

I didn't think of Sir like that. He was always so busy. I resisted the urge to tell her everything. She'd love hearing about his childhood. It would make her cry though. Plus, if she knew how much he'd spent on the bracelet she'd have a nervous breakdown.

"More coffee, darling?" She said, standing up to go to the kitchen, humming "Happy Birthday" to herself.

"Yes, please."

Some things were better left unsaid. No parent would want to hear their daughter's dream man tied her up to hotel beds and liked to be called "sir". It would be a stretch even for Mum to feel happy for me.

An hour later, when she'd left for work, I helped myself to the last of the pancakes and sank back onto the sofa to check my phone. I had one message, *Happy birthday, beautiful Tilly.* I typed back, *Thank you, Sir. The flowers are wonderful.*

Within seconds he texted, *Good. Any questions about them? I'm intrigued.* Since when did he care what my mum thought? I replied, *No questions. Just, well, it doesn't matter Sir.* I took a bite out of my pancake as I waited for his next message.

He answered, *It does matter xxx* I raised my eyebrows at his kisses and typed back, *My mum thinks I've found the perfect guy. She was super impressed with the flowers.* There was a pause. I cursed myself. I was intimating that our relationship was more than sub-dom. He wouldn't like that.

Oh, Tilly. Blurred as fuck. Now your mum's involved.

I didn't know whether "blurred" was good or not. He didn't sound happy about Mum. I should've downplayed it more. I texted, *Lol, no, it's fine, Sir. She will just think it's a guy sending me flowers and won't understand why I don't wanna get more involved. It will be a one-time blurred incident haha.*

I nodded in approval. "Haha" always made everything sound more casual.

He replied, *Tilly. You are involved. You are my sub. Nothing conventional, obviously, but you know as well as I do you are involved.* That was such a contradiction of a text. He was saying we *were* involved but I was his sub and nothing more.

Well, I wasn't going to hold back just because he was—I'd text the opposite and see what he said, *I am involved, Sir. And ironically, you're the perfect guy for me. This is exactly what I need and want. Super sexy and addictive.*

His next message made me smile. *Ridiculously sexy. I hope for one thing - that I'm always your Sir and you can realise your acting dreams.*

That had worked. He'd done a complete U-turn. He'd practically proposed. He sent another text. *Any news from your audition?* My heart fell. I wasn't doing well on the acting side of things. I replied, *I didn't get it, Sir, but it's OK, there are others.* He answered, *You will get what you want. Don't give up.* He was right, but drama schools hated me.

I stared at my phone, not sure what to say. It vibrated in my hand, *I adore you, Tilly.* I couldn't stop a smile from spreading across my face. "Adore" was one step away from "love." The idea of keeping our arrangement purely sexual felt more and more like a distant memory everyday. He sent another message, *Stay in the bubble with a little chemistry blur and all will be well, Tilly.*

I put my plate down, my smile disappearing. Why did he have to put a disclaimer on it? "Stay in the bubble with a little chemistry blur" must mean "don't break out of our contract." We had to keep our arrangement as it was and not let our chemistry develop our relationship. But why? I had a nagging feeling something wasn't right.

My phone vibrated again, *Enjoy your day, birthday girl. I'm glad you liked the roses. Dismissing you until ten a.m. tomorrow.* I finally answered, *Thank you, Sir.* I looked up at the ceiling in frustration. There was no point trying to work him out. He was a man of mystery. One minute, he was creating loopholes about other subs and getting annoyed about cardigans (which, by the way, I'd been right about all along, and we *still* didn't have the baby-blue cardigan he wanted); the next minute, he was changing my life with heartbreaking stories of his childhood and sending me roses. It was time to speak to my love gurus. They'd know what to do.

Chapter 19

"OK, go over each point slowly from the beginning," Amelia said that evening with a hint of excitement in her voice. She loved solving dilemmas.

"Take your time. We've got all night," Sarah said happily with a fluorescent pink cocktail in her hand. She was wearing a long, flowing gold dress. I'd chosen a short silver dress and Amelia was wearing a red trouser suit. She leaned against the wall of the bar, listening intently.

"We should write each point down," she said.

"Did you bring a pen?" I asked, playfully.

Sarah laughed and got her phone out instead. "Amelia's right. We need to be systematic with this and not emotional."

I sighed heavily. I'd been trying to ignore my doubts for weeks but now was the time. I had to face them. "OK, here goes. Number one. He's always on his phone. Sure, he runs a business, but sometimes it looks more personal than that."

Sir had looked so distant and serious when he was outside the spa in Tring, and he'd taken a photo of his curry later. Was he checking in with someone?

Sarah nodded and typed a note on her phone.

Meanwhile, Amelia yelled, "suspicion."

I frowned. It wasn't a suspicion, I had evidence.

"We'll start with whether it's a cold hard fact or simply a suspicion," she explained, realising me and Sarah were both staring at her.

I shook my head in disbelief. I wasn't sure whether Amelia should yell "suspicion" before we'd discussed anything. I didn't mind for now, though. We could talk details once I'd mentioned all my points.

"OK, so when he says goodbye, he always gives me the leftover condoms. Why doesn't he just take them home?"

"Fact."

Sarah nodded in agreement and started typing again. A smile spread across my face. I wanted to laugh. Their dedication to the conversation was making me feel better.

"When we're out and about in London, he says 'danger zone' when we're near his house."

"Danger zone?" Sarah asked.

"Yeah, he always looks nervous when he says it."

"What else?" Amelia said, sounding more serious now.

"Well, he has a habit of saying, *Be careful what you wish for*, and today, he texted, *Don't break out of the bubble and everything will be fine*."

"Is 'bubble' a BDSM thing?" Sarah asked, confused.

"No, it means our time together. It's his own term. A bubble is a date or a scene," I explained.

"Wait. Didn't you ask every guy whether he had a wife or a girlfriend?" Amelia brandished her now empty cocktail glass at me, excitedly. She was right. We'd asked the same set of questions to every guy who seemed promising online. The only problem was, Sir had somehow slipped through.

I shook my head sadly. "He was the only one we didn't ask."

The nagging feeling in my heart was taking over. Amelia's

face looked ashen. Sarah had put her phone away and was now pulling anxiously at the hem of her dress. I felt my chest tighten. Did Sir have a girlfriend?

I checked my phone. Sir had sent two messages. *I hope you have a wonderful evening* and, *We should do a call tomorrow if you're free.* His expression when he said we were close to his house came into my mind.

"You should ask him," Sarah said, reading over my shoulder.

Amelia nodded. "It's better you know."

I knew they were right, but I couldn't stop the hard knot forming in my stomach. There was no way I could ask him without crying. Plus, I had a bad feeling he was technically allowed to have a girlfriend. The bracelet meant we couldn't have sex with anyone else but it didn't mean we couldn't be in a relationship. Weirdly, Sir had made it clear I could date no matter what. That had to be a bad sign. That must mean *he* could too. My phone vibrated, *I totally can't believe our chemistry. You may reply, Tilly.*

I shook my head. He was in a completely different space. There was no way I could act as if everything were normal, though. I would have to ask him now. I typed back, *Sorry Sir. I thought I was dismissed. Can I ask a question?* He replied instantly, *Of course, Baby Girl.* I continued bravely, *You said earlier I should stay in the bubble and everything would be fine, Sir.* He answered, *Yes, Tilly.*

I sighed. He always made me spell everything out. I messaged, *You always say that.* He replied, *Say what?* I looked up at my friends for encouragement. Sarah was standing opposite me, willing me silently on. Amelia downed the rest of her drink.

I typed, *Don't break out of the bubble. Is it because you think I will?*

I watched the three dots as butterflies danced in my tummy. The wait was too much.

"I'm ordering more drinks," Amelia said, resolutely.

I nodded without saying anything. My eyes were glued to the screen.

Sir replied, *No. It's because we're dom and sub.* I frowned and texted, *So it goes without saying, right, Sir?* Surely, he didn't need to keep saying "don't break out of the bubble" if our relationship was clear. Why was he so obsessed with ensuring it stayed as sub and dom and didn't develop into anything else?

He answered, *Yes, totally. No wiggle room for anything else.* There was plenty of wiggle room in *my* life for something else if I wanted it. Why wasn't there any in his?

"Ask him," Sarah said, over my shoulder.

I texted back, *Why, Sir?* There was a pause. He was still online but he'd stopped typing. I looked at Sarah. She was smiling in a reassuring way.

My phone vibrated, *That's what you want? Dom totally?*

I typed back, *What do you mean, Sir? I want a total dom and nothing else?*

Another pause. I was giving him a full interrogation now. No more vague texts or hints. I needed to know what was going on.

"Well done, Tilly. Get it out of him."

He texted, *We need to have this conversation in person. Your "why" threw me. We are in a perfect place. The best place. Agreed?*

"No," I said out loud, frustrated.

"No, it's good," Sarah said. "It's better to talk in person."

I sighed impatiently. I wanted him to explain exactly what he meant now, but she was right, we couldn't discuss something this serious in texts. I replied, *Yes, Sir, a conversation in person would be good. Agreed.*

"When are you seeing him?"

"On Friday."

"That's only three days away," Sarah said encouragingly.

Three days was a lifetime away. How had I gone from having the most romantic Sir in the world to a man who was a possible cheat, in the space of a day?

He sent a final message, *Don't look too deeply if you can, but know you are a life memory for me, regardless of where this goes.* I shivered. "Regardless of where this goes". That didn't sound good. I looked around the busy bar, blinking back tears. My Hollywood film was crumbling.

Chapter 20

"My close friend is seriously ill in hospital. I will stay with you if I can. It all depends on what they need. They're an old friend, so it's important I support them."

I studied Sir's face. It was three days later, and he was standing in front of me in the hotel. The afternoon light shone through the floor-to-ceiling window, illuminating his face. His eyes were tired. I turned to look out of the window at Hyde Park. This was probably the most glamorous suite yet, but I couldn't enjoy it. The nagging feeling in my heart hadn't gone away since talking to Amelia and Sarah.

Sir was wearing jeans and a merino knit jumper. He looked more casual than normal, as if he'd not been at work. I wondered whether he was telling the truth. Maybe his friend wasn't really dying, or maybe his friend was his wife. I closed my eyes and let the sinking feeling take over. I should have checked if he was in a relationship before we'd got involved with each other. This was so typical—find the perfect guy and realise he's not even single. I smiled wryly.

"What?"

"Nothing, Sir. It's just you said we were in the danger zone because we were close to your home, and now this—" I stopped myself.

Earlier, he'd driven us to the hotel from the train station. As we'd come close to a large park with lofty trees he'd shifted uncomfortably in his seat and said we were in the danger zone again. A few seconds later, I'd recognised the pub we'd been to before, so that meant he lived nearby. I'd laughed at the time, thinking he was joking, but now I wasn't so sure. It made sense he'd want to keep his house private from his world of subs, but why was he so nervous about it? It couldn't be me. I gave off innocent, love-me vibes, not scary, stalker ones. Didn't I?

I had to tell him what I was thinking. I opened my mouth to talk, but changed my mind. He looked too sad.

"I hope your friend is OK, Sir," I said, instead.

"Yes, Baby Girl. I must go. I will see you after your audition."

In the middle of all of this, I had my second drama school audition. It was a kinder and more welcoming school than the last one. Maybe it would be perfect for me. I'd be confident this time and make sure the stakes were higher in my speeches as Mario and Ruth had advised. Controversially, I'd decided to keep my contemporary monologue—it was too risky to pick a new one so late in the process.

Sir turned to go. My heart sank. What was the point in seeing me at all if he had to go already?

"I couldn't not see you. Beautiful Baby Girl is in town," he called as he walked towards the door.

* * *

Five hours later, I walked back into the hotel feeling dazed. My audition had been a train wreck. It had lasted three hours. There'd been no time to eat. The two speeches that were normally in front of a few teachers had been in front of everyone.

I'd kept it together, though, and not forgotten my lines. The rest of the audition had been better. We'd split up into smaller groups to take part in an improvisational workshop where we played games like Dog Catwalk and Doctor's Waiting Room.

Doctor's Waiting Room involved everyone being stuck in a room for hours with different reasons for being there and different ways of reacting. Dog Catwalk was a fashion catwalk where the models were all dogs. We were told which breed we would be and the designer we were walking for. We had to convey everything in our movements.

I was a Cocker Spaniel wearing Burberry. I'd tried to look friendly and cheeky with an edge. I was thinking "dog about town," but I hadn't pulled it off. I was focused, but everyone else was amazing. Somehow, they genuinely looked like dogs wearing Dior and Chanel.

I was sure I'd done better than my last drama school audition, but I was wrong. The worst thing about the day was the end. We were told to sit down in the hall. If our name was called out, we would stay; if it wasn't, we had to stand up and leave silently. I held my breath. If I'd been successful, my name would be one of the last to be called out. A man with round glasses and a polished bald head squinted at the clipboard. My heart soared. People always struggled to pronounce my surname.

As the name Henry Scheiner was called, my heart fell and I stood up quietly to leave. I could feel my cheeks burning red as I walked through the heavy double doors. They swung shut behind me, catching my heel painfully. A white light of pain shot through my body. I was in agony, but I held in my tears and carried on walking. I refused to cry.

An hour later, I stood silently in the panelled lift of the hotel, closing my eyes as it sped up to the top floor where the suites were. Sir had said he would wait for me in our room. He must have been able to leave his friend in the hospital. I breathed out shakily, feeling light-headed. I searched in my bag for something to eat and found an old fluffy almond.

I walked down the hushed corridor before pressing my key card against our door. Relief washed over me as I saw the huge living room area of the suite with its vases of fresh flowers, velvet sofa, and spectacular view of Hyde Park. The lights were dimmed, and the delicate fragrance of the room smelt amazing. I slipped my trainers and coat off by the door, glad to be rid of my *Fame* outfit. I looked longingly at the sofa, but I crept into the bedroom, instead, where Sir was waiting for me.

I smelt red wine. He was sitting in a dark blue armchair. As I got closer, industrial restraints and a terrifying black crop came into sight. A yelp of fear escaped my lips before I could stop it. I sank into a seated position on the floor.

"Baby Girl?"

"I just need a minute." I forced myself to stand up. I turned and rushed towards the bathroom. I felt like I couldn't breathe. For some reason, I'd expected us to have a meal together and do a scene later. I'd not been prepared to walk straight into a hardcore sex session. It felt as if I was here for everyone else's entertainment. The audition had drained me, and now Sir wanted his pound of flesh too. Why did no one ever think about what I wanted?

"Tilly?"

I looked up from my place on the cool bathroom floor. Sir was knocking gently on the door.

"I'm fine," I said, feeling embarrassed. I was overreacting, I was probably hungry.

"Change of plan. Please be ready in twenty minutes."

His voice sounded cold, but I knew him well enough to detect concern. He was worried about me. He'd changed his plans to make sure I was happy. A feeling of gratitude spread through my body. I'd have a cool shower and do my makeup again. I needed to wash off all memories of the dog catwalk.

Chapter 21

Later, as we sat in a Japanese restaurant surrounded by decorative cherry blossom, Sir said, "I thought I'd lost you back there."

I smiled. "I really appreciate this."

He looked back, relieved. "You come first, Tilly. Happy sub, happy life."

I laughed. I took a bite out of a jumbo tiger prawn, practically swooning as the flavours exploded into my mouth. "Where did you say we were?"

"Zuma, Tilly."

I stopped eating and studied his face, properly. His skin looked different, like he'd had a five hour nap. Perhaps his hospital visit had gone better than he'd expected.

"How's your friend, Sir?"

He raised his eyebrows. Normally, I wasn't allowed to ask questions. I figured tonight was an exception, though.

"Better, Baby Girl. Better."

I tucked into a plate of spicy beef tenderloin. I was coming back to life.

"This is amazing, Sir. Thank you."

The food was out of this world.

"You're most welcome, Tilly."

After our mains, he ordered dessert. He *never* did that. When the dish arrived, I dipped my spoon into the creamy coconut custard and let it melt in my mouth.

"Good, right?" He said.

I nodded in agreement, closing my eyes to savour the taste.

"Now eat up, Tilly. We have one more place to go."

I ate slowly, enjoying every mouthful. Even amongst the terrible audition, starvation, and now this meal, the nagging in my heart hadn't disappeared. Perhaps, Sir would explain everything at the next place. I had to know why he didn't have room in his life for anything more than sub and dom. I had to know why he kept reminding me not to break out of the bubble. I had to know if there was someone else.

* * *

"Welcome to the Radio Rooftop," Sir said, forty minutes later.

We were high above London in the most stylish bar ever. Everyone looked older, richer, and trendier. I listened to the beat of the music, feeling like a rap star. I was wearing a faux-fur jacket —all I needed was a matching hat. The bar was busy but not crowded. I looked up to see lines of orange shining in the dark ceiling. I noticed black velvet stools with amber thread detailing. Everything was immaculate.

As soon as we managed to order drinks, Sir handed me my martini and said, "Let's go outside."

I followed him out onto the balcony into the surprisingly warm night air. Sir spotted an empty sofa in the far corner and pointed, so I sped towards it. I was in a race with a group who had walked out onto the balcony at the same time as us. As cool as they looked, they'd definitely sped up too. I slammed triumphantly down onto the sofa. I was faster, even in heels.

I watched couples kissing near the edge of the balcony. The atmosphere was electric. I was part of the happening scene of London. I pushed down the worry in my heart. My questions could wait.

"I love all the places you take me to, Sir."

"Only the best for my little sub."

I moved closer. He didn't tell me off, so I reached out and rubbed his leg.

"Tilly."

"Yes, Sir?" I giggled.

I moved my hand away but edged my body closer so our legs were touching. I loved the feel of his suit trousers against my skin. I was starting to feel tipsy already.

We drank cocktail after cocktail. Sir even joined me for an espresso martini, which was the best one I'd ever had. I savoured the strong shot of coffee combined with the syrupy goodness of the liquor. It was my second favourite drink ever.

Every time we ordered, Sir made me go to the bar alone and tap his card so he could look after our seats. I was starting to feel seriously drunk as I sauntered back to him. He was waiting for me under the glow of the strip light with the backdrop of a million lights behind him. His strong jawline and blue eyes made my heart flutter. He was so handsome. I laughed at his mock-shocked face. I'd bought four drinks this time so I wouldn't have to go back for a while. I placed our drinks down with a flourish on the glass table and sank onto the sofa next to him. I kissed him on the cheek.

"Bad girl."

He kissed my neck, before moving his lips slowly down to my shoulder. He bit down hard. I suppressed a scream as the pain hit me.

"I want to mark you, Baby Girl," he whispered in my ear.

"Mark me?"

"Permanently brand you."

There was no way he was going to permanently brand me, especially if he had a wife. I opened my mouth to speak. It was time to ask the question.

"Sir, if you want to mark me, then—"

I stopped, my bravery gone.

"Tilly?"

I let the alcohol flood my head. "Before I can consider branding, I have to ask you a question."

I turned to face him. I wanted to know if he was lying. Without looking away, I took a deep breath. "Do you have a wife?"

"No," he answered immediately.

He was telling the truth. I didn't feel relieved, though. There was more.

"I have kids," he confessed.

I shook my head, dismissively. We weren't having a relationship. It didn't matter. I'd never meet his children. At least I didn't think I would. Anyway, his confession about having children was a smokescreen. He was hiding something. Something that was much more challenging to tell me.

I continued determinedly. "Do you have a girlfriend?"

I tightened my grip on the stem of my cocktail. Wife, girlfriend, it was all the same. I shouldn't have to go through every phrase imaginable. It wasn't an English language test for all the different terms of being in a relationship. Either the bracelet and our commitment to each other meant something or he'd been lying this whole time.

There was silence. This was it. The truth was coming. I waited with a lump in my throat. Sir's eyes were shiny. I started to cry.

"Baby Girl, don't cry." He moved forward to comfort me, but I moved away. I forced myself to look at him. I had to hear him say it.

"Yes, I do." He bowed his head.

My image of a lone, devoted workaholic sitting in a plush Mayfair apartment shattered. Every last moment of our time together had been a lie. No wonder he didn't want me to be anything more than a sub. All the disclaimers in his texts were there for a reason. I'd unknowingly been part of an affair. A horrifying thought came to me.

"Did you have your children with the girlfriend you're with now?" I asked angrily.

"No. No. I split up with their mother a long time ago. Around ten years ago."

That hardly made it any better. There was still a woman out there who thought she was in a happy relationship while the man she loved was cheating on her. Sir's personal life was a web of lies. He came across as such a purposeful person who knew what he wanted, but he didn't have a clue.

"Let me explain, Baby Girl. I didn't have to tell you the truth just then. I made a choice. I wanted you to know," he said, speaking in a low, urgent voice.

I wished I'd asked him at the start. I'd wasted the last few months of my life building him up to be someone amazing. But the truth was, I *did* love being with him. The world felt magical together. He treated me like a princess - bought me gifts, took me shopping, booked five star hotels and treated me to glamorous evenings in London. Plus, he made me laugh.

And he always knew what to say to make me feel better. He looked at me like I was the only woman in the world. But, I wasn't the only woman in his world and I never had been.

"I'm perpetually disappointed," I said, tearfully.

"That's a good word."

"Perpetually disappointed. I'm perpetually disappointed by men. I'm—"

"OK. That's enough with 'perpetually,'" he interrupted.

The irony. He could have a girlfriend but I couldn't say "perpetually" a few times. I was wasting my time. I had to get a grip.

"I get it. I do." He rubbed his eyes, looking lost for words. "I wanted to be honest with you. You deserve that. That's why I told you. I could have lied."

I nodded silently, letting the tears roll down my face. Was I supposed to thank him? He'd misled me. Initially, we'd said we could have a romantic relationship at the same time as our sub-dom situation, but I'd thought things had changed. There was no point in the bracelet if we weren't exclusive.

"Was your girlfriend the one in the hospital?"

"Yes, Tilly."

Guilt stabbed my heart. I had no right to take a man away from his sick girlfriend. She needed him.

He watched me sadly for a few minutes and said, "Our time's up, Tilly. We have to go."

Our reservation must be finished. We left the rooftop together. I walked as confidently as I could through the bar. I felt embarrassed in case people saw my tears, but the lighting was dimmed and no one cared, anyway; they had their own drama to focus on.

We got a cab to the hotel. It pulled up outside. We waited

in silence together. I tapped my foot, restlessly. The sooner we got to our suite, the better. I had so many questions to ask. The rain hammered down on the taxi roof. I turned to look at Sir. The guilt in his eyes told me what I already knew. My heart sank. He wasn't coming into the hotel. He was staying in the taxi. He was going home to his girlfriend.

My mind raced as I put everything into place. Every time he'd seemed distant on his phone, it was because he was messaging his girlfriend. He must have taken a photo of his food so she'd know where he was. He'd said danger zone when we were near his house because there was a high chance she'd walk past and see us. It all made sense now. They'd been together for years. They probably had a dog and wore matching fleeces at the weekend and went on country hikes together. I wondered what they did at Christmas. I bet their families were as one. I meant nothing to Sir apart from sex and a few fun nights. I remembered his inspiring speech. He probably gave advice to everyone. What had meant so much to me, meant nothing to him. I was a fool.

"I have to go, Tilly."

I looked into his eyes. They were even more tired than before. He reached over to kiss me. His scent wrapped around me a final time. I closed my eyes so I could feel his lips on mine. I wanted to block out the world before it was all over.

Chapter 22

I stood in the rain, watching the taxi drive away. Shouldn't Sir roll out of the moving cab at high speed, sprint back to me and yell, *I love you*?

I waited, watching cars race by on the wet road in front of me. He wasn't coming back. There'd be no proclamation of love. No apology. I thought back to the night he'd pulled the heavy duvet over us and told me I was safe no matter what. Now I was alone. And he had a girlfriend. Our time was over. Nothing could save us. Leaving his girlfriend wouldn't undo the past few months of lies. It would only make me feel guilty. Breaking up a relationship wasn't on my list of aims.

I looked up at the flags waving at the front of the hotel as I ascended the stairs. I was walking into one of the grandest hotels in the world with smudged mascara and tears rolling down my face. I wiped them away and ran a finger quickly under each eye. I combed my hands through my hair and stood up straight. All I had to do was pretend to be happy for a few seconds, and then I could wail uncontrollably in the suite. I hoped the rooms were soundproofed.

The porter bowed to me as I rushed past. I forced a smile. My heels echoed on the marble floor as I walked quickly across the lobby. I fumbled in my handbag, finding the key card and tapping the lift into life.

When I reached our suite, I sank into an armchair. I gazed blurrily at a mirrored tray on a square pouffe in front of me. The tray was set with biscuits and a china teapot. What had my life become? I was a glorified prostitute for a man who was happy to spend money on me but couldn't bear to be with me longer than a night. What did his girlfriend have that I didn't have? I bet she didn't have to call him "sir" or be dismissed whenever he felt like it. She had the freedom to talk whenever she wanted. They were probably sitting together now, holding hands, watching their favourite TV programme. I wondered if it was *Bake Off*. I closed my eyes. They must share the same bed. Did they cuddle before they went to sleep?

I got up from the armchair and staggered into the bedroom. I felt the cold gold of my bracelet and pulled at it to get it off. I needed the silly screwdriver. I marched across the room to find my handbag. I searched through old receipts and almonds. I put my hand in something soft and squidgy and yelled, pulling my hand out in disgust. It was a banana. I'd left a banana in my bag. My life was a mess. I couldn't organise anything. I'd failed all my drama school auditions. And I was doomed to be in terrible relationships forever. I should give up now.

I turned my bag upside down and watched everything fall out onto the floor. With a sinking heart, I realised Sir had the screwdriver. I couldn't even take off my own bracelet.

I needed something to drink. I grabbed a half empty bottle from earlier that had been left on the table. I'd never downed champagne before. I drank it straight out of the bottle, looking out of the window as I swigged. What was wrong with me? Was I a magnet to awful guys? Each tiny dot of light in the night sky reminded me how many people had amazing relationships.

They were living their happy lives right now. Everything was easy for them. Love and loyalty was a guarantee. If other people got it right, it was possible for me to get it right too. So, that meant it was my fault. I'd been blaming guys for my heartbreak, but it was me. I was the constant.

I stood up, transfixed by the skyline. I took a step towards the window. It was a big window. It was sunk into the wall with a windowsill you could stand on. I'd be able to see the lights more closely if I climbed up. I pushed a chair against the wall and got up easily. I stood on top, surveying the hotel room. I was much higher than I'd expected to be.

I turned around and pressed my body against the cold glass, staring at the city below. I pushed hard. The glass didn't budge. In another lifetime, it would give way completely. Cold air would gush into the room. I'd fall instantly. I'd drop like lead through the night sky. Did people turn when they fell or just fall straight down? The wind would be more forceful than I'd imagined, that was for sure. It would probably hurt my face. My skin would feel like it was being stretched backwards. I'd feel alive, though. Razor sharp and clear in my mind. And the best thing? It would all be over in a few seconds. I wouldn't be a fool anymore. I'd be dead.

My funeral would be depressing. It would be the kind where people cry so loudly you can't hear the speeches. Mum would stumble into the church, heartbroken. She'd be holding onto my brother for support. A tear fell down my cheek at the thought of her pain. I shook my head. I took a step back from the window. I couldn't do that to her. The glass wouldn't budge anyway.

* * *

Are you awake?

I opened one eye and stared at my phone screen. I was shivering. I looked around the room. Light streamed in through the window. It must be the morning. Somehow, I'd made it to the bed. I was laid on the duvet with my clothes still on. I felt chilled to the bone. I swallowed. My throat was dry. I needed a glass of water and a hot shower.

I saw the empty champagne bottle on the floor. The Radio Rooftop bar drifted into my head. I remembered Sir's voice when he told me he had a girlfriend. How sad he'd looked. I thought of the window and how I'd planned my funeral. I still felt the same misery this morning but no matter how hopeless life got, I couldn't give up. Being blind drunk hadn't helped. The truth was, it would all be OK. I'd have my happy ever after, even if it wasn't with Sir.

There was no point ignoring him though, not until I'd left London. I needed to get to the train station, and I wanted to have breakfast. It would be easier with him. I replied, making sure not to say "sir." I wasn't submitting to a guy who was a big, fat liar. No more mild-mannered, submissive me. I texted one word, *Yes.* He messaged back in lightening quick time, *I'm in a session until ten. I'll bring you breakfast. Coffee?* I answered, *Yes.*

I dragged myself out of bed and walked into the bathroom. The underfloor heating gripped my feet like a big, fluffy slipper. A wave of sickness made my vision go blurry. I was badly hungover.

After my hot shower, I dressed, taking total delight in choosing my outfit. Sir hadn't told me what to wear, and if he had, I wouldn't have listened anyway. I stood back, admiring my reflection. I was wearing a grey body top, no bra, black skinny jeans, black velvet ankle boots, and my black leather jacket. I looked amazing, like Kate Moss at a funeral. This was a fuck-you outfit. I spritzed perfume everywhere to finish and found my black oversized Prada sunglasses. They were the only real designer item I owned. It was time for Sir to learn who was boss.

Six minutes later, I heard the door click open. He pushed into the room with two coffees and a paper bag of what smelt like pastries. He was wearing a dark-grey tailored suit and brogues. I smiled in spite of myself. Who wouldn't want a handsome man with bakery goods arriving at their luxury hotel?

"You look amazing," he breathed.

I stood up straighter and put my hand on my hip, defiantly.

"Is this for me?"

I shook my head, "No, Sir. No. This is for me."

"Touché." He laughed appreciatively. "Let's share a coffee and head out. You're too beautiful not to show off."

I sank into a nearby armchair and ripped a huge chunk of croissant away with my teeth. No more tiny nibbles and graceful behaviour. I would do what I wanted from now on, *and* I would speak my mind.

"Is she really ill?" I asked suddenly, whilst still chewing.

A look of disapproval flashed across Sir's face. "Baby Girl?"

"Is your girlfriend really ill?" I repeated, impatiently.

He shook his head. "She's not been well for a long time, but the operation was a good sign. She's moving in the right direction now. She'll get better."

"Is it cancer?"

"What?" he said, looking shocked, and then he shook his head vehemently. "No, no. Not at all. She's been ill for a long time."

I stayed silent. The less I talked, the better. He needed to explain himself.

"Tilly, our relationship broke down a long time ago. We just exist together. It's not what you think. I didn't mean for my situation with you to be anything more than sub-dom. I had no idea we'd have such a connection."

"What do you mean? How did it break down?"

He sighed heavily. "We're like brother and sister. I love her, but I'm not in love with her. We haven't had sex in years. It's a relationship of habit more than anything else. There's no passion there."

"So, why don't you split up?"

"She relies on me. She doesn't work, and she's been ill for a long time now. It didn't feel right to break up with her when she was so sick."

I stopped chewing. It all sounded so serious. I felt terrible.

"Why didn't you tell me about your life?" I whispered.

"I was scared, Tilly. I was scared you'd run a mile."

I looked up at the plasterwork angels engraved in the ceiling above us. I blinked back tears. I wasn't supposed to give a fuck, so why was I crying already? This was only ever meant to be about sex. I couldn't bring myself to look at him. His eyes looked desperate. The sooner I was alone, the better. He wasn't the heartbroken guy defying normal conventions of dating by becoming a dom that I'd thought he was. He was a man having an affair, which had spiralled out of control. He'd dragged me into his mess, and now I had to decide whether I wanted to be a part of it.

Chapter 23

I had a wonderful morning, Tilly. Thank you.

I put my head in my hands. I had no idea how to reply to Sir. The train was busy. The woman's box of doughnuts next to me on her fold-down tray looked inviting. I wished I could drown in a sea of sugar glaze. Breakfast with Sir had been super fun, which made everything ten times worse. The last few months of my life had been amazing, and now it was all over.

There had to be some way we could keep seeing each other. I texted back, *Me too,* hoping he'd come up with a solution. He answered immediately, *You know how deep this can go.* I sighed. Deep would never be a good thing while he was in a relationship. I knew what I had to do.

I texted, *I'll have to pause before I go deep.* He replied, *Don't pause. Jump.*

I shook my head. He couldn't tell me to let go and trust when he wasn't taking his own advice. I typed, *That's easy for you to say.*

He messaged back, *I'm jumping.*

Obviously, he wasn't jumping. I texted back, feeling irritated, *No, you're not. I'm not prepared to give everything to someone who won't give everything to me. I will pause for as long as you need to sort your relationship out. I don't want to feel compromised.*

His reply was as long as mine. *I respect your pause button. You are a beautiful human being and an incredible woman. I'll never hurt you. Remember that. Dismissing you until Barcelona. Obviously, I'd love to see you then. You may at any time ask permission to speak.*

He'd mentioned Barcelona over breakfast this morning. He wanted me to come with him to a work conference there. Clearly, he didn't respect my pause button. I wanted to stop until he sorted his relationship out. But he thought after a few days of me not talking to him, I'd get over it, meet him in Barcelona, and continue as normal. Well, he had another thing coming.

* * *

"I can't believe you're the other woman." Amelia said.

"I thought Sir was a romantic." Sarah looked more heart-broken than me.

"I was in a similar situation once," Amelia confessed quietly.

"Were you?"

"Yeah. Remember Ryan?"

I nodded. Amelia had been crazy about Ryan. He was handsome and funny and loved to party. Exactly Amelia's type.

"Oh, yeah," Sarah said, remembering too.

"It was fun at first, but then I felt guilty. I ended up really liking his girlfriend. I knew her through work."

I stuffed seventeen mini marshmallows into my mouth. It was the next day, and we'd called an emergency meeting at Sarah's house.

"I can't believe I didn't ask him right at the beginning."

"You weren't to know," Sarah said, shaking her head. "He shouldn't have been on a sex website. I can't believe how many married men are out there."

"He isn't married," I said quickly, taking a sip of my hot chocolate. "I need to understand exactly what's going on. I feel like he's hinted that his relationship is coming to an end, but I don't know if that's true."

"Yes. Get everything out on the table. He should answer all your questions," Sarah said, fluffing a pastel-pink cushion aggressively.

"So, has he actually said he'll leave her?" Amelia asked, grabbing the bag of mini marshmallows from me.

"To be honest, I'm not sure. She's ill, so it feels like he needs to look after her."

"Is it cancer?" Sarah asked, looking up from the cushion in horror.

"No, no." I shook my head. "It's something else, and he said she was on the road to a full recovery now."

I felt a pang of guilt. "I feel so bad sitting here talking about an ill woman while I'm having an affair with her boyfriend."

Amelia shook out a large handful of marshmallows on the coffee table and said firmly, "You can't be feeling bad about anything. It's not your fault. You had no idea until a few days ago. Plus, you can't think this is the first time he's cheated."

I raised my eyebrows. She had a point. Maybe he wasn't even a real dom. Dismissing girls gave him full control so he'd know exactly when to expect text messages and wouldn't get caught out by his girlfriend. He controlled when he met women, which allowed his cheating to run alongside his normal life. He was a Casanova. I'd known it from the beginning. I should have trusted my instincts.

"Maybe he doesn't even want to be a dom. It's just a way of cheating on his girlfriend," I mused.

Sarah narrowed her eyes. "He's very passionate about being a Sir, though, and he *is* good at it."

"It comes naturally to him. He's always buying you gifts and saying sexy things," Amelia joined in.

They were defending him. They were supposed to be on my side. They were right, though. He *did* love talking about his journey into domination. It wouldn't make any sense for him to be lying about being a dom. Perhaps, this was as much of a surprise for him as it was for me, and he'd told me the truth as soon as he started having feelings for me. That's why he'd said I could have a boyfriend at the start because he was trying to be fair. Plus, a lot of people didn't equate a romantic relationship with a BDSM one—they were often two separate things that ran parallel to each other.

"Imagine if he's still having sex with his girlfriend," Amelia said.

"He's not." I shook my head quickly, stealing a marshmallow from her pile. That was the last thing I needed. I had enough to worry about.

* * *

A few days later, I sat alone eating a jacket potato. I was in Leeds doing a four-day promo job. I looked around at the girls chatting and texting. Everyone seemed so happy. I missed Amelia and Sarah. They'd both booked separate holidays ages ago at the same time. They'd be back in a few days, but their timing was horrific. They'd left me wallowing in endless pots of heartbreak ice cream while they gallivanted around Italy and France, Amelia with her mum and Sarah with Dave.

After work, I walked back to Sarah's house. I was house-sitting for her. She had a lot of plants. My phone pinged. It was Sir. *Direct question. You may answer yes or no. Have you made a decision regarding Barcelona?* I typed back quickly before I could overthink it, *No.* But then I changed my mind and texted, *Yes.*

My phone pinged, *That's clear. I have to register you for the conference, that's all. I'm being pressed to do so. Either is good, obviously.* Obviously, either was good. I could decide whatever I wanted. And I could be as unclear as I wanted. This was all his fault, not mine.

I messaged back, *Can I be booked in and change my mind later? Or is that not possible?* He replied, *Yes, of course.* That was a better idea. I texted, *OK. I'd like to do that. I'm still deciding.*

He sent a final message, *Yes, Tilly. Agreed. Dismissed.* I put my phone back in my bag. He shouldn't be dismissing me. I should be dismissing him. It had been *my* decision to pause everything, but he was still gaining the upper hand.

It was a twenty-minute walk to Sarah and Dave's house. The fresh evening air made my head feel clearer.

When I arrived, I let myself in with my spare key and took my shoes off straightaway before padding across the thick cream carpet. Sarah took a lot of pride in her house. She was always tidying up after Dave and telling him off for bringing mud and leaves inside. He had a thing for leaves. I was sure he had an official collection somewhere. I put my bag down and went into the kitchen. I looked in the cupboards for something to eat. I pushed aside tubs of vitamin D tablets, tins of tomatoes and boxes of cereal to find pasta and a saucepan. I put the kettle on.

My phone pinged. It was Sir again, *Regardless of the external world, this is a life moment. I'm sure of this. You have never occupied my head so much as today.* My heart soared. I replied, *Really?*

Yes. It's a breakthrough for you to know everything. I'm slipping into you faster, but I understand I need to sort my relationship out before we can continue. He was saying all the right things. I typed back quickly, *I just want everything to fall naturally into place.*

Yes, Tilly. Have you confided in anyone?

I closed my eyes as the gravity of the situation hit me. We'd been having so much fun. Why did everything have to get so serious? I texted, *Yes, I have, but they're on holiday now.* He answered, *Try not to let your head rule your heart, Tilly. Let your heart have a say too.* I replied, *Thank you. I will.*

He texted, *Dismissing you.* I frowned. He should let me speak freely without dismissing me. It wasn't fair. I desperately wanted to see him and forget he had a girlfriend, but the only way I could do that was by talking everything through with him first. If he kept cutting me off, I couldn't justify continuing.

As if reading my mind, he sent another message, *You need space, Baby Girl. Total respect to you. And remember, it's your life, no one else's.*

I looked up from my phone to see my pasta boiling over. I ran over to save it. As I was grating cheese at full speed (the timing had to be perfect to allow it to melt), I thought of Mum. When she'd got divorced from my dad, she'd cried for weeks without stopping. Not sobs. Just tears that rolled down her face at every hour of the day. While she was eating her breakfast in the morning or cooking dinner in the evening or hoovering the living room, she'd be crying. I'd watch her, helplessly. There was nothing I could do to make her happy again.

A few months later, my brother and I had met "the other woman" for the first time. Mum had asked what she'd looked like when we got home. We'd said blonde and sporty because she'd been wearing leggings and a sports top. Mum had gone out and bought a tracksuit the next day.

I swallowed, staring hard at the melted cheese. I'd done it too early, and now the cheese was all stringy. Everything I touched, I ruined. Was I losing sight of who I was? I'd failed my auditions when all I ever wanted to do was act, and now I was considering going against my mum to make a decision she'd be ashamed of. If I continued with Sir, I'd become the other woman. Surely, that would be the biggest mistake of my life?

Chapter 24

Miss you, Tilly.

It was a few hours later. I was tucked up in bed for the night in Sarah's room, cuddling her soft toy elephant. I'd locked the doors and checked the windows. It felt strange being in a house alone, but Sarah's room was comforting. Her bed was big, and there were lots of candles and cute decorations scattered around. I listened to the gentle tick of her unicorn alarm clock. I opened one eye to look at my phone before sending a sleepy text back to Sir, *I miss you too.*

He replied, *You're trouble. I knew it from act one, scene one.* I liked recalling the first time we met. I texted back, *The moment I walked in?* He answered immediately, *Yes, Tilly.* I propped myself up in bed. *I knew this would capture me, chasing my heart's desire. I knew it would result in something powerful, Sir.*

Yes, the whole journey from Tilly Williams to Tilly Fucking Super Sub. I smiled. Tilly Williams was my made-up online name. I typed back, *Hahaha, Tilly Williams.*

You were always trouble. I find you addictive, he texted. I raised my eyebrows. Addictive was good. I checked the time: it was 11:32 p.m. I wondered if he was sitting at home having a glass of wine unable to stop thinking about me. I took a deep breath, spikes running through my heart. I shouldn't have thought of his home.

He messaged again, *Have you asked yourself, how will I ever have normal sex again?* Normal sex was the least of my worries right now. I had bigger things to think about like whether he was having sex with his girlfriend or not. He'd switched tactics from apologies to persuasion, and that wasn't about to work with me. I'd decide what to do next. Not him. I typed, *You always say that, Sir, but I won't be having normal sex again. No chance.*

His reply was quick and sounded relieved. *Of course, Tilly. As long as we play this right...and we keep the intensity. We can march forward.* I laughed under my breath. He thought I meant with him. Well, he'd be marching forward alone. He'd taught me how to be the best sub in the world, and then broken my heart. I'd find a better dom who didn't have a girlfriend, and wanted to be with me forever.

I had to correct him. *I've never thought I would go back to normal sex, Sir, even if our arrangement ended.* He replied, *Exactly. Smart little bastard.* A smile spread across my face. He sent another message. *I'm sorry about your audition, Baby Girl.* He was never this chatty. I answered, *It's OK.* He texted, *You should be a top actress. Do it. Have no fear. Anything is possible.* I closed my eyes. I knew he was right, but it seemed so far away at the moment. Two bad auditions in a row had knocked my confidence. Anyway, we were going off topic. I wanted to talk about his relationship, not my audition.

Before I had time to reply he texted, *I will catapult you.* Did he mean catapult me into success? Maybe he knew Russell Brand and Russell Brand knew Mario and Ruth. They'd change their mind and enrol me into their school, and I'd spend three years becoming an amazing actress and winning an Oscar. I asked,

Into what?

He replied, *Into your perfect state.* I sighed loudly. Now was not the time to talk in code. It sounded like he was going to split up with his girlfriend but I couldn't be sure. I typed back, *My perfect state of me and you, Sir?* A minute went by. I waited anxiously. Perhaps, I'd misunderstood what he was saying. Finally, he answered, *Yes. I know what you want, Tilly. I just need time. It will take a while for me to sort out my relationship.* I narrowed my eyes. I didn't want to have the weight of a break-up on my shoulders. I texted, *Would it have ended anyway, even if it wasn't for me?*

Definitely, Tilly. But it's complicated. We have created a life together. I have a responsibility.

I nodded. *I understand.* He continued, *In the past, it was easy to play my game and stay in my relationship. I didn't have chemistry like this with other subs. You've made me question everything. My life cannot continue the way it is. I know that for sure.* I took a moment to process his words. This was huge. *It's late, you should sleep.* I rubbed my eyes, frowning. He'd just dropped a bombshell while I was half asleep, and now he was saying good night. I looked around at Sarah's bed. Her fluffy pillows and thick bedspread *did* look inviting. It'd been a long day, and there was no point trying to decipher his messages now. It'd be better to think about everything tomorrow.

You're right. Good night, Sir. He replied, *Good night, Tilly. 100% in my head.* One hundred percent. Wow. We'd talked often about getting to this point and how significant it would be. One hundred percent meant we could think of nothing else but each other. He was a romantic. I knew it.

I sank back into the pillows and pressed my face into Sarah's soft toy elephant. I let my body relax. I hadn't slept properly for days. Hopefully, tonight would be different. I'd see Sarah and Amelia in a couple of days, so I could discuss everything with them then.

Chapter 25

"Open your arms," Amelia ordered.

There was no point in being self-conscious. It was a week later. We were standing on top of a cliff in the Peak District. There was nobody around. Amelia had insisted we drive here. The Spring sun beat down on my face, the wind blew my hair back. I had no idea what Amelia was doing but I was happy to oblige. If anything, it would be a welcome distraction from my heartache. Plus, Sarah's happiness was contagious. She was standing next to me, with her arms wide open. She loved the countryside.

"Close your eyes," Amelia said.

I closed my eyes. I was near the edge of the cliff but my feet felt firm on the ground. I had a good grip.

"You too, Sarah," Amelia ordered. "Now shout together, I am strong."

I opened one eye. "Really?"

She threw me a disapproving look. "There's no time for hesitancy. You just have to do it. No one can hear you."

I sighed. She was right. It was seven in the morning. I'd not even seen any eager dog walkers. We were totally alone. Plus, Sarah would definitely do it. I had no excuse.

"I am strong," I muttered. Thankfully, my voice got lost in the wind. Sarah's shout carried though, her joyful tones echoing across the hills.

"I am worth it," Amelia said.

I opened my eyes to roll them. This wasn't a L'Oréal advert.

"Just do it," she ordered, seeing my face. "And shout it."

"I am worth it," I yelled. This time my volume matched Sarah's and the wind amplified our noise.

"I am me," Amelia continued, pleased.

I opened my arms wide and shouted as loud as I could with Sarah, "I am me."

Amelia punched the air, "That's it girls!"

I laughed. "I am strong."

"I am worth it!" Amelia joined in with us.

We held hands in a three and called into the wind together as it buffeted us. It was the strangest thing. I felt exhilarated.

Sir's voice came into my head: *Everyone lives in a box, Baby Girl. Trapped by their own ideas of who they think they should be and what they think the world should be.* I wanted to live a different life and see a bigger world. He would show me how. If he hadn't told me he had a girlfriend, our emotions would have accelerated. And the truth was, I wasn't my mum. I couldn't compare her situation to mine. I had to make my own decisions. I was always thinking about how everyone else felt or worrying about being careful and making sure I did the right thing.

When I'd met Sir at the Mayfair hotel, it was the first time I'd focused on myself and done something *I* wanted to do, no matter what anyone else thought. And it had led to the best moments of my life. It wasn't as if he was happily married or I was ruining his relationship. As Amelia said, he must have cheated many times before he met me. His girlfriend might have even cheated too. I wasn't the other woman, I had a connection with Sir. I was sure of it. Being sub and dom meant it was different—it felt intimate and deeper. There was so much left to explore.

When we got back to the car, I checked my phone. I had two messages from Sir, *Have you ever seen The Matrix, Tilly?* Then half an hour later he'd texted, *Take the red pill, Tilly. Stay in Wonderland.* I closed my eyes. I didn't want it all to end. I didn't want to pause us anymore. I pressed my thumb on the centre button of my phone. The screen came alive. My heart was pounding. I started to type, *Do you promise to catapult me into my perfect state, Sir?*

My phone vibrated instantly, *Yes, Tilly. It will take time, but I won't be in this situation forever. I know that for sure. You have changed everything.* I took a deep breath and typed back, *Fuck it, Sir. Yes, I will.*

Everything sprang into action. It was as if he'd been waiting, ready. He sent multiple orders in quick succession. *French nails—square. Hair straight. This outfit.* He sent me a photo of a girl in white suit trousers and a dark-green shirt. *Hair wavy. I need you understated, casually beautiful. You will act as my brand manager at the conference.* I texted back, butterflies dancing in my tummy. *Yes, Sir. I will look online. Do I need to prepare anything?* He answered, *We can talk nearer the time. Show me what you come up with clothing-wise. Everything needs to be ordered immediately. I'll give you more details soon.* I replied, *Yes, Sir. Thank you.*

I put my phone down and focused on the road ahead. We were speeding over the bumpy country lane. Amelia was such a fast driver.

"The speed limit is a guideline not an aim," Sarah reminded

her from the back of the car.

"Yeah and it's sixty anyway, not seventy," I added, disapprovingly.

"Killjoys," Amelia replied. "We've just had an enlightened moment and all you guys can think about is speed limits."

I watched the speedometer go down to sixty. She'd listened. I bit my nail as I looked out of the window. I hoped I done the right thing. I'd expected him to say thank you a million times and profess his undying love for me when I'd said I wanted to carry on. This was *Sir* I was talking about though. His way of showing emotion was through instructions. His sudden stream of orders meant he was over the moon. Plus, the nagging feeling in my heart had gone. I felt relieved. My hands were still shaking though. I'd either just made the best choice of my life or committed love suicide.

Chapter 26

Two weeks later, I flew first class to Barcelona. I flew from Manchester, while Sir flew from London. I spent three hours in a practically empty VIP airport lounge where I got a one-hour body massage. This was followed by two hours on the plane eating delicious food and drinking champagne. It would have been the ultimate relaxing experience if I hadn't felt stressed the whole time. I kept my phone with my ticket on it clutched tightly in my hand in case someone took one look at me and tried to move me to economy class. I dropped chocolate twice on my white trousers but managed to dab them clean with a makeup wipe. And I said thank you a total of seventy-seven times to anyone and everyone I came into contact with.

I landed first from Manchester. As I dragged my suitcase over the smooth airport floor, I spotted Sir marching towards me. He was wearing the same black suit he'd worn when we first met. I watched, transfixed, as every inch of my body goosebumped. After our break of not seeing each other, I thought his effect on me might have dwindled but I was wrong. It'd been amplified by a thousand.

When he saw me, his whole face changed. As soon as he got close enough, he wrapped his arms around my waist, kissing me deeply in the middle of the airport. Normally, he'd never allow that. He avoided PDAs as a rule. I closed my eyes, trying not to cry.

* * *

"So, if anyone asks, you're my branding manager," Sir said in the taxi, as we sped towards the conference.

I swallowed nervously, wishing we didn't have to make up a story. I was rubbish at lying. Everyone would know instantly that I had no clue what branding even was.

When we arrived, we pulled up outside and strode through the glass doors to join the hum of business people milling about in the hotel lobby. To my horror, everyone was networking already. Hopefully, this would all be over soon. I needed to talk to Sir.

He handed me a glass of champagne. I took it gratefully and smiled. I wanted to make an excellent first impression with everyone. This event was important to Sir. I didn't want to let him down but I didn't know the first thing about branding. Anyway, all of this was one big distraction that I didn't need. We needed to be alone to talk in detail about his relationship.

"This is Martin. He's the head of Philip Graceson, one of the companies I work with," Sir explained.

"Hi, you must be Tilly." Martin was wearing a green shirt and grey trousers that looked one size too small. He was sweating profusely but smiling cheerfully.

"It's wonderful to meet you, Martin," I said as he shook my hand with so much vigour I had to dodge my own hand before it hit me in the face.

"And you, Tilly. I believe you've timed it perfectly. The food is ready," he said, beaming.

I followed Martin and Sir up a winding glass staircase to a mezzanine where ten large round tables awaited us.

"You're here," Martin pointed, proudly to a table in the far corner. It was set with silver cutlery, bottles of red and white wine and artistically decorated place cards.

"It looks wonderful."

Sir pulled a chair out for me and I sat down. As the rest of our table joined us, the food was served quickly. At this rate the event would be over and I'd be alone with him before I knew it.

I tucked into a starter of prawns as a man called Brian called across the table, "Are you married, Tilly?"

He'd been talking about his wife and their wedding for a full ten minutes and was now happily extending the conversation to the whole table. I composed myself and said with a smile, "No, I'm not, but I would love to be one day, Brian."

I stole a glance at Sir, who was hiding a smile.

"And you, Marcus? Have you ever been married?"

"No, I haven't," he said firmly.

"I'm sure you would make someone very happy," I said, overly graciously.

Brian agreed and continued to talk about his wife. Sir looked over at me with a face of mock horror, but I knew he was enjoying the marriage discussion. He pretended to hate weddings, but he loved them really.

The food was delicious. We had three courses and two options for each course. My favourite was dessert. I chose white chocolate and ginger cheesecake. I listened to two grey-suit-wearing women talking to each other while I ate. They were using so much industry-specific language, I couldn't understand one word of what they were saying. I had no idea what I was doing here. I poured myself more wine.

"Are you enjoying your meal, Tilly?"

Sir was drunker than me. We were supposed to be networking and ignoring each other, but here he was talking to me again.

"Oh, it's just delicious, *Marcus*," I said slowly, looking into his eyes.

"Tilly!" He kicked me under the table.

"Ow, Marcus," I said loudly.

He looked around in alarm, but no one was paying any attention. I tried not to laugh.

"You can't flirt with me here," he whispered.

"I don't know what you mean. I'm just being my normal brand manager self."

He looked fazed by my brazen response. This was too much fun. He turned to talk to someone else, but there was nobody. Everybody was immersed in conversation. After a few minutes, he gave up and turned back to speak to me. The truth was, no one cared—the constant flow of wine meant everyone was drunk already. Polite networking was out of the window.

Once the meal had finished, I stayed sitting down to watch people leave. Three men stumbled past us, each holding a glass of white wine. One woman with flushed cheeks walked down the spiral staircase, holding on to the handrail and her glass carefully.

"Can I tell you something, Sir?" I asked playfully.

"Please do," he said.

"Do you know my Prada bag?"

"Yes."

"It's not real," I said with a flourish.

"Not real?"

I laughed. "I bought it in Bangkok."

"Oh dear. Let's go get Baby Girl a real one."

I squealed in delight. "Yes, please, Sir."

"Come on, Tilly. No one will miss us," he said, standing up.

"Now?" I asked, in a high-pitched voice.

"It's now or never, Baby Girl. I've had enough of this place anyway."

Twenty minutes later, to my disbelief, we arrived outside the official Prada shop in Barcelona.

Sir opened the door. "Step inside, beautiful."

I shivered in excitement as I gazed at the twinkling glass cabinets and soft leather handbags all around me. I caught sight of the most perfect baby-pink Galleria handbag sitting on a low glass shelf. I knelt to look at it.

"That's the one," he murmured behind me.

He pointed it out to the shop assistant, and I watched, mesmerised, as the man began to wrap my precious bag with crisp Prada tissue paper and white embossed ribbon. My need to talk to Sir had temporarily evaporated. I couldn't focus on how confused I felt about his relationship with my dream handbag in front of me.

"It's all yours."

I clutched it to my chest as if it were a baby.

"We'll drop it off at the hotel and head out," he added.

When we walked into our hotel room, Sir strode over to the wardrobe and began unzipping his suitcase.

"I was going to wait to give you these, Tilly, but now feels like the perfect time," he said, taking a cloudy lilac shoebox out of his suitcase.

I held my breath. The baby hairs on my arms stood on end. He took my shopping bag from me and placed it next to the lilac shoebox on the side.

"Go ahead, Tilly."

I ran forwards and touched the box shakily. The silver iridescent letters made my heart sing. It was exactly what I'd thought it was. He'd bought me my very own Jimmy Choos. I remembered the way he'd looked at me when we'd first met, his eyes locking on to mine: *I'll buy you Jimmy Choos, if I'm still your sir.*

"Better late than never," he said, watching me.

I shook my head in disbelief. Not only had he bought me the world's best high heels, but now he was apologising for being a few weeks late. It was impossible to be late with Jimmy Choos. I ignored the nagging feeling in my heart. Sure, we'd not talked yet and he could be showering me with gifts because he felt guilty, but there'd be plenty of time to talk about everything later.

My heart was pounding as I lifted the lid. I peeled back the tissue paper and struggled to untie the dust bag inside. I couldn't breathe. I never thought he'd actually buy me Jimmy Choos.

I gasped as I pulled out the most beautiful diamond-covered heels I'd ever seen. I felt like Cinderella and Sir was my fairy godmother. He was waving his wand over my life, making everything magical. They sparkled in the light. I held them close.

"They're beautiful, Sir."

"Don't stop now. Keep going."

I untied the Prada ribbon on my huge white shopping bag and took out the textured box inside. I'd been waiting for this moment all my life. I ran my hands over the baby-pink leather. My own Prada Galleria bag. I held it in my hand, swinging my arm so I could see the shine of my bracelet against the pink leather of the bag.

"They go perfectly together. I can imagine you dancing the night away," He said, admiringly.

"Thank you, Sir," I said, spinning round and round with one heel and my bag clutched tightly to my chest.

I hugged them close. This was all I needed. I could wear them forever. I wouldn't need any other shoes or bags ever again. I'd wear them with all my outfits. I'd look amazing at all times and they were such exceptional quality that they'd last for years and years.

I spotted a light-blue cashmere knit draped over the dressing table. I'd been so focused on my bag and shoes that I'd not seen it. I reached for it carefully, the soft fabric unfolding in my hands. It was a cardigan.

I laughed. "You found one, Sir."

"Hobbs, Covent Garden, Tilly." He smiled, his eyes twinkling. "You were right all along. I hope it fits. I got the size you said."

"I love it, Sir. Thank you so much."

"You could wear it when we're at breakfast."

I reached to kiss him. He held my head gently and kissed me back. I could feel my heart beating against his.

"Let's go out. Barcelona awaits," he said, softly.

"Can I wear my bag now?"

"Yes." He smiled.

My bag would look amazing with my outfit. I was wearing the dark-green shirt he'd asked me to buy with the white trousers. I switched my things from my old handbag into my new bag, admiring the exquisite lining. I looked over at my new shiny shoe friends. I'd placed them back in their box and tucked them away under their tissue paper, but now they were calling out to me. They looked sad. They needed to see the streets of Barcelona too.

"Can I wear my Jimmy Choos now, Sir?"

"Go on, then."

He sat down on an armchair near the bed to wait for me. I took off my nude heels, trying to be as quick as possible, but he was busy on his phone, so it didn't matter. I picked up my new shoes and ran into the bathroom.

"What are you doing?"

"Nothing, Sir," I said, dipping my feet into the bidet. I patted them dry with a fluffy white towel and slipped my feet carefully into the diamond heels. I took off my shirt and pulled on the new blue cardigan. I admired my outfit in the mirror. The cardigan was a perfect fit. It looked amazing with my trousers. I walked back into the room with a flourish.

"Oh. You look spectacular." Sir put his phone down. "Give me a twirl."

I turned on the spot. My heels were a dream. My Prada bag felt amazing in my hand, and the cashmere of my new jumper was beautifully soft against my skin.

I felt Sir's hands on my waist as he pulled me close. "Barcelona won't know what's hit it, Baby Girl."

Chapter 27

"I found this place by chance. It was during my many days of exploring. I would walk without worrying about time or whether I was lost or not. I lived here for a few months. It has always felt like a special place. I feel at home here," Sir said.

It was half an hour later. I looked around the softly lit restaurant with its polished floors and glass cabinets of wine.

"The food is amazing. You have to give it a try, Tilly."

I didn't know if I could eat anymore after the meal we'd just had, but before I could reply a waiter appeared with two plates of deliciously smelling food. It was as if the kitchen had been expecting us and prepared our meal in advance. The waiter nodded at Sir and then disappeared before returning a few minutes later with two more dishes, a cocktail for me and a glass of red wine. He placed the glass of red wine down last, as if it were extra-special.

"We managed to get a 2005."

Sir's face lit up. "Thank you." He looked genuinely grateful. I stared inquisitively at the wine. It looked like a normal glass. I couldn't see any difference.

"2005 was a good year for wine," Sir explained, noticing my confusion.

I smiled politely but had no clue what he meant. I didn't

know wines could have good years.

The dishes were small but filling. I surreptitiously undid the top button of my trousers as I ate. I wanted to ask for a doggy bag but that wouldn't be a demure thing to do. Instead, I stopped eating and sipped my cocktail. I felt good. This was the perfect moment to ask Sir all of my questions. There was no work conference or sparkling gifts to distract me.

As soon as he'd finished eating and placed his cutlery neatly in the centre of his place, I said, "May I ask a question?"

"Be my guest," he replied.

I took a second to gather my thoughts. "Do you know your relationship?"

"Yes..." he said, narrowing his eyes.

We'd talked in riddles for way too long. It was time to get everything out in the open. "How is it possible that you're not having sex?"

He looked at me in surprise but I didn't care whether I'd overstepped the mark. I continued. "How can you live together and not have sex? You do have sex, really, don't you?" I looked at him expectantly. He *had* to be lying.

He didn't rush to answer. He took a sip of his wine, savouring the taste and contemplating my words. "It's a good question. We've been together for a long time. After a while, a lot of couples stop having sex. A month becomes two months, becomes half a year, until it's been years since you last had sex and it feels too awkward to raise the issue."

He talked calmly. I watched his eyes as he spoke—he was telling the truth, but I couldn't understand how. What kind of relationship didn't have sex in it? Would the same happen to me as I got older?

"I've never been in a relationship like that, so I can't

imagine."

"Her condition made it worse too."

My heart sank. "Is that why you stopped having sex?"

"No." He shook his head. "We'd stopped years before that."

I felt relieved. "How long have you been together?"

"Nearly nine years."

She was the super-long relationship he'd mentioned at the start. They'd been through a lot together. I wondered what her illness was. I didn't want to pry, but he hinted all the time about it.

"Is there something seriously wrong with her? I understand if you don't want to answer."

He paused and exhaled slowly before replying. "She had pelvic pain for a long time. We didn't know what it was. We tried everything. We even went private, but no one knew what was wrong. She was in a great deal of pain. In the end, they finally found a cyst."

I took a gulp of my cocktail, feeling guilty. The recent operation must have been to remove it. I was the worst kind of woman. I needed to drink more to block it all out. It was impossible to have a good night with such a serious underlying reality.

"It was a long journey, Tilly. Super stressful for her, obviously, but for me too."

He looked distant. This conversation wasn't making me feel any better at all. I was breaking up a life bond. He should stay with his girlfriend and make their relationship work. I looked down at my perfect French nails, feeling ashamed. I shouldn't be here.

"Look at me," he snapped.

I looked into his eyes.

"Do you have any idea how beautiful you are?" he asked, sternly.

"Thank you, Sir," I whispered but his compliment didn't make me feel better. "You clearly adore her. I'm a change of perspective for you, one of those experiences that makes you realise how lucky you are. In a few months, you'll have the spark back in your relationship and everything will be OK. I'm temporary."

His girlfriend was an upgraded version of me. I was a weekend in Benidorm. Soon, the dirty weekend would be over and he'd go back to Saint-Tropez forever. It was better to let him know I knew how throwaway I was. That way, it would be easier for him to get rid of me when the time came.

"No, no, I disagree. I don't adore her. I adore you." He locked eyes with me. "I care for her, Tilly. We've been together for a long time."

I looked down at the table. I couldn't think of anything to say.

He stood up. "Enough talking. Let's get cocktails."

We paid the bill and walked out into the balmy night. Fairy lights sparkled in the trees, and faint laughter and happy shouts spilt out of each restaurant as we passed by, but all I felt was the urge to cry. I should never have come.

"This is the best bar in Barcelona," Sir said, pushing open the door to a trendy-looking place with low-hung lights and climbing green plants.

As we stepped inside, a huge hand came out of nowhere to stop us.

"ID."

I looked up in a panic, it was the bouncer. He looked stern. I hadn't brought my ID out with me. I never did when I was in the UK. I thought Spain would be even more relaxed. Imagine if there was a fine for not having ID. He'd go inside alone, and I'd have to wait outside, hoping the police didn't come and ask me why I was loitering in the street.

I looked to my left and realised Sir was getting his wallet out. He was laughing with the bouncer. They must be friends. I shook my head. It was all a joke.

The bouncer looked at Sir's card and said with a bow, "Happy birthday, *señor.*"

My heart stopped. I turned to look at him but he was avoiding my gaze by taking longer than normal to put his ID back. He never fumbled with anything ever.

"Look after this one," the bouncer said, patting him on the shoulder.

I smiled and took Sir's hand. "*Siempre.*"

"Baby Girl can speak Spanish?"

"It's your birthday?" I whispered.

He ignored me and walked straight to the bar. He ordered a glass of Bordeaux for himself and a fruit cocktail for me. My cocktail had a stripy pink-and-white umbrella and a sugar-rimmed glass. I stared at it and then at Sir. I didn't know whether to laugh or cry. He'd chosen to be with *me* on his birthday.

"Problem, Tilly?"

"You wanted to be with me on your birthday." I felt my cheeks go red under my makeup. "I had no idea it was today."

"Of course." He smiled. "Why wouldn't I want this for my birthday?" He gestured at me and at the lively bar. I looked around at the people dancing and the swinging lights above us. It was the perfect place to celebrate his birthday. The conference had been a cover up. We were here for one reason and one reason only.

"Happy Birthday," I said shyly, clinking my glass against his.

"Do you have any more questions?"

I spun the stripy umbrella in my hands. "No, I don't think so, not for now."

"I don't ever mean to make you feel bad. You know that, don't you?"

His sudden switch in emotion made an instant lump form in my throat. I closed my eyes.

"Tilly?"

"It's fine, Sir," I said, opening my eyes as cheerfully as I could.

"Talk to me."

I breathed out. "There was one last problem."

"Go on," he said, looking uneasy.

"I was scared you didn't want to spend time with me."

"What do you mean?" he asked blankly as if I were speaking another language.

"Is it just about sex?" I pressed.

He should come out and say it if it was. I had a right to know.

"Tilly." He fell silent. "You have no idea, do you?"

A shiver ran through me. He was looking at me so intensely.

"No idea about what, Sir?"

He grabbed my hand.

"Our chemistry is out of this world," he said, his voice low.

I moved closer so I could hear him against the loud laughs and shouts of the bar.

"Look, I never saw this coming. How could I? How could I guess we would have such a powerful connection?"

I gazed into his sparkling blue eyes.

"Tilly."

I held my breath. Time stood still. The people around us stopped moving. The light dimmed. All I could see was Sir.

"I'm in love with you."

I took a gulp of air, as if coming to the surface of the water for the first time. I was breathless. I had no idea how much I'd wanted to hear him utter those words until this moment. I didn't wait for permission. Before I could speak, my lips were on his. My hands caressed his chest. My body pressed urgently against him.

The next morning, I squinted my eyes at the bedside clock. It read 5:29 a.m.

"Tilly's skin," Sir muttered, turning over in bed and pulling me roughly over to him.

I breathed in his scent, sleepily. How could he smell so good when we'd only just woken up? He began to rub my skin with his big hand. He rubbed my shoulders and back. I sighed, blissfully, drifting back to sleep.

His hand moved to my nipples pulling me sharply awake. He tugged hard and a strangled moan escaped me. He knew how much I liked that. I was helpless in his hands. His touch moved down, caressing my thighs gently. I relaxed my legs, opening them wide, willing him to enter me. Something about being half asleep made every part of my body feel more sensitive. I ached for him. I needed him. He pulled again at my nipples. I whimpered.

"Please Sir."

Tracing kisses down my neck, and pushing my legs further apart, he guided himself inside me. He moved slowly at first. I moved with him, my hands gripping his back. We shifted together in unison, his skin on my skin, his lips pushing against mine, slipping between awake and dreaming.

"I love you, Tilly."

"I love you," I breathed.

We were in the clouds. Soaring in the sky. Flying somewhere beautiful. Everything was rushing towards me. I had no idea where we were going. All I knew was I never wanted this feeling to stop.

"Now," he ordered.

My orgasm descended. My body melted into his. He held me close as I trembled underneath him. A ray of early-morning light shone through a gap in the curtains, illuminating the room. Sir pressed his full weight on top of me and I squeezed my legs tightly around his back, barely able to breathe. I looked towards the window where the light streamed through. I felt as if I'd become part of him. We were one.

After a few seconds, he rolled away. I moved closer and lay my head on his chest, listening to his heartbeat. We were in love, in Barcelona, celebrating his birthday. Nothing else mattered.

Chapter 28

"I knew it," Amelia said triumphantly. "No more, 'we're only together for sex' chat."

I laughed. "I was kidding myself all along."

"It's so romantic," Sarah said happily, twirling in her princess dress.

"It really is," I said, remembering the way Sir had looked at me when he'd said 'I love you'.

We were working on a two-day princess event. I had a blue princess dress, Sarah had a pink one, and Amelia had a yellow one. We watched kids colour furiously on a large pink mat in front of us.

"Barcelona is dreamy." Sarah sighed.

"What did you do the next day?" Amelia asked.

"Once we got out of bed we went to a spa," I said, with a smile, remembering the hushed atmosphere. I'd had to wear a little white hat to cover my hair and a white waffle dressing gown. I'd felt embarrassed, but Sir had worn one too. I'd stifled a giggle when I'd seen him sitting under the Gothic stone ceiling. He'd looked so different in a robe. We'd explored the pools and steam rooms together until he found the best one, a saltwater pool where we could float together. I closed my eyes and felt the water lap around my body, pushing me gently one way and then the other.

"*We* should go to Barcelona," Sarah said wistfully.

Amelia knelt on the mat to organise the colouring pads. "Are there any updates on the wife situation?"

"Girlfriend," I corrected her, opening another pack of felt-tips. "It was really good to talk. I feel like we got everything out in the open. I even asked about her illness."

"That was brave."

"I didn't want to pry, but it was good to know because it sounds like she's fine now. She's recovering. It went on for a long time, but it wasn't a disease, it was more physical," I explained.

"It's good you know more now," Sarah said as she unfolded an extra activity mat.

"They're definitely not having *S E X*," I said, spelling it so the children wouldn't understand.

"Yeah, it sounds like they're not," Amelia said.

Sarah nodded too.

Relieved they agreed, I said, "Apparently, they stopped years ago."

"Wow, I can't imagine that." Amelia looked shocked.

Sarah crossed her arms defensively. "It *does* happen. You just get busy in your lives, and a few months go by and you realise you've not, you know"—she raised her eyebrows—"for ages."

"Do you ever want to get out of it completely?" Amelia asked.

I added felt tip pens to the stationery collection on the mat and said truthfully, "All the time, but I've never met anyone like him." I sighed. "I wish he was the lone workaholic guy I thought he was."

"Dave said men like that are all the same. They're happy

with their girlfriends. They get all the sex they want from other women and then return to their girlfriends every night. They'll say anything to keep having sex with you."

I looked at Sarah. That was harsh. I hadn't realised Dave had such a strong opinion.

"I don't know if I agree though," she said, quickly. "Each situation is unique and Sir *is* in love with you."

I put lids back on pens to distract me from our conversation. It was easy to forget reality when Sir was showering me with gifts and whirling me around Barcelona, but ultimately, he had a girlfriend. Maybe Dave was right. Everything had been ruined. The only twist in my fairy tale should be that Prince Charming liked to drag me around the bedroom, not that he had a princess already.

When I returned home an hour later, Mum was at the door with her coat and shoes on, looking confused. "Hi, darling. I'm supposed to be meeting Sandra but I can't find my phone anywhere."

"I'll call it," I said.

A second later, the tone rang out loud and clear. How was it so close? I glanced around the kitchen but there was no phone in sight. Mum checked her bag and after a bit of rummaging, held it up laughing.

"It was there all along. Thanks darling. I'll see you in a bit. I won't be back late."

"Bye Mum," I said, giving her a hug.

I made myself pasta and sat down on the sofa to eat. I grabbed my phone. I had an audio message from Sir. That was unusual. He normally texted. I played it out loud as I ate.

"Tilly. Where are you my little slut? I have a plan. What's your availability like from Friday? I want to take you away."

I smiled. Hearing him call me slut in my childhood home was surreal. I put my fork down and texted back excitedly. *Hi Sir. I have a meeting at 3pm on Friday. If I can change it then it could work.* He replied straight away, *We will take the bubble abroad Baby Girl.* I raised my eyebrows. We'd only just got back from Barcelona. Plus, this time it wouldn't be for a conference. It would be a real holiday. Things were stepping up a notch.

I answered quickly, *I'll see if I can change the Friday meeting now, Sir.* He replied, *Tilly, it's important to do career things over bubble things.* There was no way I was about to go to a meeting instead of going on holiday with him. Besides, I'd only said a meeting to sound important. I was actually having coffee with Sarah. There was nothing more exciting in my life right now than a trip away with Sir. Imagine where we would go. I bet he knew all the best places in the world. He was probably a member of a luxurious hotel club, or owned a private jet.

I typed back, *Yes, Sir. I know.* He texted, *Can I call you?* I choked on my pasta. This was all so impromptu. Could we not keep texting instead? I couldn't say no though. I wanted to hear his voice and find out where we were going. I replied, *Yes, Sir.*

My phone lit up and a photo with his sharp jawline and bright blue eyes filled my screen. I could smell his intoxicating scent all around me as if he were in the room. I took a deep breath to calm down before answering the call.

"Hello Baby Girl."

"Hello."

"Sir," he corrected me.

"Sir," I said. It felt weird saying "sir" in the same room in which I watched *Bake Off* with my mum.

"OK. I'll make this quick," he said, sounding professional.

"If you can change your meeting on Friday, then do. Send me flight times to the Maldives and prices. First class, please. I don't care what airline. We'll both fly from London. If you can't cancel Friday then no stress. We can do it another time. Your career always comes first, Baby Girl."

"I'll look now," I said, unable to stop smiling.

Obviously, I was going. I'd start packing my suitcase now. The Maldives was beyond my wildest dreams. It was for celebrities. Not me. It had the most beautiful beaches in the world. I'd wear a white bikini and dip my toes into the warm turquoise ocean. My pale skin would be golden brown after hours of sunbathing. Sir would fall even more in love with me and forget all about his life in the UK. We would stay there forever. Maybe we'd even get married. *OK, that was too much.* I'd pack first and leave the wedding fantasy for another day.

Chapter 29

I cowered at the front door, struggling with the metal bolt. I'd made a terrible mistake. I'd pressed send on a message to Sir and suddenly the whole screen had changed. Right in front of my eyes, his name had become Darren's. Fear had spread through my heart. My hands shook. My breathing became shallow. I had no idea how I'd made such a fatal error. I didn't even have Darren's number.

As soon as I'd realised what I'd done, I'd sprinted downstairs. I wouldn't have long. He'd see my text as an invitation and be round the house in an instant. There'd be no escape. As I'd reached the door, my heart sank. It was too late. He was already there. He was banging on the door, furiously. I struggled with the bolt. He was inches from my face, on the other side of the door. Terror threatened to freeze my limbs and ground me to the spot, but I fought against it. I used every last bit of my strength to pull the bolt across.

I sprinted away. I had to hide. I'd bought myself an extra three minutes at least. But the knocking was even louder now. It seemed as if the door was made out of paper. I was kidding myself. I knew the truth. The lock wouldn't save me. Nothing could save me now.

I woke up in a cold sweat. A sob rattled through me. My

whole body was trembling. I looked around the room, feeling confused. Everything looked different. My nightmare had come true. The room seemed to be moving around me. I glanced at the door. It wasn't my door. I looked down at the bed. It was huge. The bedspread was white and perfect, not the usual pink, floral pattern of my bedroom.

I wasn't at home, I was in London. It was the morning of our flight. I breathed a sigh of relief. My senses sharpened. The room was still. Everything made sense now. I'd had a nightmare and I was in a hotel about to leave for the Maldives. I was safe. Life was good.

A loud bang at the door made me jump.

"Tilly, are you OK?"

It must have been Sir knocking at the door the whole time. I sprang out of bed. Weren't we supposed to meet downstairs? He'd said he'd arrive in a taxi and we'd go straight to the airport. I flung open the door. Sir was mid-knock, wearing a dark green shirt and jeans. He looked worried.

"What are you doing?"

"What do you mean?" I asked, feeling flustered.

"You're not dressed."

I looked down at my PJs. They were pink with white fluffy sheep all over them. I should have worn my sexy ones. I had no makeup on, bed-head hair and probably flushed cheeks. I bet I looked terrible.

He stared at me. "Have you been crying?"

I wiped my tears away self-consciously but didn't answer. There was no way I could explain my nightmare without sounding crazy.

"I've been waiting downstairs for twenty minutes. I was worried something had happened to you."

"I'm fine," I replied, attempting a smile but panic spread through me. I must have slept through my alarm. If I didn't hurry we'd miss the flight.

"Good, Tilly." He pushed past me into the room, clapping his hands loudly to move me into action. "Get dressed. I'll pack up. We can still make it. You don't need makeup. You look beautiful as you are."

"Yes, Sir," I said, coming to life. We had a flight to catch.

Within minutes, I was somehow showered, dressed and packed. Sir ushered me out of the room, putting my sunglasses on my head and closing the door behind us.

We made excellent timing in the taxi. The road was beautifully clear. I sat still in the back of the cab, processing my nightmare. Sir sat silently next to me. He reached for my hand. His ability to somehow read my mind, meant he knew I didn't want to talk. I squeezed his hand, gratefully.

"We'll be through security in no time," he said.

And we were. As soon as we got out of the taxi, Sir tipped the driver generously for waiting so long outside the hotel with him and strode into the airport. We were immediately guided past the queues and crowds of holiday-makers to the first class lounge, by a woman wearing a dark pink skirt suit and carrying a walkie talkie.

"Just this way sir. Madam," she said, importantly.

A man dragged our suitcases away to be checked in. The woman muttered into her walkie talkie and sped up, her heels clip-clopping on the airport floor. I felt like a celebrity. In record timing everything was done. What felt like seconds later, we stood among the designer shops in the empty first class lounge, passports in hand.

"Please let me know if there's anything you need," The

woman said, before disappearing.

"Go get food. I've got something special to buy," Sir said mysteriously and disappeared too.

I walked around the buffet area, in a daze. Everything was so abundant. I stared at rows and rows of croissants, bowls of fruit salad and baskets of freshly baked muffins. I contemplated a tiny salted caramel cheesecake in front of me. Could I eat it for breakfast? I heard Sir's voice and looked up guiltily. He wouldn't approve of a cheesecake breakfast.

"Tilly," he said, looking pleased with himself. "Sit."

He had a white-and-black Chanel paper bag in his hand. He was a quick shopper. He'd only been gone for ten minutes.

He moved us over to a table near the floor to ceiling window overlooking the runway.

"It's time you had your own scent."

He gave me the bag. I peeked inside, before carefully pulling out a heavy box. The shiny cellophane fell away. I gasped. My own Chanel perfume.

"Do you like it?"

I looked up in surprise to see a flicker of doubt flit across his face.

"I love it." I beamed.

Who didn't love Chanel? Besides, the deal was he bought me whatever he wanted. I was his to dress and do whatever he liked with.

"Good." He smiled. "Now food."

He stood up and walked over to the buffet. He got special treatment wherever he went. I watched a waitress take a hot plate out of the pile for him so he didn't have to do it himself, and another waitress sprint off to get him fresh coffee. I shook my head. It was so typical.

Later, as I sank into the soft leather of our first-class seats, I stretched my legs out and admired my private booth. This would be a flight like no other. It felt even more luxurious than the flight to Barcelona. The goodie bags were unreal. I had a black silk eye mask, expensive toiletries, and even a pair of state-of-the-art headphones.

"Why would we fly separately when we could fly together?" Sir's voice drifted over to me from the booth in front. He sounded a few seconds away from sleep. "I love flights. It's the only time I get any peace."

Chapter 30

I lay down, next to Sir, on a king-size towel. My body moulded into the warm sand. I looked up. An endless black expanse spread out above us as far as the eye could see. Billions of diamonds twinkled in the night sky. I'd never seen stars like it. The world was silent apart from a low hum of insects and the gentle lapping of the ocean waves. I felt the soft air on my face. My nightmare felt like a lifetime away. So much had happened since - Sir arriving at my hotel room to look after me, his gift in the first class airport lounge and the long flight afterwards. It'd been a total of ten hours, followed by a sea plane to the island.

"The stars are beautiful, aren't they?"

It was about six p.m., and already the sky was completely black. I nodded my head in awe. My world felt so important, but it wasn't, not really. My fears were just a moment in time. They would sink into the millions of years of the Earth's existence. I had to stop regretting my past and reliving my fears. My life was good now. Like Sir had said, I was safe. It was frustrating, though. Why was I *still* having nightmares? Maybe he was right and my brain was processing everything. I'd make sure to ask Edith next week. She would have a logical explanation. Our sessions together were going really well so far. Sure, I sobbed pretty much every time I saw her but we were making progress and I loved talking to her.

"It makes you realise we're one of billions, doesn't it?"

"Yes, Sir," I said, quietly.

There was a beat of silence and then he said, "No matter what you're feeling now, Tilly. No matter what fears you have, they will fade. I promise."

"Even nightmares?" I asked.

"Even nightmares." He found my hand in the darkness. We stayed that way for what felt like hours but was probably only minutes. I lost all sense of time as I relaxed into a deep sense of peace, marked only by the heat of Sir's hand in mine and the sound of waves lapping on the sand.

After a while, we walked hand in hand back to our room—well, it wasn't a room. It was a huge suite with it's own private area of the beach. At first sight, I'd thought Sir was joking or giving me a general tour of the place out of interest. There was no way it was ours. We had a super-king-size bed with rose petals scattered across it in the shape of a heart, a luxurious bathroom with a bath that looked out onto the ocean, a living room area, a kitchen, and our very own infinity pool outside with sun loungers and a waterfall shower.

As we arrived back at our suite, I felt an immediate sense of relief. Everything was still here. I hadn't been dreaming.

"Twenty minutes to get ready."

I sat down to empty the contents of my makeup bag out on the floor, before scooting over to the floor-length mirror.

Sir looked at me strangely. "Do you always do that?"

"What?"

"Empty your makeup all over the floor?"

I nodded, feeling suddenly young. Was that a silly thing to

do in such an extravagant place?

His eyes twinkled. "That's very sweet, Tilly. You're very sweet." He shook his head, fondly. "I'll put some music on for us."

A few seconds later, guitar music filled the room, followed by the beautiful sound of a violin.

"'Sweet Thing' by Van Morrison, Tilly. The Waterboys version," he said.

I stood up from my place on the floor and moved closer to him.

"You've got champagne eyes." He ran his fingers over my lips. I shivered, involuntarily. I watched as goosebumps spread along my arms. He traced his hand across them, slowly, making more appear at every touch. "I love the effect I have on you."

"I can't help it, Sir."

He tutted lightly in approval and without breaking my gaze he took a silky blindfold out of his pocket. He slid it over my eyes, making sure it was properly on. He lifted my floaty summer dress up and over my head, before unhooking my bra, with one effortless motion. I was totally naked.

"Sit," he said.

I felt around blindly with my hands to work out exactly where I was. I couldn't see anything. He stopped me and guided me to the bed to sit down.

After a few minutes, I felt a thick, rough material, like rope, between my legs. He moved the length of material gently against my clit. Teasing me. Rubbing me. I arched my back, wanting more. But, he stopped. I felt a flash of anger. I didn't want to be teased. The rope had felt so good. It was completely still now. I willed it to move, to rub against me again but it rested, motionless, against my pulsing clit.

He was somewhere else, now. I could hear a rustling noise. He was busy. What was he doing? The other end of the rope was moving. It was a long length of rope. Maybe he was tying a knot. As each minute passed, the rope tied tighter around my body and trapped my limbs together until I realised what was happening. He was tying me into a ball.

I was now a ball, completely unable to move. As I lay in my tight shape, blindfolded on the bed, a strange thing happened. The room became completely silent. Totally still. And so did I. I had no urge to resist. Being tied into a ball had unearthed a fantasy so deep within me, I felt calm to my core.

Sir kissed me gently. I'd never trusted anyone to tie me up like this before. I was totally at the mercy of this strong, purposeful man. He knew what he wanted and now he had me, helpless, his to do whatever he liked with. My clit throbbed against the rope, my nipples stood to attention, rubbing painfully against the rough material. I waited, my body aching, but my mind at ease.

He teased along my thigh before brushing, accidentally-on-purpose, between my legs. He circled skilfully and softly, building me into a frenzy. He bit down on my lip as we kissed, and finally, he pushed his thick fingers inside me. I tightened around him, gasping.

"Do you like my fingers, Baby Girl?"

I nodded, my eyes glazed over in pleasure. He picked up his pace inside me. He added one, then two fingers, forcing himself deeper inside. He pushed me open and just when I could take no more, he pulled away. His fingers were gone. I whimpered, craving the blissful feeling of fullness. I felt his hands on my hips. The way he'd tied me meant it was easy to enter me. I was open and ready. He ran his fingers down my slit. Pleasure took over everything. He pressed his raging cock against my wetness and with one hard movement, he pushed himself inside. I moaned. He inched himself deeper and deeper.

"More, please, more," I begged.

My climax was coming. He heard the intensity in my voice. His thrusts were harder and stronger as he slammed against my hips.

"Now, Tilly, now," he panted.

I cried out in pleasure. I surrendered every part of myself to him and that's when the most intense orgasm of my life took over.

* * *

"Come outside when you can, Baby Girl."

Sir's voice drifted through to the warm bed. I stretched, lazily. I must have fallen asleep. My body felt tired but in a good way, in a delicious, aching after- sex way. I closed my eyes. Another nap would be perfect.

A yummy smell wafted over, making me open my eyes again. I hadn't realised how hungry I was. There was no way I could sleep now. I moved the duvet aside and padded over to the French doors. As I pushed them open and stepped outside, I spotted Sir setting the table. He placed an iced jug of water down in the middle.

"You're here," he said, looking relieved.

"How long have I been asleep for?" I asked, rubbing my eyes.

"An hour, Tilly. Sit," he ordered. "Wait there."

I sat. Seconds later, he came back with two plates of freshly made food.

"This is a firm favourite with my clients," he said proudly, placing the dishes down on the table.

"Thank you, Sir," I breathed, feeling stunned. How had he had the time to cook?

I began eating immediately. I was starving. His food was full of flavour. The turkey was cooked to perfection, and the vegetables were delicious. This was one of the best meals I'd ever eaten. I felt suddenly emotional.

"Tilly?" He asked, looking into my eyes.

He didn't miss a thing.

"I think this is the happiest day of my life," I confessed.

His laugh rang out loudly across the terrace. He put his cutlery down, still laughing. "Well, that's by far the best reaction anyone's ever had to my stew."

I smiled. It was true. "It's delicious. How did you even get all the ingredients so quickly?"

"The staff are very helpful here. They know I like to cook."

I polished off my food and pushed my plate to the side.

"Are you finished?" he asked, pointedly.

For a split second, I had no idea what he meant, and then it clicked. I pulled my plate back towards me and corrected my cutlery so the knife and fork were together in a straight line.

"Better." He said, approvingly. "Let's head out, Tilly. How long do you need to get ready?"

"Thirty minutes, Sir?"

"Perfect, Baby Girl."

I stood up to clear the plates, but he shook his head. "Go empty your makeup out onto the floor. I can clear up."

I smiled and stepped back into our deliciously cool air-conditioned suite. As I showered, reapplied my makeup, and spritzed a generous amount of my new Chanel perfume everywhere, I couldn't help thinking Sir might just be my dream man.

Half an hour later, he held my hand as we pushed the hotel's restaurant doors open.

"You'll create quite the stir here."

Sure enough, every head turned to look at us. I clutched Sir's hand tightly, pulling self-consciously at my dark-blue silk dress. I couldn't see any women. It felt like a men-only restaurant.

"There aren't many women here. At this time of year, the resort is usually full of men who come to work. They prefer the smaller, more private resorts like this one."

It was just my luck.

Sir gave our name to the waitress, and we followed her through to the outside eating area. I noticed a couple sitting together and felt instantly more comfortable. They were on their own separate deck suspended over the turquoise ocean.

"Please enjoy." Our waitress smiled, gesturing towards the nearest table.

I descended the small wooden steps and waited for Sir to tell me where to sit. It was more for theatre than anything. If he pointed at the chair next to him, it would be awkward. I smiled at the idea of having to walk around the table and sit down on the chair nearest to him just because he'd pointed at it.

As expected, he pointed to the one I was standing next to, and I sank into the cushioned seat. I looked up at the stars in the black velvety sky.

Sir popped the champagne and I jumped in fright. He shook his head affectionately and motioned for me to pick up my glass so he could pour the fizzy liquid into it.

He chinked his full glass against mine. "Cheers to your beauty, Tilly and your wonderful energy."

"Thank you, Sir." I smiled. "Cheers."

Chapter 31

Sir's phone lit up. He focused intently on his steak, cutting it into neat squares, totally oblivious. I shook my head, how could he miss that? The screen was so bright and it was practically vibrating off the table. He *had* relaxed a lot over the past week, though. He was like a different man. The stress of his businesses had left him. His constant rushing around London and impatient tutting had been replaced with a relaxed stroll along the beach and a gentle tap of his foot as he listened to music.

We were sitting in the airport lounge waiting for our flight back to London. The last week had flown by. Scuba diving among the dazzling coral reef and sipping coconut water by the pool every morning already felt like a lifetime ago.

He *still* hadn't noticed his phone. I squinted my eyes at the screen. Who was calling anyway? It was upside down. I couldn't work out the letters but it looked like a female photo. My heart sank. My throat went dry. I looked around for water. I grabbed my glass and gulped the icy liquid down. His girlfriend was calling him. Of course, his girlfriend of nine years could call. It didn't mean it didn't hurt though. I felt the prickly sensation of tears well in my eyes. For a whole week, I'd manage to forget all about his messy life.

"Your phone, Sir," I snapped. I hated that our paradise had been ruined.

He looked up. I watched his face change, right in front of me. My guess was right. It was his girlfriend. The colour drained from his tanned skin as his blissed-out expression disappeared. He snatched his phone.

"Excuse me," he muttered, practically sprinting towards the exit.

He could take the call at our table. He didn't have to hide away. Where had he told his girlfriend he was, anyway? A week was a long time. Perhaps, she thought he was with a client. I wondered if she was suspicious at all, or whether she was used to him going away without her. It was painful to think of him with someone else. Someone who he was probably much closer to than me. He'd said they didn't have sex, that they were like brother and sister, but that didn't mean they didn't love each other. They probably slept in the same bed every night. He'd must kiss her on the cheek when he saw her. Maybe even, the lips. I grabbed my phone out of my handbag. I needed a distraction.

Thankfully, I had a message from Amelia, *Babe, I'm fuming. The chocolate job has been cancelled. They're not even paying us a cancellation fee. They literally called me a minute ago.*

I put my phone down in despair. My distraction technique had worked well. *Not.* I needed good news, not more negativity to ruin my quickly disappearing holiday glow. How could they cancel the chocolate job? I'd already spent my wages about fifty times in my head. I'd told Mum she'd be getting loads of free chocolate too. Without the job, there was no way I could reignite my acting career. I wanted to pay for more acting lessons so I could work out why my recent auditions had gone so badly.

"It was just work," Sir called, cheerfully, walking briskly back to our table.

As if his girlfriend calling wasn't bad enough, now he was lying about it. I thought we were honest with each other.

"Tilly?"

"It's fine." I shook my head. It wasn't worth it. I'd change the subject and bring it up later if I had to. "It's just the chocolate job has been cancelled. Amelia texted me."

He looked genuinely sorry. "That's disappointing. I know that was a lot of money for you."

He picked up his cutlery and carried on eating. As soon as he was finished, he pushed his plate to the side and opened his mouth to talk. It felt like he was about to say something important.

"I've been thinking about this for a long time. I was reluctant because of the blurred lines but obviously, it doesn't matter anymore. We're blurred to fuck," he laughed.

I smiled. "True Sir."

"Alongside my business I run an art foundation."

I nodded slowly. We'd never properly discussed his business or what he did in the little free time he had.

"I invest in up and coming young artists. It's been an incredibly rewarding venture in the past. I helped Charlie Duskins, Elizabeth Stone and Ross Livers."

"*The* Charlie Duskins?" I asked, open-mouthed.

"Yes," he smiled. "He was very different to the Charlie Duskins people know today. He was just seventeen at the time. Young, unsure and lacking any kind of financial stability. The foundation funded his first exhibition. He was a stand-out photographer even back then."

I listened, unable to think of any kind of response that would do his story justice.

"I want to get it going again but the website and social media need to be totally overhauled. You could be the person to do that for me. You're very clever. I need speed and intensity."

Maybe my fine art degree would finally be put to work. I could improve Sir's social media and even do a course on branding so I knew what I was doing.

"It needs to be streamlined and perfected. It will help a lot of young artists again if done right," he added. He stopped talking and waited for me to answer.

Was I ready for this? We were falling into each other faster now. This would be the final test. I knew work and play should always be kept separate but I was sick of how unpredictable promo work had become. Jobs got cancelled all the time. I needed money to pursue my acting dream.

"Can I take a few days to properly think about it? I want to make sure I can do the best job possible for you."

"I knew that's what you would say. You're an excellent worker, Tilly."

* * *

The next morning, as I opened the gate to our garden, I felt cold and tired. The flight had been amazing as ever, but I needed to get used to the new time zone. I always found it more challenging coming back from a holiday than going. Plus, it was freezing in England.

I walked carefully over the grass; it must have rained a lot while I'd been away. I glanced over at the now massive pile of paving slabs leaning against the shed. We needed to build the path as soon as possible. The garden was a mudslide. When I got to the front door, I put my key in the lock and pushed hard.

"Darling," Mum said, looking up from where she was sitting on the dining room floor. She was surrounded by piles of papers and unopened envelopes.

"I started tidying up for you coming back, but I got distracted," she explained, looking dazed. She must have taken the morning off work to be there for me. "It looks like a mess now, but it's an organised mess."

"I should do the same in my bedroom. I've got loads of stuff to sort out," I said.

She moved a pile of papers aside and stood up to hug me. I relaxed into her arms—it'd only been a week since we'd last seen each other but it felt like ages.

"Do you want to go for a walk?" I asked, suddenly.

"Brilliant idea." She jumped to her feet and started sifting through papers, looking for her trainers. She scratched her head thoughtfully, muttering to herself, before turning around and walking into the living room.

She came back with one training shoe. I found the other one by the front door. She pulled on her red fleece and she was ready. She'd had that jumper since forever. It reminded me of Christmas. Mum always made me and my brother go for a walk in the woods before Christmas dinner. It was the last thing we wanted to do - a freezing cold trip outside, instead of staying snuggled up in front of the fire. She said it was good for us, though, and we'd enjoy our roast chicken more.

As we walked up the lane, the afternoon sun warmed my face. Mum walked briskly alongside me talking nonstop about the garden and possibly making a driveway as well as as the path across the grass. I strolled along happily, admiring the flowers and fruit trees in other peoples' gardens as we passed.

"Did you have a lovely holiday?"

"It was amazing, Mum. We scuba dived and had so many gorgeous meals. He even cooked for me one night."

"That's very kind," She said, approvingly. "He mustn't get the chance to do that at home."

I frowned. Did his girlfriend not eat? And then I remembered. Mum didn't know.

"I guess not," I said, uncomfortably.

"It's definitely tough living alone."

Now would be a good time to tell her, but knowing Sir was in a relationship would make her feel sad. I didn't want to do that. In this situation, the truth was irrelevant.

"Definitely. He actually asked me to work with him for his art charity. I'd be in charge of all admin and social media, maybe even branding too. He'd pay me more than promo pays now, and it would only be two or three hours a day of work," I said, rushing to explain the details.

"That sounds excellent."

I raised my eyebrows. I thought she'd be more suspicious.

"He's a good guy, you'd work well together, and you'd have more time for acting."

I blinked at her. She was right, but I'd expected us to talk through the pros and cons first.

"Time for some research," she said, getting her phone out happily.

"Mum," I squealed in horror.

What if she discovered that he was in fact a dom and not the straight-laced, normal guy she thought he was? She'd be horrified to learn he was a multimillionaire who had a penchant for candle wax and industrial-strength restraints.

"What's the name of the charity?"

"It's an art foundation. It's called Foundation for the Future," I said, reluctantly. I couldn't give Mum a fake name. Not when she was looking it up right in front of me.

"It looks great. The website's a little dated. I can see why he wants you to take over," she said, scrolling busily.

I ignored my rapidly beating heart. It was fine. There was no way she'd see anything. Sir's profile on the sex website we met on was anonymous and he was always careful online. He was super professional. There was nothing to worry about.

Chapter 32

I sat down on the large oat-coloured sofa, a familiar rush of nerves running through me. This was my twelfth counselling session but it still felt like a big deal. There was something about delving deep into my innermost feelings, the ones I'd tried to push away into the darkest corner of my mind, that made me feel nervous.

"It's lovely to see you," Edith said.

I smiled. "It's lovely to see you too." And I meant it. It'd been an amazing few months together.

"What would you like to talk about today?"

The nightmare before the Maldives sprung into my mind.

"I had a nightmare," I said.

"What happened?" she asked, sitting back comfortably in her armchair.

As I launched into a detailed description of my dream, I felt emotional but not as silly as I normally would have done. I was starting to realise that my thoughts and nightmares were both a part of me and separate. I didn't have to feel apologetic or angry at myself for having them.

Near the end of the session, Edith asked me a question, "Have you ever heard of post-traumatic stress disorder?"

"Yes." I nodded, knowledgeably. That was when veterans

re-lived their traumatic experiences for months or even years after coming home from the war.

"Have you ever thought *you* could be experiencing PTSD?"

Me? I stayed rooted to the sofa, my heart pounding. The constant flashbacks and terror I felt all too often coursed through my head.

"It's possible and common to suffer from PTSD after an emotionally abusive relationship," she added quietly.

Before I could answer, a tear rolled down my cheek. I remembered Colin knocking on our front door and how terrified I'd been. I thought of my nightmares and the way unwelcome thoughts sneaked intrusively into my mind at all hours of the day.

My chest heaved as I sobbed. "I'm sorry, I don't know why I'm crying."

"Sometimes when we feel a great sense of relief we cry," Edith said gently.

"But why now? Why didn't I have it before?" I asked.

"Trauma has no calendar, Tilly. Sometimes a big life change can trigger delayed PTSD. Other times the brain waits until it feels safe before it begins to process."

I took a tissue from the coffee table in front of me.

"It's a sign your brain is healthy. You are able to respond and process. It's not easy but it's not forever. There's a small body of research into a disorder called post-traumatic relationship syndrome. This is what I believe you are specifically dealing with. I can help you through it. You've made amazing progress so far."

I grabbed another tissue. Thankfully, I'd stopped wearing makeup to counselling after the first session ages ago. As I wiped away my tears, Edith's kind smile reassured me. I could do this. Everything would be OK.

When I got home, Colin was waiting for me.

"You'll have to make a start on the path soon," he called, cheerfully over the wall. "The grass is getting muddy."

"True," I smiled, imagining how annoyed Mum would be. She hated it when Margaret and Colin got involved with the garden.

"Bob has more slabs if you need them," he said.

"Thank you. I'll let you know," I said, gratefully. He might be nosy, but he meant well.

As I pushed the front door open, the house felt eerily silent. It was Mum's day off so I'd expected her to be in sorting out more stuff or making plans for the path.

I walked into the dining room and that's when I saw her. My breath caught in my throat. Her face was pale. Something terrible had happened.

"Darling, you should sit down."

My stomach felt like a lead weight. Mum's nails were bitten down to the skin. She never bit her nails. I sat down slowly at the table, scared of what she was going to say. She pushed today's newspaper over to me.

"It looks like it happened a few days ago," she said.

I read the headline, *Man stabbed to death in city centre brawl.* I gulped. It was Darren. Dizziness took over. The room went black. The last thing I saw was Mum's concerned face peering into mine.

I woke up on our hard dining room floor with a cushion under my head.

"You fainted," She said, holding a glass of water, next to me.

Her face was blurry.

"I caught you." She sounded proud. "I thought you'd be better on the floor for a bit where it's flat. Are you OK?"

My chest was still tight but I felt lighter. A huge weight had been lifted from my shoulders. Was it bad to feel relieved after the news of a person's death?

"Do you want to go for a gentle walk?"

I laughed. I was conscious enough to find Mum's unfaltering passion for walks funny.

My laugh caught her off guard. She said, "I'm serious. It will be good to get out in the fresh air."

As I stood up to follow her outside, I felt a confusing mixture of relief, joy, sadness and fear. Darren hadn't had a good start in life, but that didn't excuse him for being abusive. Strangely enough, his abusive behaviour didn't make his death any less tragic. I *had* loved him briefly once. At least I thought I had. I focused on my breathing as Edith had shown me to. It would be good to speak to her.

"Did I really faint?"

"Out cold. For a whole minute," Mum said, patting my arm.

I'd never fainted before. Dealing with a scary ex's death wasn't exactly a normal occurrence, though.

"Let's enjoy this walk and then snuggle up at home with *Bake Off,*" Mum said.

I nodded. "That would be nice."

It felt surreal to watch *Bake Off* when someone had just died but a little normality would be a good thing. I grabbed Mum's hand as we walked. Just like Amelia and Sarah, she would always be there for me.

* * *

"Good riddance," Amelia said.

"You can't say that," I gasped.

"Yes I can. He terrorised you. He was awful when he was alive and he's awful in death. Hell has gained a new member."

I shook my head. "We have to respect the dead. Think of his mother. She'll be heartbroken," I said. It was the next day and we were in our favourite coffee shop.

Amelia shifted in her armchair, tucking her hair behind her ears. "Yes and I feel bad for his mum but that doesn't mean he wasn't abusive. We barely saw you when you were together and when we did occasionally see you, you were all pale and jumpy. Now look at you, a year and a half on and you *still* haven't recovered. I would have killed him first if I had my way."

"That's not true," Sarah said half-heartedly, taking a sip of hot chocolate but I could tell she agreed with Amelia.

I sighed. "You're right guys. He wasn't a good person and I *am* relieved. But that makes me feel guilty. I shouldn't be relieved about someone's death. It's sad."

"It's definitely sad," Amelia said. "But there's nothing wrong with you feeling relieved, either."

"Hopefully he's resting in peace now," Sarah said diplomatically.

I nodded. I genuinely hoped he was. For him to deliver pain to the people he loved, must have meant he was in a lot of pain himself.

"Come on, let's talk about something lighter," Amelia said.

"I found a good deal for a weekend in Barcelona," Sarah said, brightly.

"We've not been away together for ages." I smiled, relieved at the subject change.

As we crowded around Sarah's phone, I felt a warm glow of gratitude spread through my heart. We'd been through a lot together as a trio. When we were younger the tough times had been different. Instead of deaths and heartbreak, there'd been hospital visits when Amelia broke her leg falling off a slide and Sarah suffered a serious allergic reaction to peanuts. Then as we grew up, we'd been with Sarah at her grandad's funeral who'd been like a father to her. And of course, they'd both been there to take my mind off everything when Mum and Dad got divorced. One thing was for sure. No matter what changed in my life, we'd always be friends.

Chapter 33

The next morning, I settled on the sofa in the living room with my laptop. Mum would be at work all day. It was the perfect time to start working on Sir's art foundation. I didn't want her to get involved and suggest ideas while I was still trying to understand everything. The truth was, I had no idea what I was doing. Hopefully, I'd do a tonne of research and Sir would never know how clueless I was. We'd agreed on a one-month trial first so I could decide if it was a good fit.

As soon as I logged in to Instagram, I was met with a terrible clash of personal and professional photos. Even *I* could tell that wasn't the way to do things. At first sight, a person would have no idea what Sir's charity was about. No wonder he'd asked me to sort it. The first thing I would do was delete all the personal photos. After all, I had permission to do whatever I wanted.

As I scrolled, the same woman in fitness clothes kept appearing. She didn't look like she had anything to do with the foundation. I couldn't work out why Sir would keep posting photos of her. She had blonde hair and looked around forty. He kept saying what an amazing fitness inspiration she was. That had nothing to do with art. I frowned. She'd commented on every single one of his photos. They clearly knew each other well. This was weird. Why was he making such a fuss of her?

My heart stopped. I closed my eyes. I told myself I'd made a mistake. I always got like this when I was annoyed. I panicked and jumped to conclusions. I needed to calm down and act rationally. But as I opened my eyes again, there it was, the photo that made me want to crawl into a hole and sob for the rest of my life. On his feed was a photo of him and this fitness woman at a business event. The sun was shining down on them. His arm was wrapped tightly around her. She was smiling with her immaculate white teeth. Her hair was blow-dried to glossy magazine perfection. She wore a tailored dark-blue suit that fitted her dream body snugly. The caption read: *Lucky to have @vicky_fit with me in Barcelona.*

My stomach felt hollow. I put my coffee down and looked at the once irresistible toast in front of me. There was no way I could eat it. I clicked on vicky_fit's profile. My head was screaming at me to stop, but I couldn't. I scrolled urgently through her photos. This woman had the best life. She went to the most amazing gym. It looked like she practically lived there. I checked her posts. Who went to the gym six times a week?

When she wasn't at the gym, she was at stylish bars in Mayfair wearing Dolce & Gabbana shoes. She even had a Cartier watch. I zoomed in closer to check. I shook my head in disbelief. It was real Cartier. I looked down at my bracelet in horror.

I studied the watch in vicky_fit's perfect photos again. Her name was Victoria Crofts. She was amazing. No wonder Sir was obsessed with her. I started looking at the comments on her photos. To my surprise, his comments appeared multiple times. He'd called her "beautiful" and "sensational." He'd even called her "babe." He didn't call me "babe."

But wait, what was this? There was another guy. Harry_roycey4 commented a lot more than Sir did. It was a love triangle. And, surprisingly, Sir wasn't winning. Vicky replied more to the Harry guy than she did to him. I clicked onto Harry's profile and then stopped myself. What was I doing? This was getting ridiculous. I had a decision to make. I either told Sir I hated his social media and didn't want to work for him or I focused on what I was supposed to be doing and stopped making myself feel bad. I had to stop making it worse.

My phone pinged. Seeing Sir's name sent a surge of anger through me. With a click, I immediately wished I could take back, I pressed to see his likes on Instagram. Squares and squares of supermodels appeared. Women wearing skimpy outfits, tight fitness clothes, and lingerie filled my screen. Everyone looked impossibly gorgeous. One girl had super long legs and brown hair—she was the opposite of me. My legs had never been long. Sir had liked and even commented on every single one of her photos telling her she was beautiful. There was another girl who looked uber glamorous. She spent her life on yachts. She had twelve thousand followers. Sir kept telling her she was stunning and that they must meet soon.

Why didn't he have a personal account for his flirting? Was he so erratic and impulsive that he couldn't stop himself? This was supposed to be a charity. I thought he was professional. All this time, I'd told myself he was dedicated to his work. But I'd been wrong. I'd convinced myself he'd fallen in love with me by accident and was in turmoil because he wanted to be honest and split up with his girlfriend as soon as he could, but was worried he'd break her heart.

In reality, he flirted with every woman he met, talked to multiple women online, and was probably even having sex with other people. He was a total fraud. How he even found time to work, I had no idea. He was running some kind of dating agency here. The gifts he'd bought were probably to throw me off the scent and keep me happy so I never questioned anything. What a waste of a beautiful Cartier bracelet. His presents meant nothing and neither did his words.

I clicked on his inbox before I could stop myself. Now I'd started, I had to see everything. I knew I shouldn't look, but it was too late. It was full of women. To my dismay, a quick glance told me the most recent messages were from last week before the Maldives. I was shaking as I pressed Delete All. I'd seen enough.

I had no idea why he hadn't checked his awful Instagram before I'd logged in. He should have deleted all his flirty messages before I saw them. I was supposed to be making his account more focused on his art foundation, but it was too late. It was the most unprofessional, rubbish Instagram I'd ever seen. He'd ruined the charity by being so inappropriate.

My phone pinged. *I miss your skin, my beautiful Tilly.* I resisted the urge to break my phone in half or throw it against the wall. The word "beautiful" made me want to cry now. I thought we were in love. I couldn't believe how wrong I was. I turned my phone off and left the house to get some fresh air. I needed time to think. It felt like everything was collapsing around me. My magical relationship with Sir was ruined.

Five hours later, Sir sent another message. I was sitting in the kitchen, reading a recipe book, waiting for Mum to come home. After an aimless walk around the village, I'd cleaned the whole house and was now considering making food, but I didn't know where to start. All the recipes looked so intimidating.

I glanced at my phone. Sir's message read, *Tilly. You may talk.*

"Well, maybe I don't want to talk," I snapped out loud.

I'd been dismissed all day because he was busy. It was now 5:23 p.m. I'd been allowed to talk since five, but he could wait. I made sure I didn't click on his message so he wouldn't know I'd read it. I chose the chicken-and-leek pie recipe for Mum because it looked relatively easy and began collecting the ingredients.

At 7:50 p.m., I texted back, *Hi, Sir. I was busy.* A few minutes later he replied, *Is Tilly a happy Baby Girl?* I stared daggers at the screen, unsure how to answer. I could get everything out in the open and see what he said. Or I could text *STOP* and never see him again. My heart hurt at the thought but I knew it was the right thing to do. He deserved to feel as awful as I did.

Chapter 34

"What did you say?" Amelia asked.

"What did *he* say?" Sarah pressed. She balanced four empty champagne flutes in her hands as she waited for my answer.

They both waited impatiently, but I shook my head, unable to speak. Telling Amelia and Sarah about Sir's Instagram had been painful. I looked up at the ceiling, waiting for the urge to cry to subside.

"I wasn't as clear as I should have been," I said, finally. "I didn't mention specifics or that I'd been on his Instagram. I said I'd wanted everything to be wonderful, that I'd built him up as perfect so I felt sad. I said I wanted him to only want me."

"And what did he say?" Sarah asked again.

"He apologised. He didn't know what he'd done to upset me and said he *did* only want me. He asked if he could call me."

"What did you say?"

"I said I wanted to talk in person."

"That was the best thing you've ever said," Amelia said, proudly.

Sarah put a pile of plastic flutes in the bin and then returned to folding napkins on the floor. She looked lost in thought. Amelia took a gulp of champagne, followed by another. I stood in the middle of the room, dazed.

"So much for the dream job and no more promo work." I laughed bitterly.

"It would have been perfect," Sarah agreed from her place on the floor.

"Yeah, if your boss wasn't a massive dick," Amelia said, taking another swig of champagne.

I snorted with laughter. They never failed to make me feel better. We were working as a group of three in the VIP area of the cricket ground. Our job was to look after the VIP guests and make sure everything ran smoothly. As usual, I was the manager but it didn't feel like it. We'd shared the responsibilities equally so far. Besides, the job was easy. We'd spent the whole day talking. We were currently waiting for the last drunken guests to leave so we could go home.

Amelia went outside to clear the empty flutes from the seats, and I carried on talking to Sarah. "I don't want to jump to conclusions, but to be honest, even *I* can't find a positive," I said miserably.

"Look, maybe by some miracle he's a nice guy, but the truth is, Amelia's right. At the moment, the odds are leaning towards... big massive dickhead," Sarah said as she methodically folded more napkins.

A smile spread across my face. Sarah never called anyone a dickhead.

"Will you help me outside? There's loads of glasses. I think everyone's pretty much gone now, though, so that's good," Amelia said, popping her head around the door.

We worked quickly, collecting plastic glasses and rubbish. I was grateful not to talk for a while. My head was full. I didn't mind Amelia and Sarah calling Sir a dick. He *had* acted like one. But the man who told me inspiring stories, encouraged me to focus on the positive, kept me safe and always knew what I wanted, wasn't a dickhead. Had someone stolen his Instagram and flirted with loads of people? There had to be a logical explanation.

"So, has he admitted to messaging other women?" Amelia asked.

"We didn't get that far. He had no idea what I was hinting at. But he knew I was starting work for him this week. We'd agreed the first thing I would look at was his social media, so I don't know how he couldn't guess what I was upset about."

"That's weird." Sarah frowned. "Do you think he *wanted* you to find the messages?"

"No way," Amelia breathed. "He isn't a dickhead."

I frowned. I had no idea what they were talking about. All I knew was that there was a high chance they were about to bring up 'peacocking' again. They looked at me hopefully.

"Guys, I'm so confused right now."

"Well, surely he would have deleted all his messages and comments before you logged in if he didn't want you to know," Amelia explained.

"He wants you to know everything," Sarah added.

"We can guess he's been playing his game as a "sir" for a long time before he met you. He also said he's been cheated on in the past. So, maybe he wants to put an end to all of it and stop playing a game," Amelia said slowly.

"Showing you his Instagram is his way of getting everything out in the open so he can be committed to you." Sarah said.

"He wants to know how you really feel about him."

"You *have* become really close recently."

I frowned. "So, he's been messaging other women but

it doesn't mean anything, and he wanted me to find the messages so I'd get jealous and he'd realise how much I like him and we could live happily ever after?"

Amelia and Sarah nodded in unison, smiling, but I rubbed my head, feeling frazzled. Sir knew how much I liked him. We'd already said 'I love you' to each other. It didn't make sense. Basically, they were trying desperately to turn this situation into a positive when the reality was far from it. The truth was, I had to speak to Sir.

* * *

"I only want you."

I ignored Sir's dazzling eyes. I was not going to fall at the first hurdle. It was the next day and we were in a bar in the centre of London. I sat back on my stool to gather my thoughts. I was determined to make him explain every last detail.

"No, you don't. That's a lie," I hissed.

How could he say he only wanted me when he'd also taken Victoria Crofts to Barcelona?

"Tilly?" he said, turning pale.

I'd never spoken to him so angrily before. My fury had replaced my usual desire to be polite and stick to the rules of our game. I needed answers. The rules didn't matter anymore. I had nothing to lose.

"Why do you keep posting photos of the same woman in fitness clothes on Instagram? She's not a model or an influencer. It looks like you know her. And you took her to Barcelona."

My voice cracked when I said "Barcelona." I stopped talking. I didn't want to ruin my fury with tears.

"Oh, Baby Girl."

The gravity in Sir's voice made me look at him. It looked as if he was summoning up the right words.

"That's the anchor," he said finally.

"The anchor?" My stomach knotted. I knew what he meant, I was just stalling for time.

"Victoria is my girlfriend. I say 'anchor' because a girl I met a long time ago during my sir journey called her boyfriend an anchor. She said a person needed someone to keep them grounded in the normal world while they explored the BDSM world. Victoria is my anchor."

I zoned out. I wished he'd stop saying Victoria was his anchor. All I could think about was her. The designer clothes she wore, her perfect abs, her beautiful face, her effortless glamour. When he'd told me he had a girlfriend, one of the ways I'd been able to deal with it was by separating her from me in my head. I was the fun one who Sir liked to party with, and she was the older, more serious one. They'd watch the news together in the evenings and go for hikes with their dog at the weekend.

But none of that was true. He had a glamorous younger girlfriend and he was in love with her. I was here for sex; she was there for everything else.

"You're in love with her, Sir, not me."

"No, Tilly. I love her like a brother does a sister. I care for her. We've been together for a long time. I want to support her. It was my idea for her to get Instagram, to give her something to do. She doesn't like to work."

I shook my head. How convenient. No one liked to work. He paid for her expensive lifestyle so she wouldn't have to work ever.

"You're submissive to her."

"No, I'm not," he said, his eyes flashing in anger.

"Yes, you are. Not sexually, but socially. Like all the time," I said, pointing my finger at him.

He hated people pointing at him. I waggled my finger harder. He had a strange look on his face, but now that I'd started, I couldn't stop.

"You know, I always used to wonder how it was possible that you were dominant in all areas of your life, but now I get it. You're not. You don't know how to say no in a relationship. You do everything she wants, whenever she wants. She clicks her fingers and you come running."

I clicked my fingers.

"That's not how it goes, Tilly."

I finished my cocktail and then turned slowly to stare at him, my eyes wide. I'd been so upset, it hadn't clicked in my mind. Victoria was the love-triangle woman.

"She's cheating on you."

"What?" He frowned.

The alcohol had kicked in, so I steamrollered on. "There's a guy. He's all over her Instagram."

He nodded calmly, looking suddenly tired. "Harry?"

"Yes." I leaned in closer to him. "Harry Rocey or something."

"That's the one," he said, laughing.

I looked at him in surprise. He wasn't supposed to laugh.

"Look. Harry has been around for a while now. I don't know if they've had sex or anything like that, but he's one of many. It doesn't faze me anymore. A relationship breaks down over a long time, Tilly. I wasn't perfect, not at all, but initially, it wasn't me who cheated."

Every single last angry word left my mind.

He looked at me wearily. "Are you sure you want to hear this?"

I nodded, unable to talk.

He put his wine glass down. "We'd been together about four or five years. We hadn't had sex for a long time. It was a super-stressful period of my life. Business was bad, we were probably both depressed, and sex just didn't feel right. Nothing stays the same for long, though. So, eventually, things began to improve. I started a new business, we moved back to the city again, and she started going out a lot in the evenings—she was happier. I thought our sex life would improve too, but it never did. I tried, Tilly, but there's only so many times you can get rejected, you know?"

"You mean you tried to have sex with her and she didn't want to?"

"Yeah. Look, I won't go into detail because I know you don't want to hear it, but something had changed. She just wasn't interested."

"Did you ever play your game with her?"

"Sub and dom, you mean?" He asked. He shook his head. "No. Never. Well, in fact, we did try once when we were first seeing each other, but she couldn't stop laughing. She couldn't take it seriously. She didn't like being tied up, it wasn't her thing at all. It didn't feel right doing it with her."

"Why do you put her all over your Instagram, and why did you take her to Barcelona?"

Sir looked confused. "That was ages ago. Check the photos. I used to post photos of her all the time because I wanted to support her. We did have a good relationship at the start, but that was years before I met you. When our relationship was good, she'd come to Barcelona with me. It was never like it is with me and you, though. Everything's more fun with you."

"What do you mean? You didn't have fun with the anchor?"

"Sure, we had fun, but, with her, it was always about making a statement. We couldn't just explore and go anywhere. It had to be some amazing place that was in vogue. She had rules about everywhere we went. She was never impulsive. I can't live like that. It's tiring."

It made sense that Barcelona was ages ago. Sir *did* look younger in the photo. I took another sip of my cocktail and said, "Did you buy the Cartier watch for her a long time ago too?"

"Her Cartier watch? That was a recent present from her mum. I wouldn't spend twenty thousand pounds on a gift."

"Wow, her family must be rich," I gasped.

"Reasonably so. They've invested well."

Investing sounded grown up. I had no idea what people even invested in.

I put my drink down. I wasn't done yet. "How can you prove she cheated first?"

He sighed. "There were loads of incidents. The second phone that went off by mistake."

"What?" I asked, intrigued.

"We were watching TV and we heard a noise. I looked around in surprise, but then I saw the look on her face and I knew."

"No way. Only drug dealers and—" I began.

"Cheats have second phones." Sir nodded. "It was charging under her bed. She said it was a spare phone her mum had given her for emergencies. Then there was the Agent Provocateur lingerie under the bed in her suitcase. I've never bought her Agent Provocateur."

"You've never bought *me* Agent Provocateur," I said, raising my eyebrows.

"You're La Perla, Baby Girl, you know that," he said, squeezing my thigh.

I smiled. He sipped his wine slowly. I knocked back the rest of my cocktail. I needed the courage. I couldn't stop now. I couldn't get sidetracked. I hadn't got to the worst part yet.

"It wasn't just the anchor," I said hesitantly.

He looked at me.

I continued bravely. "You've messaged loads of women. You've told women they're beautiful." I tried to steady my breathing. Now was the moment. If Sir couldn't explain himself, this was the end.

Chapter 35

Sir was temporarily speechless.

"I'm sorry," he rubbed his head. "This is the last dregs of my messy life coming out." He looked straight into my eyes. "I've got nothing to hide. Why would I give you access to Instagram if I did?"

That was a good point. He would never have given me his passwords if he wanted to sneak around. That's what Amelia and Sarah must have been talking about.

"I've lived the past six or so years in a relationship where cheating was normal. It became a habit. Just something I did." He paused. "I'm tired of it."

"But you did it recently."

"Tilly?"

"Some of the messages were as recent as last week," I said, unable to look at him. There was a beat of silence. Then another one. This was painful. He had to talk soon. He took a breath and reached out for my hand but I shook my head. I couldn't touch him right now. I was scared I'd cry.

"It's time I did what I'm always telling you to do," he said, finally. "I need to trust, to jump into you. You deserve all of me. Our week in the Maldives changed everything. I'd never touch Instagram, now. It's part of the reason I asked you to take over. I'm ready. It takes time to trust, to give in to our connection. I have to be brave."

I nodded. We'd spent every moment of the day together in the Maldives. Sunbathing, swimming, exploring the island. Being with him had felt so easy, so natural.

"Instagram is a game, like having a card up your sleeve. A backup plan in case it all goes wrong."

I knew what he meant. In the past, I'd always had a backup plan. It made me feel safe and less vulnerable.

"You have my account now. I don't need it. In fact, you should take it over completely."

I frowned. I wasn't here to stop him from having social media, I just wanted to know I could trust him.

"I fell in love with you the first time I met you, Tilly," he said, his eyes softening. "This conversation tells me where you're at and that means a lot." He pulled me close. "Let's leave. We need to be alone."

We held hands as we walked out into the cool evening air and along the bustling road. People drank on the streets outside busy bars, clutching pints of beer and talking animatedly. Normally, the happy mood would be contagious, but my mind was racing. It hurt that Victoria Crofts was Sir's anchor, but the truth was, it didn't matter whether she wore a fleece jumper or a ball gown—they were clearly not happy. I wasn't breaking up a relationship, that was for sure. And the good thing was, my whole perspective had changed. Victoria was a cold go-getter who took all of Sir's money, and he was a romantic pineapple. Spiky on the outside, soft on the inside. He'd once said that he didn't let people in easily, but when he did, he did for life.

The Instagram issue was still gnawing away at me, though. I felt sick at the thought of Sir messaging other women. It was the opposite of who I thought he was. It ruined our fairytale forever. I'd never be able to trust him.

He squeezed my hand. "I love walking through London with you, Tilly."

I liked that he didn't feel guilty. He genuinely seemed relieved to get rid of his backup plan. I could relate. It'd had taken me ages to trust him enough to meet him. It'd been a big deal for me. Maybe this was the same for him. He knew he was going to fall in love and so he'd held back for as long as possible because he was scared of getting his heart broken. He didn't want to drop his guard, in case it all went wrong, but now he knew just how much I cared, he was ready to jump in headfirst. Had he not realised that when I'd said 'I love you' though?

"Here we are."

I looked up. For once, I'd not gone to the hotel first before meeting Sir. It was nearly as big as the Hyde Park hotel and just as grand. I pushed away my nerves. I didn't have time to feel intimidated. I needed to work out a way to get into his mind. If he was telling the truth, I was in a good situation. Not only did he love me but his anchor had cheated on him first so I didn't have to feel guilty. But, if he was playing a game and his cheating went further than just Instagram messages, I'd have to pluck up the courage to end it all now.

We walked through the glossy lobby and into the lift without saying a word to each other. When we arrived, Sir opened the door to our suite and said casually, "I thought we deserved some extra room."

I gasped. It was a mini apartment. It looked just as I'd imagined his house to be—effortlessly stylish, polished parquet flooring, panelled walls, and tasteful pieces of artwork everywhere. The lamps and cushions were more expensive than all the furniture in Mum's house put together. We had a luxurious bathroom, bedroom, walk-in wardrobe, desk, and an open plan living and dining area, all in separate rooms.

I walked into the bedroom and stood in the middle, looking around speechlessly at the mirrored triple wardrobe and super-king-size bed.

"Sit on the edge of the bed. Take your knickers off."

I slipped my thong off automatically and sat down on the edge of the bed. Now wasn't the time for a scene, though. Hopefully he had another plan. He left the room. I stared at the light above me, waiting for him to come back—it wasn't a chandelier this time. It looked like a sculpture. Who knew lights could be such a focal point of a room?

Sir came back a few minutes later with a big bottle of champagne. "We're celebrating, Tilly."

He dragged a dark-blue armchair over to the bed. He popped the champagne. Bubbles poured out of the bottle and into the waiting flutes. He handed me mine and placed his on the dresser. Before he sat down, he took his clothes off. I watched him, feeling bewildered. He'd never got naked in front of me before. Normally, I'd be blindfolded by now.

"I'm going to be naked with my Baby Girl."

He pressed Play on a remote control, and soft music filled the room.

"Put your feet on my thighs, please."

I hesitated. He'd be staring directly between my legs if I did that. He may as well shine a torch down there. I felt embarrassed at the thought. It felt like a night to do things differently though. I was being braver than normal. In one quick movement, I moved to the edge of the bed and placed my feet on Sir's strong thighs. He gazed down, slowly. I closed my eyes, feeling impossibly shy.

"The most beautiful girl in the world," he said. "And she's right here in London with me."

I blushed.

"I'll tell you a story, Tilly. You have all of me now."

He picked up his champagne. I relaxed my legs. A story would be perfect. It would take the attention away from me. I focused on his handsome face, relieved to have a distraction.

"When I was in my early thirties. Older than you are now." He stopped to look at me as he contemplated his words. "I was living on Beethoven Street in Kensal Rise, which is a bit of a shit area in London. I was acting in a way that wasn't me." He looked distant and a little sad as if recalling a memory from another lifetime.

I studied his eyes intently. I couldn't imagine him living anywhere other than Mayfair.

"I was doing a lot of things that were learned behaviour and not my true self. I'd left Naomi for Jade, and it wasn't a good relationship for me. I'll always remember sitting outside Jade's apartment, trying to see through the window. She was having a party and she hadn't invited me." He studied the bubbles in his glass.

"I couldn't work out why, or what I was doing wrong. I was— You'll be surprised at this, Tilly." He interrupted himself, mid sentence. He looked into my eyes, and as if he were apologising, he bowed his head briefly before continuing. "I was needy and jealous. I remember sitting on this cold wall outside her apartment."

He took a sip of champagne. "A light bulb went on. I wasn't put on the earth to be that way. I'd simply become that way."

He let his last sentence sink in. "I decided that where I was wasn't where I wanted to be. So, one day, I was sitting at a bus stop. It was a miserable day, the rain was lashing down. I felt as if I had no purpose in life. Everything was shit. I said to myself, *Make a change.* If I didn't like who I had become, then I had to become someone new."

His voice was more serious now, his eyes locked on to mine. "So, I got on the bus and thought about the person standing at the bus stop. That person wasn't serving me, they didn't make me feel good. I decided to wave goodbye and not look back, and wherever the bus was taking me, it would take me there as a new person. Less fear, more trust, more happiness."

A gap between the songs created a hush in the room. Sir hadn't always been so effortlessly confident. He'd worked through need and jealousy to get to a point of security and freedom within himself. I felt a deep love bursting in my heart. I understood everything now. I could see the vulnerability in his eyes. He was finally letting go. He was finally trusting me.

I looked around the dimly lit bedroom and back at Sir sitting naked, waiting for my response. He scratched a red patch of skin above his pubic bone aggressively. His nails made a rasping sound against his skin. His itch didn't fit with his 'sir' persona. I shifted forward from my place on the bed and went down on all fours in front of him.

"You don't have to— " he began.

I kissed his patch of red skin gently. It felt warm under my lips. I kissed it deeply and softly, imagining all the redness being pulled out of it. I stayed there for what felt like an age with my mouth on his skin. I sensed a deep hush in the room as if the music had stopped playing, but I knew it hadn't. I returned to my position on the bed.

He looked lost for words. “You didn’t have to do that.”

“I wanted to.”

“I would never expect you to do that,” he repeated. “Fuck, that’s super intimate, Tilly.”

Chapter 36

I lay in a tight ball on the cold floor. I gripped hard, making sure it was the perfect shape.

"And release, come alive. You're an angry ball."

I opened my arms energetically and shot up onto my feet to walk before bouncing back into my ball. I had to remember I was still round. Really, I should be rolling, but rolling felt fluid and happy and I was supposed to be angry. I made each step sudden and decisive as I walked past the panel of judges.

"And now you're a peaceful roof."

Interesting. I created the roof with my hands and then strolled loosely with a gentle expression to symbolise peace. I went past the judges the other way, resisting the urge to look up to see what they thought. That was a cardinal sin. I was supposed to be a focused actor who was completely immersed in my role as a peaceful roof, not obsessed with impressing the judges.

"And relax. Some amazing shapes there, guys."

I breathed a sigh of relief and shook myself free. I'd put a lot of effort into it. It was the final exercise of my audition. I wanted to do my best. I'd seen the listing a week ago and realised it would be a brilliant opportunity for me. I could get an acting job while waiting to audition for drama schools again next year. The only downside was, if I got the job, for three months, I'd be nowhere near London. It was a European acting tour, so we'd travel across France and Belgium performing educational plays in different schools. Sometimes the locations would be so remote that there wouldn't be public transport or any possible way to get to airports. It sounded impossible, but Sir's logic was: don't close any doors. Do the audition and then decide what to do. I could always say no.

Afterwards, I went to a nearby pub with Daisy. Most people had left immediately, but I'd noticed Daisy hanging about. She'd made me laugh while we'd been waiting for the audition to start—plus, I'd caught sight of her angry ball. She was a good actor.

"I only hope I get it." She sighed, playing with the salt and pepper pots on the metal table in front of us.

"Yeah, me too," I said, nodding passionately.

I had a good feeling this time. At the end when the head judge had said he'd contact successful people within a month, he'd looked at me. I'd finally impressed someone with my acting. My solo audition before the angry ball workshop had been particularly good. My rendition of "Happy Birthday" was a standout memory.

"Do you want to get some food?" Daisy asked.

I smiled. "I'd love that."

She took out her lime-green purse. I noticed a Pikachu charm attached to it. I loved her style. Maybe we'd both get the job and travel Europe together sampling fine wines and becoming best friends. When it was over, I'd introduce her to Amelia and Sarah and we'd all get an apartment together in New York City and recreate *Friends.* I'd be Joey or Chandler, Sarah would be Monica and Amelia would be Rachel. That left

Phoebe for Daisy. I'd have to ask her if she agreed or would rather be Ross.

My phone vibrated. It was Sir. *How's my Baby Girl?* I texted back, *I'm super good, Sir. I'm all finished now.* He replied, *Good, Tilly. Can you be at Bond Street in two hours?*

He'd booked a hotel in London for me as soon as I'd told him about my audition. We'd had breakfast together that morning before he'd left for work and I'd gone to my audition. I looked up at Daisy. She was checking her purse to see how much money she had. I answered, *Can we make it three hours, Sir? I'm just having something to eat with my new friend.* He texted back, *Of course, Tilly. See you then. Enjoy xx.*

I put my phone down and ordered a special main course offer, two for ten pounds, with Daisy. It was fish and chips. Hopefully, it would be a generous portion. I was starving after my audition. It felt right to celebrate. I was sure we'd both get a place on the tour.

"So, a roof?" Daisy smiled, raising her eyebrows.

I burst out laughing. "I did a lot of prep, but I didn't plan for that workshop."

* * *

A few hours later, as I strode down the street to the hotel to meet Sir, I saw a round mirror on the ground in the middle of the road. It was otherworldly. I noticed several perfectly manicured trees around it. As I got closer, the glassy surface caught the light from a street light. It wasn't a mirror. It was water. It was a perfectly round expanse of water. It looked like a piece of art.

The hotel wasn't as big as normal, but it somehow looked

grander than the other ones we'd stayed in. Two men in top hats bowed as each person walked in. A glossy black car pulled up at the entrance. A woman stepped out wearing sunglasses and a hat pulled down over her eyes. She had to be famous. I clutched my Prada bag close to my chest. I hadn't had time to change after the audition. I was wearing plain black leggings and a pair of flat pumps. At least my cardigan was nice, though. Sir had bought a pink cashmere one for me from Selfridges that looked like the baby blue one he'd given me in Barcelona. It fitted perfectly and felt so soft.

"Good evening," said one of the top hat men with a stern smile.

"Hello," I said as confidently as I could.

I stepped into the lobby. The floors were polished to perfection. I could see a grand piano, armchairs, and a winding staircase in front of me. Waiting at the stairs was Sir. He bowed briefly. I thought of the scene in *Titanic* when Jack bows to Rose.

"Sir." I giggled.

"My lady." He winked. "Your suite awaits."

Upstairs, we pushed open the heavy carved doors into our room and walked down the cream corridor. What kind of hotel suite had it's own corridor? Sir sat down on a chair by a large window in the bedroom while I spun around in delight.

"There's a dressing room," He said, sounding amused. "Turn right. Go and look. You only have thirty minutes though, Tilly. I want to be downstairs as soon as possible."

I shook my head to myself as I sailed away to look. He was always rushing. The dressing room alone was as big as a normal hotel room. It even had an ensuite bathroom. The wardrobe space took up two walls. I only had three outfits. I gazed at the roll-top bath in the ensuite, wishing I had more time. I'd love nothing more than a hot bubble bath but I walked back to my suitcase. I had to focus. I'd do my makeup and hair and then go find Sir.

Twenty minutes later, I heard his voice. "Come and see, Tilly."

I was ready for our night out, but totally lost.

"Where are you?" I asked.

"Walk down the other corridor," he replied, his voice distant.

I left the dressing room through a second door and sure enough, there was another corridor. I turned left and gasped as I found myself in a spectacular living room. I gazed up at the arched ceiling. "This is incredible, Sir."

"Wait till you see it in the morning. The light is amazing," he said from his place on one of several dark blue crushed velvet sofas.

I walked over slowly to show him my outfit. As instructed, I was wearing a little black dress, a g-string and no bra. I'd applied smokey eyeshadow carefully and curled my hair. I came to a stop in front of him with my hands behind my back.

"You are sensational, Tilly."

I moved to kiss him but he shook his head. "Stand for me."

I looked at him blankly, unsure what he meant.

"Stand there," he repeated. "Hands behind your back please."

I clasped my hands together and pushed my shoulders back.

"Close your eyes."

As soon as I closed my eyes, my legs began to shake. My body swung slightly forward. I felt as if I was falling. It was impossible to keep still. I wanted to open my eyes.

"Open your eyes."

He was standing in front of me holding up two blindfolds.

"Which one?"

I never normally got to choose. I knew immediately which one, though. My choice was between a marl grey headband or a thin dark grey scarf that he'd had for years. I was sure he'd used the scarf on countless women before me but strangely, I didn't care. I'd grown extremely fond of it. It looked more elegant than the headband and it was probably silk. It held many happy memories.

"That one Sir," I said, pointing at the scarf.

He nodded, as if he approved of my decision, before tying it carefully round my head.

"Stand up straight."

I stood up tall. It was a good blindfold. I couldn't see a thing. I felt shaky again. I started to sway forwards. I listened to my breathing to keep still. The darkness made my heart pound. I heard a movement on the floor and I flinched. Nothing happened. I flinched again, but nothing. As each second of darkness ticked by, the tension inside me built. The beating of my heart was so loud, it was starting to make me feel sick. My legs were shaking more than they had during our second meeting but this time it was due to effort *and* nerves. The physical exertion of staying still was more than I could take.

Sir's scent drifted over to me in the darkness. I breathed in deeply. Suddenly, I felt his breath on my neck. His hand warmed my thigh. He pushed it up further so his knuckles brushed between my legs. I moaned, softly.

"Do you like that, Baby Girl?"

I ached for more but I knew not to say anything. His thumb gently rubbed my clit. With every stroke, I felt my knees get weaker. There was no way I could keep standing for much longer.

"That will be all." His hand left my body. The blindfold came off.

I blinked my eyes open, my heart heavy with disappointment. Had I done something wrong?

"Sir?"

"That will be all," he repeated, his voice final.

It was impossible to be dragged out of a moment like that and *not* want it to continue. I considered begging him. I needed his touch. I didn't want to wait.

"Sir-" I began.

"It's time to go." He looked pleased at my reluctance but clearly he wasn't about to change his mind. There was no point in arguing. I pulled down my dress and checked my reflection in the floor-length mirror in the corridor before following him out of the suite and downstairs to the bar below.

Chapter 37

I exhaled sharply in frustration, glancing over at Sir. He was standing in his tailored grey suit by the bar, displaying no hint that he'd just made me gasp in pleasure. My tummy did somersaults as I admired his strong hands. I wanted to be naked with him. The more I waited, the more I needed his body on mine.

"Sit."

Sir gestured subtly towards a burgundy armchair. Normally, he didn't care what people thought, so I guessed this was the most exclusive place we'd been in so far. I sat down. I could hear the soothing noise of a crackling log fire and a gentle murmur of people talking around us. It was still Summer but the evenings were chilly. The fire was welcome.

"This is one of the best hotels in London."

"It's wonderful," I said, pressing my legs together. I tried to quell my sexual tension by admiring our surroundings. The obligatory chandelier hung above us, over-stuffed armchairs stood in private corners of the bar, and billionaires discussed their lives in hushed tones. It felt like a secret club.

As soon as we'd ordered drinks, Sir sat back in his chair. "We don't have long," he said, apologetically.

"What?" I asked. There was no way we didn't have long. We

were staying in the biggest suite of the hotel. We could stay in the bar all night if we wanted to.

He didn't correct my "what" to "pardon". He looked distracted. He pressed his lips together. "I can't stay tonight. I didn't know when to tell you. I'm sorry. Let's try and have a good night if we can. Victoria was supposed to stay at her mum's. She normally does. She cancelled at the last minute. There was nothing I could do."

My horniness evaporated. I tried to steady my nerves. The idea that he only met me if the anchor was busy made my blood run cold. Victoria always came first. I ran my finger along the mahogany table in front of us. None of this glamour was worth anything if I couldn't be with Sir tonight. I was sick of being alone.

He paused. "Also, I have something to tell you."

What was he going to say now?

"It's funny really."

Sir's idea of funny was usually far-out. I swallowed nervously.

"The anchor tried to have sex with me."

I blinked. That wasn't funny.

"I said no," he said, quickly.

I narrowed my eyes. You wouldn't say no to sex with someone you'd been with for nine years. Even if it'd been years since they'd last had sex, it would be second nature to them. They shared a bed every night. It wouldn't take much to inch over and run a hand over Victoria's naked body. I studied Sir's face to see if he was telling the truth. Was he telling a half-truth, where you reveal some of the story but not the worst part? My hands were sweating.

"But, why now?" I asked.

"I have no idea."

I frowned.

"But the horse has bolted."

"What do you mean?" I asked, hopefully.

"Well, she can't refuse to have sex with me for years and then try out of the blue just because she's drunk. It doesn't work like that."

I shouldn't jump to conclusions. I looked around the luxurious bar as I attempted to gather my thoughts. I loved being with Sir. I just wished we weren't talking about his anchor again.

"I wonder why now?" I pondered out loud.

"Why now? Maybe she can tell something has changed. It could have been a way of testing her suspicions or a last resort to see if there's anything left in our relationship."

"That makes sense."

"Instagram was the final straw, Tilly. I'm in love with you. I'm loyal to you. You're mine." His eyes flashed with passion. "Even if the horse *hadn't* bolted, I would never go near her. Not now. I have you."

"I trust you," I said, surprising myself. It normally took me a long time to trust but I had said it without thinking and the truth was, I *did* trust him. Although the odds had been stacked against us recently, I knew deep down he was loyal. Instagram had been a defence mechanism. I was sure of it. I looked across the table at him. He seemed relieved, like he'd been waiting to tell me. His face was happier. He was so handsome.

"You've got love eyes, Tilly."

I blushed, wishing I could see my eyes. "Have I?"

"Be careful what you wish for," he said, shaking his head, affectionately.

Suddenly, a glass of red wine appeared in front of Sir.

"2005 Bordeaux, Sir," The waiter announced.

He nodded, "Very good."

I raised my eyebrows. That was the same year as the wine he'd had in Barcelona.

A cocktail landed in front of me, "And a passion fruit martini for the lady."

"Thank you," I said. Passion fruit sounded more demure than porn star.

After the waiter had gone, Sir's mouth set into a straight line. "We'll have one more drink here, Tilly. Then we'll go upstairs. When you enter the suite, you'll take off your dress and-" He stopped mid sentence. "Oh, who am I kidding? I'm coming in with you. It's my job to take your clothes off."

I giggled, feeling my shoulders relax. I took a sip of my sweet cocktail. I preferred it when he came into the room with me. I got so nervous when I had to go in first.

He studied my face while he savoured his wine. "What are you thinking?"

"I'm thinking I prefer when you come into the room with me, Sir. I can't cope with the tension alone."

He tutted gently. "Oh Baby Girl, that's the whole point. That's why I use a blindfold. Tension makes your senses sharp. It creates a heightened experience of pleasure."

"Yes Sir," I said, remembering the way he'd made me ache for him in the hotel room.

An hour later, we left the bar and walked upstairs. Sir guided me to our suite's dining room. He peeled off my little black dress as soon as we got inside and pointed to a dark wooden chair. I sat down, obediently, naked apart from my tiny g-string. I rested my hands on the wooden arms.

Sir tied his silky scarf around my head and darkness descended. He tied me tightly to the chair. It felt as if he was using the new ties he'd bought recently. They fastened with a sharp metal clasp. I could feel the metal against my skin as he pulled hard. I heard a sound of appreciation from him. I imagined him stepping back to admire his work. I arched my back and pushed my chest out. The silence of the room made me acutely aware of every movement. I detected his footsteps on the carpet as he walked away.

Minutes later, he came back with a bottle of wine. The flow of liquid hitting the glass was unmistakable. The strike of a match made me tense. I held my breath. Silence. My heart hammered against my chest. I tried to work out what was happening. Did Sir have a candle?

A second later, I yelped in agony. Yes, he did. Wax landed on my left thigh. It was burning hot. He dripped the candle repeatedly onto my skin, keeping to the exact same part of my thigh. The sensation was agonising. I clamped my mouth shut and bit my lip down hard. I was determined not to make another sound. I didn't want to give him the satisfaction. Adrenaline coursed through me as he continued. My fists were squeezed tight by my side. Sir tortured the same patch of sensitive flesh over and over again. The closer he got with the candle, the more painful it became.

Finally, I smelt fire again as he blew the flame out. It was all over. I breathed out shakily. The uninterrupted darkness felt like a welcome friend now. There was no sharp pain to break the peace. I took a moment to gather my senses. My skin was on fire.

I heard a new noise. The clink of ice cubes. The shock of cold on hot hit me as Sir poured ice all over my blistering thigh. My breath caught in my throat. A bottle of champagne popped close to my face. I jumped. He was playing with me. Amplifying my senses. Teasing me. It made me angry. I flinched suddenly as a spurt of cold champagne poured down my body. I pictured it shooting out of Sir's mouth like a fountain. The icy liquid made my skin goosebump everywhere. I pushed my head back as my hot skin finally cooled.

Sir kissed me, before untying me. He took the blindfold off gently. "Welcome to the room."

I didn't want to be welcomed into the room. Not yet. I squeezed my eyes shut to block out the bright light above us.

"Open your eyes," He demanded.

I wasn't ready. I sat with my eyes closed.

"Tilly."

I squinted them open, reluctantly. The room was bright. Sir was sitting naked before me. He motioned to me to pass him my knickers. I obeyed, pulling them over my heels, feeling dazed. He checked I was watching before wringing the material out slowly onto the dining room carpet. I knew it wasn't just the champagne that had made my knickers so wet.

"Suck my cock."

I fell to my knees immediately. My tipsiness made me brave enough to look into Sir's eyes. It was my time to tease *him* now. I licked gently, before picking up speed. I moved hard and fast. I stopped completely. I returned with the softest of lips, the slowest of licks. I darted my tongue around the most sensitive part, imagining the pleasure he must be feeling.

"Enough," he said, his breathing heavy.

He took me in his arms and pushed me onto the dining table. He thrust inside me. My back felt cool against the smooth wood as he pressed harder and harder. I gripped his arms for dear life. The relief of him finally entering me was too much. Sir flipped me over and dragged my feet to the floor. My head was now on the table. My hands held onto the edge. I could hear him panting in my ear, as he pushed roughly inside me.

"Yes, Tilly. Now, Tilly," He shouted. He bit down as he came, sinking his teeth into my shoulder. I tightened uncontrollably around him, shuddering as I lost all sense of myself.

Chapter 38

"There's too much going on. Victoria is fighting for her man. Meanwhile, you're getting left in luxury hotels alone," Amelia ranted.

"It's not what you signed up for," Sarah said, from above us. She was perched on top of a huge decorative piece of Red Leicester, dressed as a mouse. It was nine a.m. We'd been at the cheese festival since seven. It was empty. There'd been a trickle of people when the gates first opened, but nobody else since.

"Enough is enough," Amelia said, taking a bite of Stilton.

"It's time," Sarah joined in, adjusting her mouse ears.

"Time for what?" I asked, confused. I thought our night together had gone well in the end. The sex had been possibly the most amazing yet. I *had* cried in the hotel room when he'd left, though.

"You need a plan," Amelia announced.

"A plan?"

Sarah nodded. "You need some kind of timescale so you know when they'll split up."

They were right but I felt nervous even at the thought of asking Sir for a plan. He'd been with his girlfriend for so long. Did I have the right to ask him for a timescale?

"Do you think they'll end up staying together?" I asked, quietly. "What if they *did* have sex?"

Amelia shook her head, vehemently. "No. Absolutely not. They didn't have sex. You'd know." She popped a pickled onion in her mouth. "He's in love with *you*. You're everything he's ever dreamed of."

I breathed out in relief. I trusted Amelia's opinion. I waited, apprehensively to hear what Sarah thought. She'd climbed down from the plastic Red Leicester and was now standing next to me stroking her mouse's costume tail, deep in thought.

"He'll stick to his word," she said finally. "No two situations are ever the same. Sir is loyal deep down. I know it."

I glanced at Amelia holding the plate of pickled onions and Sarah, in her furry mouse costume. I loved them dearly.

"Did you tell Sir about Darren's death?" Sarah asked, tentatively.

I shook my head. "It didn't feel right. We've never talked about him specifically before. Why start now?"

Amelia nodded. "Keep it simple."

"Anyway. You have a timeline to focus on," Sarah said, letting go of her tail.

* * *

The next morning, I arrived in London to see Sir. Shops were opening around me. People were rushing past on their way to work, carrying briefcases and laptop bags. As I stepped onto the escalators, I heard a loud clap. It was Sir. He was waiting for me. His blue expensive suit stood out amongst the crowd of commuters.

"Look lively, Tilly," he called, cheerfully.

He *never* parked the car and came into the train station to meet me. I walked straight into his strong arms. His stubble brushed my skin as he kissed me.

He released his embrace, grabbed my suitcase and walked quickly into the nearest shop. I followed behind him, feeling dazed. It was a chocolate shop. Maybe he was buying chocolate to melt on me later.

"One for the lady, please."

The man behind the counter started dipping strawberries into thick milk chocolate. It smelt delicious. This must be a snack for now. I *was* hungry. I hadn't had breakfast. I couldn't argue with eight chocolate strawberries. I'd ask Sir what was going on once I'd eaten them.

He walked out of the shop and made his way to Chanel, which was two doors down. I ran behind him, eating a strawberry along the way. When I joined him, he'd already found a shop assistant and was asking her for red lipstick, lip liner, and nail varnish. She showed him three shades. He picked one and then waited for each item to be wrapped carefully in tissue paper and ribbon.

His shopping frenzy was making me feel uneasy. Had he done something wrong? Perhaps he'd ended up having sex with Victoria. Or he'd realised he was still in love with her. He wanted to split up with me and thought presents would soften the blow.

"What's the world coming to if a man can't treat the love of his life?" He said happily as we walked out of the shop. He handed me the Chanel shopping bag. I took it carefully, clutching the bag of chocolate strawberries in my other hand.

"Thank you so much, Sir."

"You're welcome, my gorgeous Baby Girl. You deserve only

the best. Always remember that."

I took a bite out of my second strawberry and walked faster to keep up with him. He was speeding towards the exit. We reached his Mercedes and jumped in. As the car's engine hummed quietly to life, he placed his hands on the steering wheel and focused on the road ahead. I looked over at him, admiring the fit of his suit, new Rolex and polished brown brogues. Perhaps, he'd won a huge business contract and was celebrating.

"Now, I have to warn you, the plan has changed slightly."

I knew it. Here came the reason behind the gifts.

"My apologies. I thought tonight was a definite full bubble. I have until eight p.m."

"It's OK. I understand, Sir," I said, immediately.

I looked out of the window at the sea of traffic. What was I saying? It wasn't OK. These sudden changes of plan had been happening for weeks now. We couldn't carry on like this.

"I really appreciate your patience."

"I don't know how much longer I can do this for."

"What's 'this'?"

"You know, Sir. You know what I mean. *This.* Your situation," I snapped.

He didn't say anything. I sat still, my arms crossed tightly. I refused to speak until he'd given me a solution. I was happy to wait for hours.

"Do you know what?" He said.

I turned to look at him, pressing my mouth closed tight to make sure I didn't speak.

"You're right."

I frowned. The argument I had poised in my mind like the next moves in a game of chess fell away. I was lost for words.

Sir agreed with me.

"I can't imagine how I would feel if it was the other way around," he continued. The car stopped at a traffic light, and he turned to look at me. "I will sort it, Tilly. I will. This is all temporary. I know what I want."

I nodded. I trusted him, but I would bring it up again later. Amelia and Sarah were right. It was time for a plan.

* * *

Hours later, Sir swiped the key card against our hotel room door. The button turned green.

"I'll have to go soon," he said, apologetically.

Instead of replying, I kissed him. If he left now, I'd be alone again, unable to order room service because I couldn't answer the door sobbing and naked with hot chocolate powder all over my mouth. When I was sad, I had a habit of knocking back spoonfuls of hot chocolate powder like it was sherbet and getting naked because I didn't want to feel constrained.

I could make Sir forget everything by being extra fun and sexy so it'd be too late to leave and he'd *have* to stay the night with me. I had a plan, and it was going to work.

He pushed me hard against the wall and kissed me back. It was working already.

"Tilly," he warned, "I will not fuck you and leave you."

"Then don't leave."

"Baby Girl. I have to go," he said, moving away.

"Why do you have to go so soon, though? It's only eight. Can't you stay out later?"

He laughed. "Are you taking the piss out of your Sir?"

"No, Sir, I would never do that," I said, my eyes wide.

He moved closer. I jutted my chin, defiantly. He tutted and then, without warning, pushed me onto the bed hard. He spanked me three times, his hand making sharp contact with my skin each time. I called out in delight, wanting more, but to my disappointment, he pulled me up onto my feet immediately.

"Come on. I'll order you room service on my way out. Let's get on with this."

I'd been sure his spanks were the start of something, but my plan was failing. It was time for my last-ditch resort.

"Sir, I want a timeline," I blurted out.

"Baby Girl?"

"We need a plan. I have to know what you're thinking. I don't want to share you. I don't want this."

"I appreciate that. I would never share you, so I can't expect you to either. I need time to think. I want to give you a proper answer."

It looked like he was getting ready to go again. Couldn't he think here?

"Can I have a rough idea of when you might split up?"

"Well, the real question is, when do you want it to happen?"

I took a deep breath. That was a big question. The idea of ending a long relationship made me feel sad. Sir's life was intertwined with Victoria's. They must have so many memories together. Their families would know each other really well. What about their dog? They definitely had one because Sir's Instagram password was Desmonddog99. The fact that mine and Sir's happiness relied on making the anchor and a dog sad didn't feel good. I frowned. I shouldn't have to decide. It was his decision to make.

"I want it to happen when you naturally would have split

up. Forget about me. When would you have stopped living together?"

"Well..." He sat down on an armchair to think, and I resisted the urge to celebrate. Finally, he was staying. We should order a bottle of wine and a meal to the room.

"Obviously, I would have ended things ages ago, but then she got ill. So, if I didn't know you, I would wait till she was better, and I definitely wouldn't do it at Christmas."

For once, he wasn't being clear. I wanted a one-word answer, not a vague reply. We couldn't create a timeline if he didn't give me a definite date.

He noticed my expression and announced resolutely, "December."

That was five months away. That was a long time to wait. I *had* asked when they would have naturally split up, though. I couldn't have it both ways. If I wanted it to be sooner, it would be more upsetting. It would feel like my fault.

"I can do that but I won't be able to cope with any longer, Sir."

"I understand, but it has to be right for everyone."

He was much more caring than he liked to admit. Wanting to split up with his anchor in the most considerate way possible had to be a good sign. Surely, it'd be a red flag if he ran off without a thought for his girlfriend of nine years? Or maybe he always put Victoria first and was saying five months to get me off his case. Sarah's advice ran depressingly through my mind: *They always choose their partner. They'll never leave them.*

"I have to go," Sir said sadly, standing up to leave.

As he left, a tear ran down my cheek. I cursed myself.

"Oh, Baby Girl. Don't cry," he said, brushing it away.

"I'm fine." I smiled as more tears fell.

"I'll be here first thing tomorrow morning." He held my head gently. "I love you."

I forced another smile, bigger and brighter this time. "I love you, Sir. I'll be fine."

I watched him walk away down the corridor. He called back to me before he disappeared from view, "You're a game-changer, Tilly. Five months."

I blew him a kiss. I couldn't talk. A sob choked me. I closed the door and sat on the edge of the bed staring at the dark-green sofa and balcony. We had a view over the gardens, but I couldn't see anything. It was too dark outside.

Sir would walk through the front door of his house soon. He'd call hello to Victoria. She'd look up comfortably from her place on the sofa. They'd probably share a glass of wine and watch their favourite TV programme together. I bet they had a nice house. I still lived with my mum. I was twenty-five. Why was I such a loser? I collapsed back onto the bed. It was time to eat hot chocolate powder and cry alone at the TV.

Chapter 39

Check your emails.

I looked at my phone screen, confused by Daisy's text. It was an hour later. I was sitting tucked up in bed crying at a property programme. It was a transformation of a barn in Tuscany. It had been an emotional episode. I wiped away my tears. I never got any good emails and I couldn't work out how Daisy would know anyway.

I opened my inbox. Instant butterflies. There was a message from the acting tour company. I held my breath as I read the last line: *It is our pleasure to offer you a place on tour.* I punched the air in joy. I flung the duvet aside. I danced around the room. I'd been sure it was all over. They'd hated my audition, thought I was a terrible actress, and cringed at my rendition of "Happy Birthday," but I couldn't have been more wrong. I was on my way to Europe. Daisy must have got the same email. Our adventure of sampling fine wines around France and Belgium could begin. It would be my first ever paid acting job. I'd win an Oscar in a few years' time. I knew it.

Sarah and Amelia would be so excited. Hopefully, I'd be able to bring them *both* to the Oscars and not be forced to pick one of them. But what about Mum? I'd have to ask the committee for extra tickets. It was all so sudden. One minute, I was a terrible actress; the next, I was on my way to an acting tour and probably the Oscars. My phone vibrated. It was Sir. I stopped dancing.

I looked at the screen. *Please don't be upset, Tilly.* I came back down to earth with a bump. The acting tour was four months in total. That was a long time. It was such a pivotal moment in our relationship. What if he forgot all about me and kept with the anchor? I'd be stranded in some house in the middle of France, totally unable to reach him. Maybe the location would be so remote, we wouldn't even be able to text. I sat down wearily on the bed. The acting tour could be a step too far. I needed to be close to Sir to make sure the plan unfolded as it was supposed to.

I messaged him back, *I never thought I'd be the other woman. I never thought I'd be in this situation.* He replied quickly, *I don't like my situation.* When he was as clear as that it made me feel hopeful. Maybe, he'd stick to the plan and we really *would* be together in five months. He sent another message, *It's a matter of timing and making sure no one is unduly hurt.*

"I'm unduly hurt," I cried.

I texted, *Don't you think that's unavoidable? Won't she be hurt no matter what or do you know how to avoid it?*

He answered, *Money will help. It's a bizarre situation I've created. The clean lines of my previous games made it easier. You have, as I wanted, torn it up.* Because we had so much chemistry, we'd seeped into his normal life, which meant he no longer had clean lines or an arrangement that fitted in with his relationship. Maybe he felt pressure to carry on supporting Victoria financially. Perhaps, he'd said five months so he could make sure she was all set with money.

He sent another message. *Trust me, energy and perception*

have shifted dramatically. The universe is pushing. It will deliver and I'll move forward. It's who I am. I typed back, *The energy in your relationship?* He replied, *Yes. Exactly. I'm finding it more and more challenging to step back into my normal life after seeing you. I'm in love with you, Tilly. The anchor isn't stupid. She knows something has changed.*

Maybe, I'd got it wrong. They didn't watch TV together in the evening; instead, it was a tense atmosphere where neither person wanted to speak the truth, and only Desmond the dog made it easier.

I sighed. *Sometimes I wish I didn't know about your situation.* He texted, *I know, Baby Girl, but I have to have purity with you. I want to be honest always. You are like a dream. Life is short and precious.* He was so romantic. I felt an urge to tell him about my acting job, but I hesitated. I knew he would be supportive—he would tell me to go. But I wasn't sure if I *could* say yes. I'd be away from him for months. Without me there as a reminder, would he ever actually leave Victoria? It was too risky.

* * *

The next evening, I arrived home, my mind still in turmoil. I was desperate to ask Mum for advice. There was no way I could, though. She'd hate to know I was part of an affair. I pushed the heavy gate open automatically but my hand met thin air. It was already open. That was unusual. I ducked to avoid the low-hanging branch, but that was gone too. As I stepped onto the grass, I saw Mum. She was breathing heavily and pulling a paving slab across the mud.

"If I don't do it, no one will, Tilly."

She dropped the slab into place to join the seven others that were already there.

"Only five to go," she said, breathlessly.

A surge of emotion ran through me. She'd always done everything herself since Dad had left. She was a force of nature. I felt tears well in my eyes and blinked them away. I couldn't cry because Mum was doing the garden. But, it was more than that. She'd been meaning to do it for months. Instead of sitting back letting the world happen to her, she'd gone out and sorted it. She'd not complained about the mud or the fact there was no one to help her. She'd made her path happen.

Holding back tears, I helped her with the next paving slab. I braced myself as we picked it up together. It was much heavier than I'd expected. My legs buckled under the weight. I didn't know how she'd managed to move seven by herself.

We methodically placed each stone down onto the muddy grass. Tears rolled down my cheeks, but I didn't care. The rain would disguise them. Mum wasn't wearing her glasses anyway. I was safe to cry. She wouldn't notice. The truth was, I had to follow her example. If I didn't do something drastic, I'd be stuck in the same place. I wouldn't lose Sir by going away. I'd secure him. Besides, he had to know what he'd be missing. He needed space to work everything out for himself. If I kept hanging around letting him cancel bubbles all the time, he'd have no reason to break out of his comfort zone and keep to the timeline we'd created. He was preparing to end a nine-year relationship. That was a big deal. I couldn't sit back and wait helplessly for that to happen. His situation made me feel terrible.

I didn't want to feel sad for the next five months. I didn't have control over his relationship, but I *did* have control over my own happiness. It was time to take action and say yes to the acting tour.

I waited until we were inside and warm and dry before I got my phone out to text Sir. I had one message from him. *Let me know when you get home please.* I replied, *I'm home now. By the way, I got the acting job.* A few minutes later he texted back, *Why didn't you tell me? This is amazing, Tilly. We need to celebrate.* I smiled. *Thank you, Sir. I only just found out today.* He replied, *I knew you could do it. You're super talented.*

"Would you like something to eat?" Mum asked. "I could make toast."

"That would be lovely," I said, looking up from my phone.

She walked into the kitchen to get the bread, so I sat down on the sofa in the living room and replied to Sir. *It's four months in France and Belgium, and the locations are super remote. I might not even have a phone signal sometimes.*

He sent a long message back. *Tilly, your dreams will always be more important than me. It's important you live your life. We can make four months work. We can make anything work.*

I held my phone tightly to my chest. He believed in us, in me. I felt a surge of confidence. I was finally starting to believe in myself too.

Chapter 40

"OK, you're a flirty table and I'm a dangerous box," Daisy yelled, taking a glug of wine.

I snorted with laughter. It was three months later. We were snowed in at the first house of the tour. It was an old French cottage with a log fire and no TV. There were a few puzzles and board games kicking about, but that was it. Hopefully, in a few days time, the snow would clear enough so we could travel to the next school to perform our plays, but until then, we'd have to keep ourselves entertained.

"It's gonna be better with four. Me and Sean will be angry gnomes," Patrick said, looking up from his phone.

"What?" I screeched, looking at Daisy in glee.

"That doesn't even make sense," she said. "You've got to be an inanimate object combined with an adjective."

Patrick's face went blank. "What's an inanimate object?"

"Hang on, what kind of gnome are you thinking of?" I asked.

"The decorations in gardens," Sean said, walking in from the kitchen with a cup of tea.

"Well, that would work, then." I said.

"Oh yeah," Daisy said. "That *does* work."

"Because a gnome is the same as a roof or tree or decoration in the garden. They're all inanimate objects," I agreed.

Patrick frowned. "Mate, we're the magical kind."

I suppressed a giggle. Patrick had no clue as to what was going on.

He looked blankly at all of us. "Your improv game is going to be better with two angry gnomes."

"Let it go, mate. You've got the wrong end of the stick here," Sean said quietly, shaking his head.

I exchanged a look of delight with Daisy. The aim had been to create an improvisation game based on the angry ball exercise from the audition, but this was way better. If Patrick kept getting confused, we'd be entertained for hours.

"So, he's not even texting you?" Daisy asked later when we were tucked up in bed.

We'd won a game of rock, paper, scissors to secure the better bedroom, which had two double beds. It was bigger and warmer. Hilariously, the boys were stuck at the other end of the house with single beds and a tiny heater.

I sighed. "I'm not sure what's going on. For the past two days, he's been so quiet. He doesn't text at all apart from a heart emoji every few hours."

Daisy knew everything about Sir. I'd told her the whole story one evening over pizza when Patrick and Sean had gone to bed. She'd loved everything about it. She was the ideal person to tell because she was as romantic as Sarah but clued up like Amelia.

My phone vibrated. I checked it quickly without touching it. It was Sir again.

"Just another heart," I said out loud.

"Are you ignoring him?"

"Yeah."

This was the strangest thing in the world. Ever since the

tour began, we'd texted non-stop all day, every day. Why had he suddenly stopped?

Suddenly, a bad feeling spread through me. I clicked onto Instagram. I had to check. I went straight onto Victoria's profile. I scrolled through the usual glamorous selfies. There was nothing new to report. But then I saw it, a recent full-length photo of her on a night out. I checked the caption quickly, my hands shaking. My hunch was right. Yesterday was the anchor's birthday. Sir had gone silent because they were celebrating. He'd probably spent the whole week preparing, shopping for her and booking the best restaurant in London. He still loved her, I knew it.

A colourful photo caught my eye. It looked artier than the rest of Victoria's feed. It was a painting of a dog. It must be Desmond. It was amazing. Maybe Victoria had had it commissioned for her birthday. I checked the caption. As I read the words, I felt a weight press on my heart. I put my phone down before I could cry. I didn't want to get upset, not again.

The caption had read: *A special present from @47_Marcus.* I didn't need to check. I knew that was Sir. Sir had bought the anchor a beautiful painting. Desmond was like their child. They were a family. I was invading their relationship. As soon as I'd discovered he wasn't single all those months ago, I should have stopped seeing him immediately. Maybe, Victoria's birthday had made him realise how much he loved her, and me not being around had made it easier. Perhaps, he'd even changed his mind and wasn't going to come and see me in France at all and didn't know how to tell me.

My phone lit up. Sir was calling me. Despite my horrible discovery, my heart soared.

"Hi, Baby Girl. Apologies. It's been so busy."

As his voice filled my ears, I found myself smiling. He sounded so cheerful, I couldn't help but feel calmer.

"It's fine. I can imagine how busy you are," I said softly.

"You sound beautiful, Tilly, and very relaxed."

I laughed at the irony. "Thank you."

"So. I've finished packing." He paused, waiting for my response.

I smiled in relief. He was busy with his business and moving out. He'd been sending hearts because he was focused on getting everything organised, not because of Victoria's birthday.

"That's wonderful. It's a big job to do."

"Well, I've been packing gradually over the past few weeks, so it's been easy. Everything's done now. I'm ready."

I felt a wave of admiration. There must be a lot of logistics involved in moving out of a house after so many years, but he was being methodical. It sounded as if leaving would go smoothly, just like everything Sir did in life. It was only a month away now. No wonder he'd not been texting me.

"You're the best."

"Thank you, Tilly. I must go now. I just wanted to check you were happy and well."

"Thank you, Sir."

"Bye for now," he said and hung up.

I felt relieved, but then the painting came rushing back into my mind. *You're the best?* What was I thinking? I was no further forward. I should have asked him what was going on instead of getting impressed by a few suitcases. Sure, it was good he was preparing to move out, but it didn't explain Instagram. If anything, it made it worse. He was hiding the anchor's birthday from me.

A few days later, I stood in the bedroom I shared with Daisy looking out at the snow.

"We have no hope of going anywhere," She said angrily, marching into the room in her dinosaur onesie and flopping down onto the bed.

Everywhere was still covered in a thick white blanket. She was right. We were stranded. We'd been able to get to the schools to perform our plays, but that was because we'd had a van that was equipped for heavy snow. Now, we had two days off with no access to the van. Everyone would be stuck in the house. Meanwhile, I was supposed to be meeting Sir.

"No hope. We're in the middle of nowhere," I said, gazing sadly out of the window.

Any moment now, my phone would ping and Sir would apologise for not being able to come. He was supposed to be picking me up to go to Basel, which was an hour away. His flight had probably been cancelled. I bet he was pacing up and down in a London airport wondering how he was going to break the news to me. Or he'd arrived in France and was hopelessly lost in the snow. Maybe he'd broken down and was waiting for a rescue team.

"I thought two days off would be the perfect chance to see Sir."

"Has he cancelled?" Daisy asked, stunned.

"Not yet, but he will."

The snowflakes looked huge. They were the kind of size I'd hoped for at school so none of the teachers could travel and classes would be cancelled. But now, I was willing them to stop. I looked up at the white sky. At this rate, we'd be snowed in completely and wouldn't even be able to do our performances.

My phone pinged. I rushed to pick it up. Here came the apology. I could feel a lump forming in my throat already. I'd wanted to see him so much.

Chapter 41

I think I'm here.

There was no way Sir was here. I looked outside. All I could see was snow. I ran to the window on the other side of our bedroom and yelled happily. There was a brand-new car outside. It was Sir. He'd braved a snowy flight, driven in the thickest snow, navigated the confusing roads, and managed to get up our narrow hill to park directly outside the house.

"He's here," I squealed.

Daisy rushed to the window.

I ran downstairs to grab my bag and put my shoes on. Even though I'd been sure he'd have to cancel and stay in London, I'd laid everything out ready so I'd be able to leave immediately if he did, by some miracle, show up.

"I can't believe it."

"Have the best time," Daisy said, giving me a hug as I grabbed my coat.

I ran outside. I waved goodbye to the boys as I left. I could see their faces pressed against the living room window, trying to get a look at Sir. It felt like Christmas. I stepped over the ice carefully in my black stiletto boots. I was wearing a black faux-fur coat, my baby-blue cardigan, black jeans, and a black hat and leather gloves Sir had bought for me.

"Careful as she goes!" he called out of the car window.

I laughed. The road *was* super slippery. It had transformed into an ice rink. I opened the boot carefully, slid my suitcase into the freshly vacuumed interior, and skidded around the side of the car.

It was cosy inside. I could hear music playing. I flung my handbag down, jumped on top of Sir, and kissed him full on the lips. Gone were the days when I needed permission. Straddling him was probably going a tad too far, but he didn't complain, and I was excited to see him. The dog painting was still looming in my mind, but there was no way I was bringing it up now. He'd come all this way for me. That had to mean something. I could ask him later.

"Baby Girl." He laughed in surprise.

I climbed over him to sit down in my seat.

"What a welcome," he said as the engine hummed to life.

"I have no idea how you got here, Sir."

"It was actually really easy. The flight was great. I picked the car up from the airport, and it was a straight road all the way here."

I shook my head in disbelief. He'd made a snowstorm sound like a summer's breeze. Nothing was impossible with Sir.

When we got to Basel, we got out of the car and crossed the icy road to the hotel. As we walked up the steps to the entrance, I felt like pinching myself. Sir squeezed my hand. We were staying in a palace. How did he find places like this? I'd daydreamed about seeing him every night for weeks, and now it was finally happening. I'd almost forgotten just how gorgeous he was and how magical he made everything feel.

"Straight to reception," he said, ushering me up the stone steps.

I walked quickly and confidently. I knew the drill. No matter how scared I felt, all I had to do was smile and walk with purpose.

As we entered, I held my breath as hundreds of women in sparkling ball gowns and men in black tie and tails milled around the lobby. It looked like a press event or royal wedding. I glanced down at my jeans. I hadn't received the ball gown memo. I gazed up at the ceiling. Three floors above me was a huge chandelier that looked heavier than the whole building. I had no idea how it stayed up. What if it came crashing down and killed us? We were getting so close to our happy ending, I didn't want anything to ruin it.

"Sir, this way, please," a woman behind reception said as soon as he gave his name. She guided us over to the lift with a big smile. "Everything is ready for you. Please let us know if there's anything we can do. It's our pleasure to welcome you."

"Thank you. That will be all."

He had such an effect on people. The lady pressed a button inside the lift, beamed at Sir, and walked away, her heels echoing on the marble floor.

When we arrived on the top floor, he clicked open our hotel room door. I hesitated. There had to be some kind of mistake. There was no bed. Just a flight of stairs.

"Please continue." He gestured for me to walk forwards.

At the top of the stairs, it all made sense. The room opened out into the biggest suite we'd ever stayed in. It was even grander than the London hotels. It was a penthouse. I could see a lavish bouquet of flowers in the centre of a marble table in the dining area, the windows looked out onto the river below, and the living room's plush sofas were gathered around a real, roaring log fire.

"Wait until you see this, Tilly," Sir said, guiding me up another flight of stairs.

We walked through the master bedroom, and I made appreciative noises, but he ignored me and opened the door to the balcony. The cold night air whipped around us as we stepped outside. We were on the roof of the hotel on a jaw-dropping balcony with a hot tub and a magnum of champagne waiting in a silver ice bucket. The lights of Basel lay below. I turned to look at Sir.

"Only the best for my Baby Girl," he said, holding his hands up as if to say, *I can't help it.*

I shook my head in disbelief. No wonder the woman had been so attentive at reception.

"We'll be back to enjoy it later. For now, we have a town to explore."

Basel was set on a steep hill next to a lazily winding river. There were thousands of fairy lights in the trees and glittering Christmas decorations hanging across the bridge. As we walked up the hill, I gazed longingly at all the wine and cheese bars. Maybe we could have a night sampling cheese. Sir could have wine and I'd have endless cocktails.

We passed by lots of jewellers, and I resisted the urge to point. He was always wearing new watches. He loved being on time. This was the ideal place for him. Maybe Sir was actually of Swiss descent and this was his childhood home. I swung my bag out in front of me as we strolled along. I held on to his arm and nestled into his wool coat, breathing in his scent.

"Tilly?" he asked, noticing my bloodhound impersonation.

"I've missed you, Sir."

"Yes, Baby Girl." He smiled.

A few minutes later, he stopped on the hill to read a menu

outside a restaurant. My stomach rumbled. I was starving.

After a quick inspection of the menu, we walked in through the narrow door. The heat from the fire greeted us. I'd forgotten just how easy it was to be with Sir. He always made sure everything was perfect. Amazing food. Beautiful places. And most importantly an effortless connection between us that made everything magical.

I removed my hat and gloves, putting them away neatly in my handbag, hoping he would tell me to take my coat off soon.

"Sit." He pointed at a table near the window.

I sat down and waited impatiently. I'd gone from freezing cold to boiling hot in a second.

"You may take your coat off."

I unbuttoned it and hung it on the back of my chair, feeling relieved. As I watched him read the menu a second time, the day's events played themselves out in my head: being snowed in with Daisy, the surprise of Sir turning up, the beauty of Basel, and the impossibly luxurious penthouse suite. There wasn't room for bad news, but the dog painting was still niggling away at my heart. How could he be this amazing but also ignore me for two days while he gave a painting to the girlfriend he wasn't supposed to care about?

Sir ordered our food and I looked dreamily into the crackling flames. I watched them dance in the fireplace as rosy cheeked, relaxed people tucked into delicious meals around us. Winter coats hung on wooden stands near the entrance of the restaurant. Tempting smells of food wafted around us. Plates clattered happily. He'd picked an excellent place to eat. I'd be ruining the evening if I brought up Instagram, but I had to know.

"I didn't expect this," he said as our food arrived. He pointed to a dish of potatoes, looking irritated. "I clearly had no idea what I was ordering."

I giggled in delight. Sir never made mistakes. Ever. The dish was basically cheesy roast potatoes and looked nothing like his normal Michelin-star diet. He'd also ordered three meat dishes, a sandwich, and fries.

"I've ordered Swiss tapas," he said, looking puzzled.

I nearly spat my champagne out as I laughed.

"More drinks?" he said, his eyes twinkling.

"Yes, please, Sir."

I put my drink down. I couldn't let this wonderful night go on any longer without addressing the big issue. It was time to get it out of the way.

Chapter 42

"May I ask a question, Sir?" I said bravely, looking into his eyes seconds later.

He laughed easily. "You will, anyway, Baby Girl. Go ahead."

"It's about Instagram."

"Uh-oh. What's Sir done now? I'm not even on it anymore."

Jokes must be a good sign. Maybe everything would be OK.

"Why didn't you message me for two days?"

He opened his mouth to speak, but I rushed on. I didn't want an apology.

"I couldn't work it out. You always text me, so—"

"I sent heart emojis, and I *did* ask how you were twice," he said, interrupting me.

I stared at him. Was he for real? In many ways, the random heart emojis had made it worse. Plus, all he'd said was, *Hope you're OK.* That wasn't enough for me. He should have said, *I'll be busy packing for the next few days, and I'll talk to you properly in Basel.*

"The point is, Sir, it all seemed strange and not like you, so I went onto Instagram and—" I paused. "Well, I went onto the anchor's profile."

I fell silent. He waited for me to carry on.

"I didn't realise it was her birthday."

A look of recognition flashed in his eyes. "It *was* her birthday. I didn't think it was worth mentioning, though. Nothing happened."

"She went to lots of nice bars."

"Did she? I wasn't invited. She went out with her friends. You probably know more than me at this point." He took a sip of his wine. "Funny story, actually. I wrote a card and got her a bottle of wine, and for the first time ever, I didn't put kisses in the card, I didn't say, *I love you*. I couldn't do it. I couldn't lie." He looked into my eyes. "She went mad about it. She said, *You're not my uncle*."

I laughed. "Why did she say that?"

"Because I said 'all my love,' instead of 'I love you.'" He shook his head. "She said it was an uncle thing to say. It's fine, I batted it off."

I bit my lip. It was now or never. I launched into it. "What about the dog painting?"

He looked at me blankly.

"You gave her a painting of a dog."

He stared at me. He didn't have a clue what I was talking about.

I sighed heavily. "It was a dog. The picture was big, painted on canvas with a red background. The dog was black and white."

"Desmond," He said suddenly. "Her dad has a dog called Desmond. Well, he was ours, at first, but Vicky felt like her dad would give Desmond a better home because I was always out and she spent all her time at her Mum's."

Hearing Sir say "Vicky" was a dagger to the heart, but, of course, he had a nickname for her. They'd been together for years. I liked how he was explaining their dog to me—he clearly didn't realise how much I knew about Desmond. Maybe I *had* been stalking Victoria's profile page a little too much.

"We still have him over for occasional weekends and when her dad goes away for holidays." He smiled fondly. "He's a good dog. When we were first together, I painted him as a puppy. The whole family loved it. It was the first time I really felt a part of her family. They still talk about that painting now."

"*You* did the painting?"

"Yeah, I like to paint. I don't do it enough, really," he mused.

Was there no end to his skills? He was a successful entrepreneur, an amazing storyteller, a sex god and now Picasso too.

"How do you know about it?"

I looked into his eyes. He was genuinely interested. He wasn't pretending.

"Victoria posted it recently on her Instagram. It looked like it was her birthday present for this year. She said it was a special present from you."

"Baby Girl, it was years ago, and it was a Christmas present, not a birthday gift. I wouldn't be surprised if most of her photos are out of date. You should stop paying attention. Your time is precious, Tilly."

I nodded. He was right. It was all too easy to jump down a rabbit hole of possible scenarios. Nothing bad had actually happened. I'd been feeling sad for no reason. The anchor *had* looked different in her photo with the painting, and she'd posted one a month ago of Barcelona saying she was there with Sir when he was with me. I definitely couldn't rely on the accuracy of her posts.

When we got back to our palace, the royal function was still happening. We walked through the lobby. My heels clicked loudly on the marble floor. I kept my head down in case I was asked to leave because of my jeans, but then I remembered Sir had spent thousands on the biggest suite here. We probably had a higher status than the ball-gown people, so I strode along confidently with my head held high.

The bar at the back of the hotel, overlooking the river, was a tranquil place to be after the chaos of the lobby. Sir motioned for me to sit down. I steadied myself on a high stool at the bar, wondering whether I should drop my bag on the floor. It would be a long way down.

"Shall I take your coat?"

"Yes, please," I said.

As he hung my coat up, I looked for a hook for my bag under the bar and found one. That was better than dropping it. It was the kind of thing Sir would do.

"Let's order cocktails," he said, reaching for a thick leather menu.

We browsed the pages together. The choice was endless. Luckily, the menu was in English and there were artistic sketches to help us with the fancy names. The best thing to do was pick the cocktail that sounded the most like a porn star martini. That way, I'd know it'd be fruity and sweet.

Once we'd ordered, I sighed happily. The night had been amazing. I still couldn't believe Sir had braved a snowstorm to get here *and* made it seem effortless. Being whisked away to Basel was exactly what I'd needed. I'd been feeling trapped and tired of the constant performances and painfully early mornings on tour. It was a relief to be back with Sir and let go of all responsibility. Plus, seeing him in person had assured me everything in his life really was OK. Our timeline was on track.

"All I can see is your Disney love eyes and the river behind you."

"Oh, I forgot about the river," I said, excitedly.

"Switch places. You need to see."

I jumped down from the stool, and switched seats with him, taking in the view through the floor-to-ceiling windows. The river was nestled next to the town, a shine of red and green lights shimmering in the water.

"Sir, it's beautiful."

"Exactly."

A hush fell between us. It felt natural to take my time and allow silences now. I never rushed our conversations. Everything was always considered with Sir. I was definitely on my way to being truly Zen.

"Have you ever talked to your friends about our age gap?"

I hadn't expected that question. I'd thought he'd be thinking about how peaceful I looked, not about the difference in our age.

"How would it work? What would our friends and family think?" he asked.

I'd talked to Amelia and Sarah about our age gap at the start, but it didn't feel relevant anymore.

"How many years *is* it, Sir?"

"Twenty-six."

"I spoke to Amelia and Sarah ages ago when we first met."

"What did they say?"

"Sarah thought it was a big difference. She said I had to think about the future and whether I would want to have kids or not, and Amelia said I wouldn't want to be looking after you when you're old."

He looked aghast and said defiantly, "No one will ever be looking after me, that's for sure. And as for children, I clearly have no problems there."

I laughed. I loved the flashing anger in his eyes.

"I'm not Sarah and Amelia."

"Maybe they have a point, though. We have to realise this might not work in reality." He shifted in his seat. "Imagine what my kids would say."

It would be awkward, that was for sure. I must be closer in age to his kids than him. I liked to think it didn't matter, though. True, I couldn't imagine introducing him to my mum or brother and definitely not my dad, but did we have to?

"People can't be prejudiced, Sir. It's only age. Surely, everyone who loves and cares about us will want us to be happy."

"Yes, Tilly," he said, but he didn't look convinced. I waited for him to say something else, but he stayed silent.

"I don't doubt your fertility, by the way," I joked, trying to lighten the mood.

He laughed.

"I don't agree with Sarah. I'm sure you could give me children if I wanted them. Men can have kids at whatever age they want can't they?" I continued.

Sir smiled. "I think so. Pretty much."

Feeling encouraged, I carried on. "Anyway, children are a long way away for me. I'm only twenty-five."

"That's true. You're young. You don't have to think about it yet. It's a challenging time."

"What do you mean?"

"It can get intense. Having children as a couple is impossible sometimes. There's a lot of compromises needed."

I sat silently for a few minutes, processing what he'd said.

"Do you think that's why my mum and dad got divorced?"

"No, Tilly. It's always more complicated than that. How old were you?"

"I was five and my brother was seven."

"Just through the woods. That's when it gets easier with kids."

"And my dad did cheat, so that's obviously the reason."

"There's always more to it, though," Sir said, shaking his head. "When you have babies, the love that was there between you and your partner gets halved and divided between the children. It can feel lonely for the man."

"Why?" I asked. He'd have to explain his point in more detail. I didn't agree. Love didn't get reduced when you had babies. You couldn't ration love.

He picked up a pen from the bar and sketched a diagram on the napkin in front of him. "See, here's the love from the woman to the man. Then here it is broken down and split into two for the children. Now it's shared in the family."

I looked closely at his tree diagram before turning it over and starting afresh. "How about this?" I asked, drawing different lines to show the love multiplying. "The love isn't divided when the children come, it's multiplied."

He looked seriously at it, noting my amplified love lines, before nodding in approval. "That's an excellent diagram."

"Thank you," I said, putting my pen down triumphantly.

"That looks like the perfect situation," he added, half joking, half serious. "Let's go up to our penthouse suite and take this into the hot tub."

I giggled. "Yes, please, Sir."

Chapter 43

Sir wolf-whistled from the hot tub as I stepped out into the cold night air wearing a red bikini that clung to my body. I laughed. He was definitely drunk. He wasn't the wolf-whistling type. I climbed into the deliciously hot water and shivered in pleasure. He popped the magnum of champagne with a flourish. I looked down at the river far below us. I could hear music. I smiled. Sir had brought his favourite blue speaker. He took it everywhere. "Fix You" by Coldplay was playing.

"Chris wrote this for Gwyneth when her dad died. It was really tough for her. His death really hit her, you know?"

"I never knew that," I said softly, listening to the lyrics. I imagined my own dad and everything we'd shared together. I wouldn't want to be alive without him.

"I guess it would be super tough. I wouldn't know. I never had a dad," he said thoughtfully.

I looked at him, confused. He must have had a dad.

"He left when I was young."

I waited for him to continue, but he didn't. I looked up at the sky, feeling emotional. Everything was perfect. The dog painting had been nothing to worry about. Sir had kept to his word. He'd packed his suitcases and was ready to leave his old life.

"This track is a big one for me. It saved me many times."

I sank deeper into the hot tub to warm my shoulders. I listened carefully to the song so I could imagine how Sir was feeling. There was no music yet, just a woman talking. He mouthed along to the words. He nodded his head, and then the music kicked in. I'd never heard anything like it. The haunting sound of an organ synthesizer rang through the night air.

"'One of My Turns' by Pink Floyd. It got me through some interesting times, Tilly—OK, here we go. I'll tell you a story."

I sat back in the water, letting myself completely relax.

"I used to sleep rough."

Not one inch of me had expected him to say that. He'd been homeless? I remembered the way he'd knelt down to talk to the man on the street at the very start of our journey together. The night we'd gone to The Savoy.

He saw my worried eyes and said, "Only for a bit. It was an unusual time. I didn't get on with my mum's new boyfriend. He moved in, and, in the end, I moved out to his bedsit. Great story, actually," he said, stopping to smile.

Only Sir would make the tragedy of being homeless into a great story.

"So, Mum had said she'd packed me plenty of food to start me off."

He began to laugh. I smiled, his laugh was contagious.

"But, when I unpacked the box with my best friend, Paul, inside were just two things - An out-of-date tin of spam and a box of dried Paxo. We crawled around the floor laughing. We couldn't stop. What was I gonna do with Paxo?"

"How old were you?"

"Fifteen or sixteen."

"Wow," I breathed. That was young to leave home.

"Why did you have to move out?"

"It was me or him, really," Sir said. "The bedsit wasn't much bigger than the hot tub we're sitting in now."

I looked around. It was huge for a hot tub but tiny for a person's house.

Sir carried on speaking, quietly. "My mum went through a lot. After the attack she basically became an alcoholic. So much happened."

I took a tentative sip of my champagne, not wanting to put him off.

"It's one of the reasons why I tell you you'll always be safe."

He turned to me and I looked into his blue eyes. I hadn't expected him to bring the conversation back to me.

"I know your previous relationship still haunts you. I know you blame yourself for even being in it in the first place. But the truth is, we all have our own journeys. It's our responsibility to own what happens to us, to learn and not to blame. And most importantly, to move on. Each moment in your past led you to where you are now, so ultimately it's all good."

"He died Sir."

"Your ex-boyfriend died?"

I nodded. "A couple of months ago. There was a story in the local newspaper."

"Are you OK?" He asked, aghast.

I looked up at the starry sky. I *was* OK. Wherever Darren was now, he was in a better place. Maybe, in death, he'd finally be able to heal and become the good person I'd always known he was. In my heart, I believed heaven existed and that everyone was given a second chance, no matter what they'd done in their life.

I nodded and gave Sir a little smile. I watched his face. His eyes were alight with love. I sank further into the bubbles, feeling for the first time in a long time, completely happy. I felt light and without a care in the world.

"When you say so much happened after your mum's attack, what do you mean?" I asked, delicately. I didn't want to pry but I loved hearing about his childhood.

"Well," he smiled, sadly. "Where to start?"

He took a sip of his champagne and continued. "There was the classic not-turning-up-at-my-art-school-interview. The tutors said I was good enough but needed to show I had financial support because I was the only student not living at home. My mum had to come in to say she'd support me. It didn't matter if she could support me or not, she just needed to say yes."

He looked away. "I remember sitting in the dusty, high-ceilinged reception of the art college. Two o'clock went past, then three. By four o'clock, I got on a bus to where she lived with him to find her lying in a bed with a bottle of vodka."

The music stopped playing. The night silent.

"I think it's the first time I shouted at my mum." His voice cracked.

I wanted to reach out for his hand, but I held back. He was still lost in the memory.

"I didn't speak to her for years after that. But as I got older, I realised, you can't change someone who doesn't want to be changed. You can will them to change all you like, but ultimately, you have to accept people for who they are and learn to love them."

"How long did you stop seeing her for?"

"Years. Probably four or five. Then, she started visiting me in London. I used to feel embarrassed about her falling off the train drunk. She'd tell me she'd stopped drinking for good, but I knew she'd be sneaking off to the toilet, having a swig of whiskey."

He sighed. "I learned I had to let go of my past to grow. And part of letting go of the past is to forgive and love rather than to hate. I remember the last time I saw her. We had an amazing day in London. She was still drunk, but I put everything aside, held her hand, and took her shopping. She was like a kid in a sweet shop. She loved the glamour of it all. We visited her favourite shops. I had money by then, so I bought her everything. She'd look at me nervously like it was too expensive," he said, with a chuckle.

"We went to Keats House. She loved his work. We looked at the quotes on the wall and books in cabinets. She stopped at one cabinet for ages. Inside was her favourite quote. Even now, I remember it word for word."

He took my hand. "'I almost wish we were butterflies and liv'd but three summer days—three such days with you I could fill with more delight than fifty common years could ever contain.'"

His voice broke with emotion as he quoted from Keats' letter. I couldn't take anymore. A tear rolled down my cheek.

"Doing whatever she wanted that day, going with her to Keats House, I could see the little girl in her coming alive like she was escaping life. That night—I had a nice house by then—we sat on the rooftop together. She climbed into my hammock and I poured her a glass of wine. Then she laid back, rocking gently. I raised my glass to her and she thanked me for a lovely day. And that was it. She said nothing more, just stayed quietly looking at the stars."

He looked up at the night sky above us. "It was the nicest

silence I've ever had. I didn't know it at the time, but it would be our last moment together."

I could see deep sorrow in his eyes and something else - Vulnerability. Just a glimmer.

Chapter 44

A week later, I woke up feeling as if I was about to be sick. The nerves had got to me. I'd hardly slept. Today was the day Sir was supposed to deliver his news and break up with the anchor. I'd stayed awake until three a.m. wondering what he was doing. Was he asleep? Maybe Victoria's long, graceful arm was casually draped across him while he slept. Or maybe he was awake, letting her scent drift around him a final time. A tiny doubt would creep into his mind. He'd wonder what he was doing. He'd suddenly cancel everything and stay with Victoria.

I glanced at my phone on the bedside table. The worst part about being stuck in the middle of nowhere was that I had no idea what was going on. I was out of touch with everything. Sir had dismissed me until we were due to meet at the airport. But that was a whole two days away. If I broke the rules and called him, at least I'd be able to hear his voice and work out how he was feeling. It would annoy him, though; plus, it was disrespectful. I had to give him space to break up with Victoria in his own way. They'd been together for nearly a decade. I had no right to intervene.

I sank back into my pillow. I'd give myself another five minutes. It was freezing in our room at the cottage. I swore I could see my breath. I wasn't ready to face the day yet. I looked to the left to see Daisy in her tiger onesie, still asleep. She had an endless wardrobe of onesies. I smiled. I shouldn't overthink anything. There was nothing I could do. I had no control of the situation, so it wasn't worth obsessing about. I had to keep focused on each moment and not create worst-case scenarios in my head.

A few minutes later, I dragged myself out of bed, put on my fluffy lilac tracksuit, and ate my fruit and granola alone in the kitchen downstairs. The stone floor was icy cold under my feet. I checked my phone even though there was no way Sir would have messaged. He'd be busy. France was only an hour ahead, so it'd be five a.m. in the UK now. He'd be sitting in his Mercedes sipping a coffee, stuck in London traffic on his way to work.

He'd probably break the news to his anchor later when they were alone. I had to believe it was going to be alright and he would do it. He'd always delivered in the past. There was no reason why he wouldn't keep his word.

In the van on our way to the school for the day's performances, I closed my eyes and pressed my head against the window. It was snowing outside again. It was probably raining in London.

Later, Sir would sit down with Victoria in their massive Mayfair apartment. I bet they had a chandelier in every room. Rain would pitter-patter on the windows outside. He'd look at her fondly, opening his mouth to speak, his eyes shining with emotion. They'd hold each other in a tight embrace. They'd wonder if there was still time to repair what had gone wrong.

"You're quiet today," Patrick said as we assembled the heavy metal poles of the stage.

Instead of a normal wooden stage or the permanent one that each school already had, we, for some reason, travelled around with a DIY one. It was like a test of character every morning to set it up. It wasn't self-explanatory either. It'd taken us ages to get the hang of it.

"Am I?" I snapped.

It was seven in the morning, what did he expect? We weren't on a chat show.

"Sorry," he mumbled, busying himself with the stage.

I felt a flash of guilt. He looked hurt. My tone had been harsh. Patrick had no idea what was going on. I couldn't take it out on him. I helped him with his side of the stage to say sorry.

"I'm just tired, that's all."

He nodded cheerfully, rubbing his eyes. "Me too."

Once the stage was finally up, we met behind it to wish each other luck. The students were filling up the school hall fast, yelling and laughing at the sight of the stage. We did our usual group high five and then waited for the lights to go down.

When we'd first started touring, I couldn't cope with my nerves. My legs visibly shook before a performance. I'd been even more nervous than I was for drama school auditions, but now, it felt normal. I didn't feel scared at all. It was just a job, like any other.

As the room was pitched into darkness, the audience fell completely silent. I waited at the edge of the curtain. The lights went up, and Patrick and I marched out to begin the opening act. I was a cartoon-style evil character who got angry about everything and couldn't work out how to trick the good guys. I yelled all the time and rubbed my hands together like Mr Burns in *The Simpsons* when something went wrong. It was an exhausting character to play. I strained my voice and kept my body constantly tense to show how angry I was. The director had drilled the importance of my character's fury into me during rehearsals, so I didn't want to let him down. I always imagined he was watching in the audience.

At lunchtime, we ate our sandwiches together cheerfully, discussing the two shows we'd done so far.

"The boy at the front was loud." Daisy laughed.

"Oh, he loved it, didn't he? He couldn't stop shouting." I said with a mouthful of cheese sandwich.

"The girl at the back was making me laugh," Patrick said.

Sean smiled. "She was your number-one fan."

She'd been somewhere near the back and kept shouting helpful tips and encouragement at Patrick.

My heart dropped. I had a message from Sir. I took a deep breath. I crossed my fingers. *Please tell me it's good news. Please tell me he's done it.* I looked at the screen. His message read, *Breakup delayed.*

My body went cold. My stomach felt hollow. I put my sandwich down. I couldn't see properly. Everything was blurry. The moment we'd been building up to for months had been delayed in a second as if it wasn't a big deal. His text was so brief and unapologetic.

Sarah had been right all along. Sir had clearly postponed the breakup because he didn't think it was right for Victoria. Everything was always about Victoria. She cheated on him, didn't have sex with him, and made him work all the time to fund her lifestyle, but everything had to be perfect for her. He didn't care about my heart or how I felt. I'd been so naive. They'd been together for years. Of course, he loved her. They were practically family.

The only choice I had left was to text *STOP*. It was time to end it all and take control back. I thought of Mum and her paving slabs. No one was going to do anything for me. I was the creator of my own happiness.

"Tilly, we're starting in five," Sean said, quietly.

He was standing with Patrick, who was arguing with Daisy about something. Sean was the shyest one of all of us and always polite.

I smiled. "Thank you."

"Are you OK?" he asked, looking at me with his earnest green eyes.

I suddenly wanted to cry. I blinked away tears angrily. I couldn't start sobbing on stage. Sir had already ruined my life. I couldn't let him ruin my performance too.

"Yeah, yeah, I'm fine. Tired, though," I said, forcing a casual laugh.

I moved away and busied myself with my costume and props.

As I shouted my way through the first scene of our last performance, I felt like a shell of my former self. I was running on autopilot. The audience was laughing, but I couldn't hear them. A montage was running in my head: London and the Savoy Bar, the way Sir's eyes had danced with mine when I unwrapped the Cartier bracelet. Barcelona and his voice when he told me he loved me for the first time. His laugh when I twirled round and round, clutching my Jimmy Choos and new bag to my chest. The Maldives and holding hands in the silence, looking at the stars. Basel, sitting on the rooftop in the hot tub sipping champagne as he told me about his mum and their final moments together. It was all over. The most unbelievable time of my life was over.

The last scene of the play finished dramatically, and the audience gave us a thundering round of applause. We walked on together as a cast, holding hands. I looked along the line at Patrick, Daisy, and Sean as we stood proudly on stage to take a bow. We'd been an amazing team. I'd never thought I'd make such good friends, become a whizz at putting up a stage, or be so confident performing to students every day. And the truth was, no matter what happened with Sir, I could do anything. Even if I decided to end it all, I'd be OK. I could get through anything now.

As soon as the hall was empty, we disassembled the stage. The exhaustion on everyone's faces was obvious. We'd put everything into the last four months. Daisy's voice was hoarse. Sean looked pale. Patrick was quiet and he was *never* quiet. He helped Sean put the last things into the van, and we jumped in.

As the doors closed, silence fell. I was finally able to close my eyes without anyone wondering what I was doing. Tears rolled down my cheeks. I didn't stop them. As long as I cried without sobbing, no one would notice. In the darkness of the van, I had a decision to make: I could ditch the rules and phone Sir in a desperate attempt to save our relationship or I could take my happiness into my own hands and end our situation as I should have done months ago. I grabbed my phone and typed *S* and *T* quickly. I stopped before *O*, my heart in my mouth. The screen flashed in front of my eyes. Was I ready to end it all?

Chapter 45

"Congratulations," Amelia shouted, releasing a party popper in my face.

Confetti showered down around me as I stepped out of the van with Daisy. Sarah sprung out of a bright white rental car with a bottle of champagne in her hand. She joined Amelia by the van.

"One step closer to the Oscars."

I looked at Amelia's happy face and Sarah's excited grin. And that's when I sobbed. Loud cries rattled through my body, making Sean and Patrick move quickly. They busied themselves unpacking the van and unlocking the front door of the cottage. Meanwhile, Amelia, Sarah and Daisy crowded around me in confusion, pulling me into a big group cuddle. In-between sobs, I explained what had happened with Sir.

"We thought we'd surprise you," Sarah said woefully, breaking out of the hug.

"I'm calling him. Stuff his stupid no initiation rule. It's time he was finally put in his place," Amelia snapped.

Daisy looked overwhelmed, confused and charmed all at the same time. She'd been wanting to meet Amelia and Sarah for ages.

"Daisy, this is Amelia and Sarah, my best friends," I said,

still crying.

"We've heard so much about you," Sarah gushed, giving her a hug.

Amelia pulled her in for a cuddle too and said, "It's great to finally meet you."

Despite the fact my heart had been wrenched out of my chest, I took a moment to survey my wonderful friends. This was a moment to be cherished. All of my closest friends together in one place.

"What are you guys doing here anyway?" I asked, feeling dazed. I knew they had my address but I had no idea how they'd found the house without getting lost or how they'd managed to resist the temptation to tell me they were coming. It was the best surprise ever.

"We were supposed to be celebrating your last night of the tour," Amelia said. She pushed through the front door and into the cottage, calling bossily, "Boys, get the wine."

"Don't turn your phone back on," Sarah said, turning round to me. She waited for my nod of response before following Amelia inside. I'd turned my phone off in the van before I could text 'stop'. I had no plans to turn it on ever. I'd sink into a hole and stay there forever instead.

"You're forbidden," Amelia shouted, somehow hearing us.

"Why didn't you tell me?" Daisy asked, turning to look at me. It was just us two left outside.

"I had no idea how to say it. Plus, I didn't want to distract you from our last performance," I said, wiping away my tears. I couldn't cry all night.

"Surely, it's some kind of misunderstanding," she said, as we walked into the house together.

I loved Daisy's optimism but as the evening progressed, I

became sure of one thing – Sir was *never* going to choose me. It had always been Victoria and it always would be. He'd let her into his life and he didn't plan on leaving anytime soon. His loyalty ran deep. I had no right to think I could take him away from her anyway, but he had no right to make me fall in love with him. If I'd known from the beginning that he'd had a girlfriend, I never would have got involved.

* * *

The next morning, we all woke up in a heap squashed together on the sofa in the living room. Sean and Patrick had called it a night as soon as Amelia began a loud rendition of Beyonce's *Run The World* but Sarah, Daisy and Amelia had stayed up until the early hours of the morning with me, refusing to let me turn on my phone and forcing me to join in with their Strong Woman Karaoke.

I had to hand it to them, despite my tired, bloodshot eyes and numb heart, I felt the tiniest bit better. I had come a long way recently. I didn't need love and if Sir had been going to choose Victoria all along, then I didn't need him either.

A few hours later, it was time to say goodbye. Amelia and Sarah grabbed breakfast at the airport while Daisy and I met at the security gates with Sean and Patrick. Daisy was off to Mexico on a solo travelling venture and the boys were going back to Dublin. We'd lived in each other's pockets for months and now we were going our separate ways. I'd miss them so much.

I hugged Sean and Patrick and then turned to Daisy.

"Don't have too much fun in Mexico."

"Keep me updated on everything," she said at the same time.

We laughed. I hugged her close.

"See you soon," she whispered. "I'd love to be Phoebe."

I smiled. I'd told her about my *Friends* idea. She'd loved it. We would all live together in New York one day.

"Phoebe *is* the coolest," I said, fondly.

My last image of Daisy was her waving, happily as she walked away, in a bright green dinosaur jumper and jeans.

I joined up with Amelia and Sarah who had saved me a croissant for breakfast. I shook my head at it, my throat dry. "I can't eat that."

"You have to eat," Sarah said, disapprovingly.

"How about a champagne breakfast?" Amelia asked, with a flourish.

Sarah shook her head. "Absolutely not. Tilly needs fresh fruit and vegetables from now on and plenty of water and exercise."

I laughed, sadly. "You sound like my mum."

She was right though. No more alcohol for me. My plan was to spend a few weeks detoxing and focusing on getting money. I'd increase my promotional work over the next few weeks to make sure I had enough money to get by. After all, I'd no longer be working for Sir's charity.

While Sarah read a book and Amelia watched a film on the flight, I began automatically applying makeup. I had no one to impress anymore but I found it therapeutic. It took my mind off the constant stream of painful thoughts. I kept thinking about the way Sir's eyes shone when he was emotional or the way he looked me up and down in admiration when I was ready for a night out. My heart ached.

I was wearing black skinny jeans and my fine-knit light-pink jumper that matched my Prada bag perfectly. Every time

I glanced down at the soft fabric of my top and bag, I thought of Sir but there was nothing else I could wear. Everything in my suitcase needed to be washed.

"Security guards are so sexy aren't they?" Amelia said as we cleared security.

Sarah rolled her eyes.

"They used to be," I agreed, miserably. Their self-assured authority was no longer enough to turn me on. I was officially heartbroken.

As we walked through the arrival lounge, I couldn't help but scan the crowds for Sir. I knew I was being stupid. He'd be at home with Victoria or busy working. All the same, I found myself desperately searching through the groups of family and friends in front of us. No Sir. Obviously.

As Sarah dragged me towards a food shop to buy my body weight in fruit, I caught sight of a familiar dark wool suit. My heart stopped.

"Sarah, wait," I whispered.

She hadn't heard me.

"Sarah," I shouted.

Sarah and Amelia both turned round. I pointed wordlessly towards Sir. He'd not seen me yet. He looked exhausted. He was standing a little way off, carrying a bunch of red roses wrapped in expensive black paper and ribbon, urgently checking the faces of people arriving. For the first time since I'd met him, he looked nervous.

His eyes locked onto mine. All colour left his face. He dropped the flowers. I started to run. I didn't care if someone raised the alarm thinking I was a terrorist because I was running in an airport—I had to be with Sir. I was crying before I reached him. He wrapped his arms around me. I buried my head in his suit. His familiar scent filled my nose. I sobbed in his arms, the stress of the last day hitting me all at once.

"Why are you here?" I asked, wrenching myself away to look into his eyes.

"Baby Girl?"

"Why are you here?"

He looked lost for words.

"I thought you'd be with Victoria."

He frowned. "Victoria?"

"You said the breakup had been delayed," I said, impatiently.

"Delivered Tilly. Delivered. It was a predictive text error."

I still hadn't turned my phone on.

"I messaged straight away to tell you but you didn't reply. I was scared you didn't have any signal."

"We told her to keep her phone off." Amelia's apologetic voice appeared out of nowhere.

Sir turned around.

"It's lovely to meet you," Sarah smiled shyly, appearing next to Amelia.

It was utterly surreal to watch Sir hug my best friends. The relief on everyone's face was apparent. It'd been one terrible misunderstanding. The breakup had happened. I should have guessed. Of course, it'd been a predictive text error. Of course, Sir had delivered as he always did. He was officially single. I jumped on him in joy.

"Tilly," he laughed in relief, spinning me round and round.

"We'll get going," Sarah said, hastily.

"We love you," Amelia called, her face alive with excitement. She mouthed, "Big hands" as Sarah dragged her away. I laughed. I'd meet up with them tomorrow. We'd have breakfast together. They probably had a whole London shopping trip planned for us.

"What did your friend just say?" Sir asked, curiously.

I looked at his hands and smiled. "Oh nothing, Sir."

He pulled me close. "I'm so so sorry. I didn't know what to do when you didn't reply. I tried calling but there was no answer. I would never have delayed the break up." He released me slowly and took one step back, holding my head in his hands. "It was always you, Tilly. Always. You have all of me now. I will never let you down."

He kissed my forehead. And then my lips were on his and the airport disappeared. The crowds around us fell away. The constant announcements on the Tannoy became muted. A love song, by Frank Sinatra, played across the world. Birds sang. The stars and the sun came out all at once. Fluffy white clouds drifted by. My happy ever after had arrived and it was every bit as magical as I'd hoped.

Chapter 46

We left the airport in a taxi and drove to the centre of London. I stared out of the window at the now-familiar streets, feeling delirious. It was like a dream. The acting tour was over. I was finally with Sir, and Sir was with me. No more cancelled bubbles. No more heartbreak. No more Victoria.

"I have a special surprise for you," Sir said, as we pulled up outside a house.

I'd been so wrapped up in my own head, I'd stopped paying attention to where the taxi was taking us. We were now in a leafy residential area. Streetlamps shone. Lofty trees lined the roads. All was quiet. There were no bars or restaurants or even people.

"Sir?"

He shushed me. "No questions, Baby Girl. Just follow me."

He skipped up the steps to a front door, with a brass handle and shiny letterbox, as if he'd been here many times before. I looked up in bewilderment at the tall four-storey townhouse.

He took a key out of his pocket. "Welcome."

Oh my god. Was he showing me his home? I looked around anxiously for the anchor. This was entirely inappropriate.

"Victoria doesn't live here," he assured me, noticing my expression. "This is my house from a long time ago. Funnily enough, she's never actually been here. No one has."

The heavy front door swung open. I held my breath. A stunning hallway with a chandelier came into view - *I knew it. I knew he'd have one.* But what did he mean, this was his house from a long time ago? I automatically started taking off my shoes but Sir shook his head.

"No need beautiful. We're going outside."

He pointed towards a wide wooden staircase. I followed behind him, my heart racing. We passed three more immaculate floors and I couldn't help daydreaming about the little feminine touches I would add. A few candles here and a tasteful scatter cushion there. His minimalist decor would look wonderful teamed with my pretty, girly choices.

Sir opened a door and led me out onto the rooftop.

"I couldn't let it go, Tilly. I couldn't sell it."

I saw a wooden table and chairs, climbing greenery, sparkling fairy lights, prettily potted flowers and... a hammock. Emotion took over. My chest felt tight. I closed my eyes. He'd brought me here. One of the most special places in the world where he'd spent the final moment with his mum.

"I've never taken anyone here before." A flash of doubt ran through his eyes. "It's not The Dorchester."

I stopped him before he could say another word. Five star hotels, first class flights, Cartier, Prada, Chanel. It was all fine. Amazing, even. But it meant nothing without Sir. I didn't want The Dorchester. I wanted him. This rooftop meant more to me than all the chandeliers and roll-top baths in the world. It meant he was letting me in, he was finally trusting. He was giving me everything.

"Please make yourself at home. I won't be long," He said, before disappearing inside.

I sat down at the table, ignoring the hammock as a mark of respect. I looked up at the fairy lights. This was quite possibly the most special place in the world.

* * *

"Let's party," Sir shouted joyfully, returning ten minutes later with two cocktails. "I thought I'd join you for once." He smiled, holding the glasses up. "It's time to try Tilly's favourite drink."

As soon as he placed them down onto the table, I took a sip of mine gratefully. The fruity delicious liquid filled my mouth. Like everything Sir did, he'd excelled. He was practically a mixologist. His porn star martini was divine.

"How is it?" He asked, checking my reaction.

"Divine."

He looked genuinely relieved. "Only the best for my Tilly."

I looked around in awe and admitted, "I never thought we'd actually be here."

"I always knew we would be," He said confidently, looking straight back at me.

I smiled. How could he know that? He was so romantic. Maybe he really *had* been in love with me since act one scene one. He'd stuck to the plan like he'd said he would. My heart fell as I thought of Victoria. I had to ask the question. I had to ask how she was.

"How did Victoria take it?"

Sir cleared his throat. He shook his head. The sorrow in his eyes was evident. "She was much sadder than I expected. She cried for a long time. She said she knew it was over years ago but she never thought it would *really* be over."

I nodded, feeling a sharp twinge in my heart.

"She has someone else in America, Baby Girl. She is sad for me and her, but it doesn't mean I didn't do the right thing. We had formed a routine together. She will miss the routine more than anything. We were friends living together for many years, always avoiding the truth."

I watched his face as he spoke. Behind the pain, the stress had gone. He'd made the right decision. I wasn't naive enough to think the end of a long relationship wouldn't be tough, though. I knew it was a long process.

I took a deep breath. "I understand if you remain friends, Sir. She shouldn't be out of your life for good."

The colour returned to his face and he opened his eyes wide as if surprised. "Thank you, Tilly. I really appreciate that."

"You're brave, Sir. You did what you said you would do."

He ignored my last comment, and said, "I'm just glad I'm here. I'm a man of my word. I wanted to wait until the time was right, but I fell in love with you the first moment I met you, Tilly. You were trouble from the very beginning."

"Be careful what you wish for," I whispered.

A playful twinkle returned to his eyes. I smiled happily and looked around the rooftop. The view of London was breathtaking. This was an amazing place. The night air was cold, but I barely felt it. I was so happy to be sitting with Sir. As a biting wind whipped around me, I shivered.

"I'll get you a coat."

He came back a few seconds later with a huge parka. I pulled it on. Warmth spread throughout my body. It felt like a big duvet.

"Thank you Sir."

"You're welcome."

We fell silent.

"This is one of the places I come to when I need to think." He paused. "I came here when my mum died."

I held my breath, not wanting to put him off.

"It was the strangest feeling. Princess Diana died one day after. It felt like the whole world was mourning for my mum. It was the most surreal experience of my life. I had to escape the masses of people crying. I couldn't deal with it. I stayed on this rooftop alone for hours, looking up at the sky."

He sipped his cocktail, wistfully. "Mum loved Diana."

I stayed silent.

"And *ABBA*," he added, more happily.

I laughed, softly. His mum sounded amazing. I found myself wishing I could have met her.

A contented silence fell between us. I admired the pretty green plants and sparkling lights above us. Although I was wearing jeans and Sir's coat, I'd never felt more glamorous or beautiful than I did tonight.

Sir sat in front of me, nursing his cocktail, his expression gentle as he looked at the stars above us. "The universe has spoken. We are a paragraph into a novel of universal timing, Tilly."

"Yes Sir."

The stars had aligned. We'd found each other. We were finally able to give ourselves to one another entirely. I was safe to jump, safe to let go, safe to trust because this wonderful man, sitting opposite me, would always be there to catch me. No matter what happened. I'd never felt more connected to another soul on this earth. Seeing the emotion in my eyes, he reached over and clasped my hand in his.

Chapter 47

Thank you for reading my debut novel and supporting me. I hope you loved it, if you did leave me a review and sign up to my newsletter https://pages.thegirlwhojumped.com/ for lots of fun content and news about my next book: Victoria's story - The Other Side of Love. Read on for an exclusive preview!

* * *

In the evening light with his head tilted upwards slightly and his eyes emotional like they always were when he told a story, was the moment I most wanted to kill my fiance. It was the way he smiled fondly as he recalled the same story about his childhood best friend. The quiet satisfaction he got from telling the same story seventy seven times was infuriating. His neck was exposed. Thin skin tilting towards me. Dangerously thin. It would be easy to kill him. I'd smash my wine glass down against the mahogany coffee table my parents had bought for us years ago and lunge across the sofa. The tough part would be stopping.

He coughed. I took a sip of my drink and relaxed my fists.

"More wine?" I asked, sweetly.

"Yes please, Vicky."

I walked through into our tiny, spotless kitchen admiring the shine of the worktops. I kept our house immaculate. It was part of my daily routine. Every morning, I'd sit on the sofa opposite the bay windows in the living room stirring my cup of tea, enjoying the sun streaming through. I'd take at least an hour to wake up before jumping into action with a jog around Primrose Hill, a super-food vegan protein smoothie and a one hour cleaning frenzy of our apartment. I had life nailed. Our place was spacious, apart from the kitchen, but it was only two bedrooms. It didn't take long to clean it from head to foot. It was a satisfying task to begin the day. The cleanliness of our house and my fitness routine were the only two things I truly had control of.

As I pushed open the living room door with my hip, two wine glasses in hand, Marcus put his phone down guiltily.

"That was quick." He laughed.

I ignored him. There was nothing more annoying than a guilty man.

"How's your world?" He asked, with a big smile.

I dismissed his over-the-top cheerfulness and sat down on our cream sofa to consider his question. I swilled the wine, thoughtfully. The wine was good. Could be better. The house was clean. Couldn't be cleaner. I had pilates tomorrow with my best friend, Sienna. Marcus wouldn't be back til nine or ten at night. I'd head to my favourite bar, Whisper, instead of waiting around for him. It would be a fun day.

"It's good. Sienna got a new dog."

"Oh, did Oscar die?"

I nodded. "They buried him on the Heath. A quiet spot under the tree."

Marcus nodded, gravely.

I felt my throat tighten and took a gulp of wine. "Such a beautiful soul."

"Yes, he always sounded lovely. How's Desmond?"

"He's good. My Dad loves having him. You've not seen him for a week have you?"

Desmond was our pride and joy. A velvet grey French Bulldog with the biggest eyes in the world and a loyalty to last a lifetime. I walked him everyday but I did miss him in our bed.

"No. Work's been really busy lately." He shifted happily in his seat the way he did before launching into a long ramble.

"Right, I'm off to sleep." I yawned. I was too tired to fake interest in his businesses.

Marcus bowed his head but managed a smile. "I'll be through in a bit." He picked up his phone.

I nodded. The deal was, I left him in peace while he texted whatever woman he was currently messaging and he gave me the space to have a long hot bubble bath alone. I'd rather that than listen to an endless spiel about his work. It was an unspoken deal. Hence the guilt. It would be easier if we talked, got it all out, but that was never going to happen.

Before I got in the bath, I pulled my other phone out of it's new hiding place in the alcove behind the carefully folded fluffy towels. Harry had texted five times. I rolled my eyes. I'd see him tomorrow. He could wait. His desperation reeked. It turns out money can't buy you love. No matter how many handbags and shoes you throw at someone, and he had given me a lot.

As the water tumbled out of the shining chrome taps, I squirted an overly generous amount of foam into the bath and messaged Sienna. *Has Harry texted you?* Her reply was instant. *Four times.* I laughed and typed back, *Wanna get ready at mine tomorrow before we head out?* My phone vibrated before

I could put it down. *Yes. I'll come by at seven. Don't forget pilates is at two.* Conversation over. Sienna wasn't a fan of long text conversations.

The grouting in the tiles looked pink. I opened the bathroom cupboard and took out the strong cleaning spray and hard bristled sponge. When the bath was finally full, I was sweating and the grouting was still pink. I turned off the taps and wiped my forehead. I'd stop for today and enjoy the bubbles. I could work on it tomorrow before pilates. Maybe, I'd need industrial strength stuff.

About the Author

Matilda Swinney is a devoted romantic who believes in unicorns (or camels as her daughter calls them). She lives with her dream man and two children in a cosy spot over the rainbow.

You can connect with me on:

- https://www.matildaswinney.com
- https://thegirlwhojumped.com

Subscribe to my newsletter:

- https://pages.thegirlwhojumped.com

Also by Matilda Swinney

The Other Side Of Love

Coming in March 2023.

Victoria's boyfriend is out of control.

Victoria is out of control.

Someone is going to get hurt.

And it's not Victoria.

Printed in Great Britain
by Amazon

85444831R00181